Modern Foreign Languages 5–11

The need to introduce pupils to learning languages at an early stage has been widely acknowledged, with MFL now a core part of the primary curriculum. Fully updated to support busy schools and teachers in planning, teaching and delivering the new primary MFL entitlement for all primary pupils, this user-friendly guide covers significant pedagogical issues and is a key point of reference for all MFL work in the primary classroom.

Now fully updated to include substantive writing about planning and introducing the new assessment scale, this book contains:

- comprehensive coverage of resources and planning;
- valuable new cross-curricular links;
- ready-to-use activities that are anchored in research;
- advice on assessment, SEN and the use of technology;
- a development of the broader issues of leadership, learning strategies and continuing professional development.

Modern Foreign Languages 5–11 will help practitioners to teach MFL as a dynamic, stand-alone subject while retaining a cross-curricular focus. It builds upon core principles of cultural learning, differentiation, language awareness and transferable skills by providing practical strategies that can be easily implemented in your setting. Offering comprehensive guidance on the pedagogy that underpins language teaching and covering everything you'll need to teach effectively, this book delivers a range of practical ideas and examples of best practice to help integrate effective language learning, teaching and assessment into the curriculum.

Written to support the needs of trainees, practising teachers and school leaders as they develop their foreign language provision, this guide is key reading for those seeking to enhance their professional practice in primary MFL pedagogy.

Jane Jones is Senior Lecturer in Modern Foreign Languages Education at King's College London.

Simon Coffey is Senior Lecturer in Modern Foreign Languages Education at King's College London.

The 5–11 series combines academic rigor with practical classroom experience in a tried and tested approach which has proved indispensible to both trainee PGCE students and to practicing teachers. Bringing the best and latest research knowledge to core subject areas, this series addresses the key issues surrounding the teaching of these subjects in the primary curriculum. The series aims to stay up to date by reflecting changes in government policy and is closely related to the changing curriculum for the primary core subjects.

Each book contains lesson planning guidance and methods to develop pupils' understanding as well as offering creative and innovative ways to teach subjects in the primary classroom.

Titles in this series include:

Physical Education 5–11, Jonathan Doherty and Peter Brennan

History 5–11, Hilary Cooper

Modern Foreign Languages 5–11, Jane Jones and Simon Coffey

English 5–11, David Waugh and Wendy Jolliffe

Modern Foreign Languages 5–11

A guide for teachers

Third edition

Jane Jones and Simon Coffey

Routledge
Taylor & Francis Group

LONDON AND NEW YORK

Third edition published 2017
by Routledge
2 Park Square, Milton Park, Abingdon, Oxon OX14 4RN

and by Routledge
711 Third Avenue, New York, NY 10017

Routledge is an imprint of the Taylor & Francis Group, an informa business

First edition published by Routledge 2006
Second edition published by Routledge 2013

British Library Cataloguing in Publication Data
A catalogue record for this book is available from the British Library

Library of Congress Cataloging in Publication Data
Names: Jones, Jane, 1951– author, illustrator. | Coffey, Simon, author.
Title: Modern foreign languages 5–11: a guide for teachers / Janes Jones &
Simon Coffey.
Description: Third Edition. | Milton Park, Abingdon, Oxon ; New York, NY :
Routledge, [2016].
Identifiers: LCCN 2016022871 (print) | LCCN 2016026429 (ebook) | ISBN
9781138645653 (hbk : alk. paper) | ISBN 9781138645677 (pbk : alk. paper) |
ISBN 9781315628028 (ebk : alk. paper) | ISBN 9781315628028 (ebk)
Subjects: LCSH: Language and languages—Study and teaching (Secondary)
Classification: LCC P51 .J57 2016 (print) | LCC P51 (ebook) | DDC
418.0071—dc23
LC record available at https://lccn.loc.gov/2016022871

ISBN: 978-1-138-64565-3 (hbk)
ISBN: 978-1-138-64567-7 (pbk)
ISBN: 978-1-315-62802-8 (ebk)

Typeset in Bembo and Helvetica Neue
by Florence Production Ltd, Stoodleigh, Devon, UK

Printed and bound by CPI Group (UK) Ltd, Croydon, CR0 4YY

Contents

Acknowledgements

This book would not have been possible without the suggestions and ideas of a great many teachers, headteachers, consultants, researchers, colleagues in higher education and children, all of whom, too numerous to mention by name, have made contributions in many ways in the light of their interest in primary Modern Foreign Languages (primary MFL). The authors would, however, like to thank the following colleagues for their very precious support: Stephanie Adamou, Chris Andon, Nick Andon, Rachel Aukett, Daryl Bailey, Lis Bundock, Professor Margaret Cox, Andrew Edwards, Jane Garrett, Sue Gibbs, Muriel Grosbois, Rym Haddam, Margaret Haste, Rachel Hawkes, Neil Hillman, Alison Hurrell, Joseph Jones, Lynne Jones, Jane Nimmo, Nicola Reynolds, Liz Scott, Bridget Saul, Michaela Thomas, Emma Towers and Marc Van den Brande. They have all contributed generously in different ways, such as providing drawings, graphics, teaching ideas and plans, research support and critical insights.

Introduction: developments in primary MFL learning

Primary MFL started out as an experiment initiated by teachers who, quite some time ago, saw benefits in early foreign language learning. We give credit to those enthusiasts, who laid the foundations for children to have an enjoyable learning experience in today's tightly packed curriculum. In recent years, we have seen a series of burgeoning primary school early foreign language learning experiences and initiatives across the nation. Government initiatives, a plethora of official frameworks for learning and teaching and targeted funding for primary MFL all resulted in a seriously high profile for the whole enterprise. This is nothing short of a paradigmatic change in attitude on the part of leaders and, indeed, other stakeholders – a change reflected in the place now afforded foreign language learning in the curriculum provision of primary schools for all KS2 children.

The then Department for Education and Skills (DfES) recognised these developments and this enthusiasm and invited practitioners at all levels to contribute to a roadmap for the subject. This resulted in the National Key Stage 2 Framework for Languages 2005, which subsequently matured into the 2014 National Curriculum for KS2 (referred to in this book as KS2 NC). These have provided the early language learning adventure with a structure and thus turned it into a project by offering clear guidelines, measurability and accountability in terms of progress and assessment. The parameters of the primary languages project have allowed schools and language teachers to build on previous experiences with primary MFL as well as to develop and experiment with ideas.

Researching for this book, we have identified ongoing issues facing schools and questions that they face when implementing the National Curriculum in the planning of effective language teaching and learning. We are of the opinion that the development of a soundly principled primary languages pedagogy is a work in progress. Our book, whilst acknowledging the impact of the National Curriculum, goes beyond it in that we use research and snapshots from the world of primary MFL teaching at large to translate policy decisions and theoretical discussions into practice. These we present to teachers and parties interested in primary MFL as suggested planning and teaching approaches. Although we have had to be selective in our coverage of key areas and in the numbers of examples we incorporate, we have integrated feedback and the views of teachers and pupils from a large number of primary schools we have visited around the UK. Through our work on EU projects, we have observed practice in other countries where primary

MFL has been successfully embedded in the primary curriculum, and for some time now, a number of countries have quite independently commissioned their own research into learning and teaching modern foreign languages at primary level.

Each chapter of our book begins with a brief summary of the content and key questions to be explored. We present examples of practice from Key Stage 1 and Key Stage 2 teachers who do not make any great claims for their teaching other than that they enjoy their primary MFL experiences and try their professional best to make an appropriate challenging provision for their pupils and colleagues. We have analysed the practice of these teachers in order to establish indicators of 'practice that works' and 'in what conditions it works' to consider what can be transferred into other teaching and learning contexts. Each chapter concludes with a summary of key points and questions to the reader on what the authors believe are key issues for deliberation.

Our discussion of primary MFL begins in Chapter 1 by considering reasons for an early start, drawing on a range of research findings and on areas of consensus in the community. Those responsible for the early start need to believe in and be able to articulate its benefits. It is within a school community that primary MFL will be implemented and to do this successfully requires a strongly supportive leadership of the shared or distributed kind, as discussed in Chapter 2. The role of the subject leader/coordinator is crucial to the project. Leadership is considered essential to develop and firmly embed primary MFL into the fabric of the whole-school provision as enthusiasm, which can wane as well as wax, cannot alone sustain the project. This is then followed by practical discussion of how MFL can be implemented, and Chapter 3 deals with planning issues that concern teachers' choice and deployment of time and resources. We suggest ways to plan, what to take into account and what could be included in long- and short-term planning (schemes of work and lesson plans). The teacher focus on planning continues in Chapter 4, where choices about the effective use of MFL-specific and improvised materials are discussed and exemplified with reference to teaching the four skills of listening, speaking, reading and writing. We explore the issues surrounding the teaching and learning of specific skills, such as how and when to incorporate reading and writing into MFL to support language awareness, both in terms of speaking in MFL and first-language literacy. The theme of cross-curricular learning and embedding MFL into the curriculum is emphasised in Chapter 5 and we provide case study examples of how MFL can be integrated into other areas of the curriculum. We link this to successful whole-child learning and advocate the hugely important motivational aspect of language learning through 'meaning-making' rather than rote-learning foreign language phrases out of context.

We then highlight children's learning needs in Chapter 6 and consider learner and learning strategies that can promote and support learning to enable pupils to become competent strategic language learners. In Chapter 7 we emphasise that primary MFL, like any other subject, needs to assess children's learning, particularly through formative assessment in a supportive, enabling and forward-looking way.

Technology constantly offers new and exciting opportunities to support MFL learning for individual work, group work and teacher-led classwork. In Chapter 8 we discuss some simple and some more challenging ways in which technology can support the teacher and enhance pupils' language learning. One of the major benefits of technology use is in opening the classroom door and bridging children's experience to target language communities; indeed, developing cultural awareness and genuine intercultural understanding is a key objective of primary MFL (an objective enshrined in the Framework). Chapter 9 considers what exactly we mean by 'teaching cultural awareness' and how we can encourage pupils, many of whom have rich cultural and linguistic heritages, to embrace difference and otherness. We give some snapshot examples of how we have seen cultural input integrated into MFL teaching across Key Stages 1 and 2 and how whole-school initiatives can raise intercultural awareness.

It is crucial that primary MFL is not perceived as an isolated enterprise but is seen in the context of the whole school. In Chapter 10 we explore issues of primary–secondary transition, emphasising the importance of planning MFL provision on a cross-stage dialogic basis to ensure progression in learning and across the different school phases. Progression is equally important with respect to the professional development of teaching staff. In our discussion of this topic in Chapter 11, we focus on general principles and look at questions arising from it, but we do not promote any specific course provision, material, website or other source. We find teacher research and collaboration around teachers' own practice a particularly valuable way to support teacher learning in the field and to promote the development of a sound and well-defined pedagogy.

The purpose of this book, then – drawing on previous debate, research and discussion with primary MFL teachers – is to contribute to the hugely stimulating debate about the issues of early foreign language learning and to involve all those who have an interest in and responsibility for the subject. This is not a parochial debate but one that engages with language learning across the whole of Europe and the increasingly globalised context of learning. Our book takes forward the assumption, and a justifiable one, that the project is inclusive and provides a fruitful and enjoyable learning opportunity for all children to engage in.

1

Starting early: what do younger language learners do better?

This chapter considers the rationale for an early start to language learning since it is important that this is made explicit; it cannot simply be assumed. There are many reasons for beginning learning a language early, not least of all the greater openness of early learners to new sounds and their natural curiosity to engage with new activities. MFL teaching and learning in the UK has redefined itself for the twenty-first century. Children are now being taught to be able to speak a given foreign language, as well as to be equipped with a range of foundational language-learning skills that reinforce whole-curriculum learning and encourage increased social and cultural awareness of difference. The emphasis in this chapter is very much on promoting what can be an enriching learning experience for pupils and teachers and articulating a rationale.

Key issues

- MFL learning needs to go beyond the mimicry stage of parrot-fashion learning to encourage creative use of language and experimentation.

- Popular opinion suggests the younger the learner of a language, the more effective their learning. Is there real evidence for this assertion and are there real long-term benefits?

- Failure to engage with MFL learning represents a myopic view of language education and a missed opportunity at many levels.

- Progressive cross-phase learning between primary and secondary school is essential to a child's successful school-based language learning trajectory.

- Is one language easier to learn than another? Which language(s) should we be teaching?

Introduction – can parrots talk?

Parrots are birds of immense fascination, given their natural curiosity, varied personalities and propensity for mimicry. It appears that a certain African grey parrot of some renown – Alex – was trained to use words to identify, describe and count objects, and even answer questions about them such as 'How many red squares?' seemingly with some 80 per cent success. The parrots on the cover of the book can be seen as a symbol of these skills and remind us of much that we observe in children who show inquisitiveness as well as learning capacity. Primary MFL learning provides an opportunity for all children to demonstrate more than their powers of mimicry. While teachers sometimes talk of children parroting words and phrases – a natural part of the early stage of language learning – children have the cognitive flexibility and physiological apparatus to become competent and creative language users. Babies visibly enjoy babble and infants thrive on constant chatter and verbal interrogation of their world. As toddlers grow into children and their language use becomes more sophisticated, they retain the flexibility to unconsciously absorb and 'parrot' new words in their mother tongue or in any language that they come into contact with, as any parent who has spent some length of time abroad with young children engaged in social contact in a foreign language can testify.

Children aged 5–11 are focused on the nature of the communication afforded by language use and are not concerned with the cultural load of which words and which language they are using. This natural, uninhibited use of language makes early learners particularly receptive to learning in MFL classes, and it is a foundation to build upon.

The intrinsic motivation to learn foreign languages cannot be assumed, even with younger learners. We know that play and creativity are natural resources but that motivation to engage in particular activities depends on messages modelled by significant others, including teachers, and that feedback should include 'praise [for] effort rather than performance' (Goswami and Bryant 2007: 2). It is essential, therefore, that younger learners develop positive attitudes to languages and that these are maintained throughout

FIGURE 1.1 Parrot

the entire primary phase and into the secondary-school phase of learning to ensure the success of the primary MFL project. One of the concerns expressed in the MFL community of practice – that is the group of professionals interested in and committed to the promotion of skilled MFL teaching – has been about the decline in interest that is often characteristic of the secondary stage of learning. After many discussions with secondary teachers and interviews with Year 7 children, it appears that there is some justification for this. Let us, by way of illustration, consider comments from two groups of Year 7 pupils (11-year-olds). Year 7 children in a school with a strong tradition in languages in the London area gave the following answers when asked to describe the differences in the way MFL is taught at secondary level:

> Here the teacher just says it without explaining and expects you to understand.

> At primary school we did colours and answered questions. Here the words are harder.

> It's ace. The teacher's accent is amazing.

> We have gone from almost nothing learnt to soooo much learnt.

> More homework here. [When asked what sort of homework] Just revision.

Given its previous history as a former language college and the funding that allowed it to develop excellent resources, MFL clearly enjoyed an important place in the curriculum at this school. However, the children's views were not necessarily more favourable than those of pupils in a comprehensive school where languages did not have such a high profile or record of success. We interviewed another group of Year 7 pupils attending such a school at the same time during their first autumn term. One pupil – supported by others in the group – expressed enthusiasm for the French and German teacher and the languages:

> I just love it. I can't stop speaking French! *Ça va? Tu vas bien?* [to the author in the interview]. Miss gets us to sing and move around all the time [seat-dancing movements]. It's not embarrassing as we all do it. The PowerPoints are excellent. Miss gets us to work in teams and we get points when we say something good. If you are not sure, she helps us then comes back to us and asks us again. The German lessons are fun too [group bursts out into a volley of German phrases]. I can't wait to do Spanish.

This comment is a testimony to particular primary and secondary teachers who, working together, have succeeded in maintaining cross-phase interest, motivation and progression in language learning, arguably the cornerstones of this book. Without continuity and coherence of learning on a progressive basis, primary MFL is likely to be perceived as a failed project (see the report by Burstall *et al.* 1974 on the perceived ineffectiveness of primary MFL, whose findings hang like a cloud over primary language teaching to this day). If this is the case, an evident lack of success could lead to considerable disquiet on the part of secondary colleagues, and probably sceptical primary teachers who might feel inclined to challenge the rather over-generalised, albeit contested, notion (see, for example, the National Curriculum Review (DfE 2011)) that provides the basis for primary MFL: 'the younger the better'.

The younger the better? The 'optimum age' issue

Age-related issues have been discussed extensively and reviewed by, for example, Bland (2015), Johnstone (1994) and Martin (2000). It seems that decisions about when to introduce foreign language learning depend, in different countries, on politically variable local and national school contexts. In various European countries the 'optimum starting age' for language learning has been researched, yet there is contradictory evidence on almost every count. Across Europe we can find starting ages ranging from five to 11 – even younger in some countries and in many private schools. For example, children learn (usually) French in UK independent schools from the age of three. Neurobiologists have been involved in research on the optimum age to start learning an additional language, and results have led to an ongoing debate. For example, the Swiss linguist Georges Lüdi, from the University of Basel, working with colleagues in neurobiology on brain activation and the capacity for the development of early bilingualism, has asserted that the optimum age for the development of early bilingualism is before the age of three. Lüdi does, however, stress the need to be conscious of children's individuality and their flexibilities in different areas of acquisition and at different ages. While the neurobiological research of languages has yet to come to a conclusive result, and while the Swiss context is somewhat different to the primary-school classrooms under discussion in this book and our language-learning aims rather more modest, such research continues to fuel the 'optimum age' debate.

In view of the discussion of the 'earlier the better', Martin rightly questions the meaning of 'better' in respect of children's learning: is it 'proficiency and the ultimate level of attainment' or 'the rate of acquisition . . . and . . . which aspects of language learning are they best at?' (Martin 2000: 10). However we choose to interpret 'better', the key lies, according to Martin, in the planning of an appropriate age-related programme that capitalises on what younger learners can do better and with the greatest enthusiasm in order to maximise their advantages. Similarly, MFL provision at the secondary level needs to be planned to exploit the advantages of the secondary-aged learner by consolidating and building on, but not repeating, terrain already covered. It can be seen from this that the case for an early start is not so much age-dependent but rests on a range of other more influential factors. These are reflected forcefully in the following statement from Jurgen Meisel of the University of Hamburg (cited by Georges Lüdi in an address to the Education Department in Basel, 16 June 2004), according to whom 'monolingualism can be regarded as resulting from an impoverished environment where an opportunity to exhaust the potential of the language faculty is not fully developed.'

Primary MFL provides – assuming training, funding and support for teachers and schools – added value in the primary classroom and indeed the whole-school environment. It offers language-learning opportunities for all children on an equal basis, whatever their ability or language background, and can make the most effective use of children's full language-learning capital and potential.

What, then, are the advantages of an early start?

Throughout this book, we address KS2 teaching and include KS1, as we believe, in line with Sharpe and Driscoll, that 'foreign language learning should begin at the start of compulsory primary schooling' (2000: 83). However, we recognise that the gains of such an early start may not always be clearly quantifiable linguistically. Much of the research looking into the nature and benefits of early language learning has tried to measure the success of children's 'acquisition rate' compared to peers who did not have an early start. The most famous example of this was the Burstall *et al.* NFER report (1974), which ultimately led to the disintegration of the pilot Primary French Project started in the 1960s. When children who had studied French at primary level were compared to those who had not, and to older secondary children who had studied French for the same period of time, it was found that children who had started learning earlier did not demonstrate greater proficiency. It could be argued, though, that the research data were flawed as they were based on testing linguistic gains when children had already moved on to secondary school and so had started learning French 'again' as beginners in Year 7, along with peers who had not previously learnt any foreign language in their primary school.

In linguistic terms, there is some evidence (Singleton 1989; Tierney and Gallastegi 2005; Vilke 1988) to show that an early start helps to improve foreign language listening skills and pronunciation. Johnstone's review of evidence in Scottish primary schools related to early learning indicated some 'positive effect on auditory capacities' (2003: 15). These studies seem to resonate with Lenneberg's (1967) 'critical period hypothesis', which claimed that the brain of a child before puberty was more receptive to imitating native-like pronunciation. However, the critical period hypothesis has been widely challenged as evidence shows that acquisition and learning gains vary enormously across all age groups (see Herschensohn 2007). Contentious gains in linguistic proficiency cannot be the only reason for advocating an early start for language learners, for we would maintain that the main benefits that early MFL learning engenders lie rather in:

- enjoyment of languages
- mutual reinforcement of first-language development
- cultural awareness and enhanced understanding.

The debate about the optimal learning age will certainly continue, as different research projects have yielded mixed findings relating to the long-term effectiveness of an early start. In the long term, a more formal investigation confirming connections between early language learning and these advantages is required. This needs to take into consideration that the learning must already be embedded in a progressive trajectory that crosses the school phases both vertically through the years and horizontally across the curriculum. Language learning provision for KS1 learners is very patchy in the state system (a *fait accompli* in the independent sector often from the age of three). An early start or at least sensitisation to language is both possible and desirable, as case studies in this book show.

Which language?

There is much popular wisdom propagated about which language should be taught in schools. Most of the ideas exchanged are based on the concept of maximum 'usefulness' of a given language. This usefulness is sometimes understood in relation to the language with which we have the greatest contact (in tourism or business), or even in terms of the language with the largest number of speakers (Mandarin Chinese) – though, historically, sheer numbers of speakers have never motivated learners to learn a language unless there is a commensurate prestige or utilitarian value.

Many adults in the UK associate language learning at school with French only and this can reflect negatively or positively on the attitudes they convey to their children. Some parents continue to enjoy learning and rekindle their own French through their child's experience of language learning, whereas others may have an entrenched dislike for French and encourage their child to learn another language. Parental attitudes and other 'learnt' ideas are clearly visible when asking children which language they prefer; for example, a child cited in Chapter 4 commented 'French is hard to pronounce' – an attitude that is more likely to come from a parent/an adult than from the child himself/herself.

French has always been, by far, the most taught modern foreign language in the UK and this picture looks set to continue for the time being ('offered by 89 per cent of primary schools in 2008', Wade and Marshall 2009: 3) although the KS2 NC (DfE 2014) gives schools the freedom to choose. French remains the obvious choice for several reasons:

- it is the language of our nearest neighbours and most countries have a tradition of familiarity with their neighbouring language and culture;
- there are important historical and cultural links between Britain and France;
- French is ingrained into our education system and into our psyches as 'the' foreign language, with most MFL material aimed at French and French attracting the highest number of students, thereby language-qualified staff;
- although now no longer comparable with English, French retains international prestige as an international language of culture;
- as a mother tongue or second language, French connects a wide range of different societies around the world (*la Francophonie*);
- the linguistic effects of history have resulted in enormous lexical congruity between English and French.

There is an increasing interest in other languages, especially Spanish. Some schools are able to offer two languages, either concurrently at KS2 or sequentially one after the other across KS1 and 2. In certain areas, community languages are taught as MFL as well as 'second language', e.g. Portuguese in South London. Perceived easiness was a reason that the authors were given for the choice of a particular language. This was particularly true in the case of Spanish and Italian. Several MFL coordinators and headteachers mentioned that they would like to adopt Spanish because children, they considered, find it easier than French, especially in writing. Some local areas (e.g. Hackney) have adopted Spanish as a collective enterprise. One MFL coordinator, a Germanist, commented:

We're largely led by staffing and material factors though we would like to introduce Spanish as well as French. Although I don't really speak Spanish yet I know that pupils find Spanish easier because of the regular phonetic spelling and also they're more motivated to do Spanish and parents sometimes ask me why we don't do it.

A headteacher in a London preparatory school with an intake that included children from local French families justified her choice of Spanish as the first foreign language for children starting in Reception, to be followed by French for all children in Year 2, thus:

Spanish is easier for the [French] native speakers and all the children function at the same level. It is phonetically easier and I can teach Spanish myself. It all starts with the opening of a box with a dolly from Spain that has just arrived in England and, we tell the children, cannot speak English. (See also Chapter 7.)

The view of the headteacher, parental attitudes, the teachers themselves and their preferences for teaching styles clearly influence the choice of one language in favour of another.

We (the authors) recognise that there are practical limitations concerning the implementation of a 'no constraint' policy that include the availability of specialist teachers in particular languages. It is not unheard of for a school to drop a second language when a teacher with that specialism leaves. In the light of such vagaries, the inclusive language-learning policy of the European Commission poses a considerable challenge, with its expectation of a '1+2 languages' policy to start in EU primary curriculum provision:

The EU's objective is for every citizen to master two languages in addition to his or her mother tongue. In order to achieve this objective, children are to be taught two foreign languages at school from an early age.

(European Parliament 2015: no page)

There is little evidence of this being provided systematically other than in Scotland, where a commitment to 1+2 is being developed (to replace the old model of a language at the KS2 age range) by the end of 2020. With government funding and extensive professional development support from the Scottish Centre for Information on Language Teaching (SCILT), Education Scotland and teacher education institutions, *inter alia*, Lynne Jones, PD Officer (Primary) of SCILT Scotland's National Centre, explains this aspiration:

L2 from P1 (equivalent Reception) to S3 (equivalent Year 9) with L3 introduced no later than P5 (equivalent Year 4). There is an expectation that L2 has national qualification status in the Senior Phase (S4–S6, equivalent Year 10–Year 12) to encourage continuation/uptake of examination courses. Gaelic Medium primary schools aim for parity of Gaelic and English (L1/2) with L3 coming in no later than P5. In some English Medium primary schools Gaelic is taught as an additional language and is L2. Most, though not all English Medium primary schools (the vast majority of primary schools in Scotland) have French as L2 with Spanish,

Italian and German the L2 in some primary schools. The aspiration is that when the 1+2 approach is embedded from P1, most children will achieve Curriculum for Excellence (CfE) 2nd Level in L2, which broadly equates to CEFR A2.

The long-term planned management of change, with funding and support and built-in plans for transitional learning, underpin this bold initiative. The vision is one of a belief in the equality of languages, and the 'presumption of inclusion in the policy, "languages for all" and valuing home languages' (Lynne Jones). We are also of the opinion that *all* languages have the capacity to enrich the lives of children through the enjoyment, curiosity and greater sense of understanding engendered by encountering a different cultural space.

Continuity, progression and cohesion in language learning: the wider context

MFL provision can no longer be delivered in an unsystematic, incoherent way, dependent on the goodwill and enthusiasm of a few teachers; it needs joined-up whole-school organisation such as that evidenced in the case studies in this book. Primary MFL is not an isolated entity and any debate on the subject needs to take account of the secondary-school stage of learning, which we discuss at length in Chapter 10. Our main concern in this book remains to discuss questions about the 5–11 age range, which need to be considered within the context of a primary to secondary continuum of learning. Transfer at 11 merely reflects the organisation of schooling in England and functions as a stepping stone from one stage of learning to another, where one stage consolidates and builds upon the learning of the earlier stage. This requires planning that is progressive in content and addresses the development of skills; for example, building on the extensive 'learning through the ears' approach at KS1 advocated by Eric Hawkins (2005: 10), through song and rhyme (also appropriate for Foundation Stage children), towards 'a wider, richer concept of literacy' at KS2 (ibid. 2005: 10).

We have seen simple but very effective planning of this kind, for example a three-colour-coded mind map, indicating previous learning objectives, learning intentions for the present and learning expectations for the immediate future (see Chapter 3 for more about planning). Erika Werlen's extensive research on primary MFL (Werlen 2005), carried out in Baden-Württemberg in Germany and discussed in Chapter 10, stresses the importance of cross-phase planned continuity and progression to avoid truncating the child's language-learning experience. Werlen emphasises the need for elements of continuity (for example, of teaching approach) in both phases as well as challenge in new but connected learning in order to avoid demotivation, to recognise the strengths of both the younger and older learner, and to progress learning. Without attention to cross-phase cohesive provision and sustained progressive learning opportunities, the rationale for early learning in school might well serve to increase the divide.

Cohesive primary MFL learning enables children to learn in such a way that they understand content and contexts relating to their own experiences. When this is embedded across the whole curriculum it provides a powerful way to develop basic communicative and intercultural competence as well as a range of language and social skills. In this way, primary MFL is an integrative, inclusive, authentic and emancipatory learning experience that can also be fun, challenging and enjoyable learning, whatever the language.

Conclusion

There is, as discussion in this chapter has indicated, evidence that children are capable of far more, even at an early stage, than mere copying of sounds and symbols when learning modern foreign languages. Their language-learning skills are independent of a specific language. Many children are already bilingual and bring immense linguistic capital to their learning. The efforts of enthusiastic MFL primary-school teachers have been rewarded with the elevation of primary MFL to the status of a subject in its own right. Given the now mandatory requirement to teach a foreign language to KS2 children and the guidelines of KS2 NC, there is a genuine opportunity and need to build on and maintain children's natural interest in languages. There must, however, be sufficient support and well-trained teaching staff so as to ensure the best language-learning provision, based on a whole-school approach. The most recent report on language trends (Tinsley and Board 2016) shows that almost all primary schools responding to the survey are on board with KS2 provision and almost a half of them have some provision at KS1.

It is the right of all children to have an opportunity to engage in language learning and to have 'an engaging and enjoyable experience' (Bland 2015: 9). Primary MFL is arguably the only subject where all children, including children with special educational needs, can, with the necessary support, learn on a level-playing-field basis, especially where children learn in a collaborative, dialogic classroom and the voices of all the learners are supported, as Jones (2014a) asserts. Tinsley and Board (2016) showed that schools with a high level of EAL (English as an additional language) children saw delivering primary MFL less likely to be a challenge than schools with a high intake of monolingual children. Well-trained and confident teachers can, with their enthusiasm and with appropriate support, exploit the children's cultural and linguistic capital. Teachers can capitalise on pupil enjoyment of language learning to promote self-development in primary classrooms and to open doors to a broader world-view.

Comenius, some three-and-a-half centuries ago, also had parrots in mind when he emphasised the inclusive nature of language learning and saw it as inseparable from the development of the whole person: 'The study of languages . . . should be joined to that of objects, that our acquaintance with the objective world and with language . . . may progress side by side. For it is people we are forming and not parrots' (Comenius 1657: 203–4, in the translation by Keatinge 1967).

Questions on which to reflect

■ What is your own general view in the debate on 'the earlier the better?' and why do you take that position?

■ What are the factors shaping the language of choice at your school?

■ Do you have a preference for a particular language? If so, can you analyse the origin of this preference?

2

Leading the way: the importance of a shared-leadership approach

The vast literature on change management indicates clearly that any curriculum change, innovation or mandate needs the active support from the headteacher to be successfully sustained. Although the role of the head is central, however, it is insufficient in itself. If such change, specifically in the case of primary MFL, is to become embedded in the curricular fabric of the school and to be a sustainable option that will endure and continue to develop, the support of leadership in the broadest sense is required. Alongside the headteacher, the role of the subject leader and other parties interested in primary MFL is central in establishing a school community ethos of language learning. Success needs to be sustained and we need to explore issues of sustainability and the nature of a school culture that can nurture a whole-school perspective on primary MFL to this end. This chapter identifies what seem to be the key supportive factors for primary MFL in the school culture.

Key issues

- Leadership is crucial in the implementation of curriculum innovation and development.
- Radiating from various pulse points and not just from the top, leadership is more effective if it is a shared endeavour.
- Subject leadership is vital for quality subject provision.
- Shared leadership is a powerful tool for collaborative staff learning and professional development, including the development of trainee teachers.
- Sustainable provision for modern foreign language teaching and learning needs to be planned for as part of the ongoing school development or improvement plan.
- An international mindset is central as part of the leadership vision and an identifiable part of the leadership factor where primary MFL is concerned.

Introduction

A now retired primary-school teacher told us:

> I am a language specialist and taught French in primary schools in the 70s when it was in vogue. Part of the reason for the decline was the lack of specialist teachers, lack of coherence across and even within schools, and teachers who tried to deliver a secondary model to young children.

Some of these issues still ring true today, especially the need for adequately qualified and trained teachers and suitable transition arrangements from KS2 to KS3. Leadership is an essential factor in driving and supporting successful change management and is, therefore, fundamental to an effective and sustainable primary modern foreign language provision. The DfES Research Report 572 (2004: 103) made three recommendations specifically in terms of leadership, asserting that:

1   Key personnel were needed in each local authority to promote primary MFL and to develop networks.

2   Leadership from central government was needed to support schools in the target to meet the entitlement.

3   Schools themselves needed to take a lead on planning for a minimum time allocation for the learning of the foreign language to include 30 minutes protected time per week.

The implementation of these has been variable. The support role provided previously by local authorities has been assumed in some cases by subject leaders/leaders of learning in school learning trusts. Successive governments of the day have blown hot and cold on support for primary languages. Establishing the principle of protected time is important as it gives primary language learning status as a core subject within the whole primary curriculum provision. Leadership, as understood in a broader sense, is essential for this to happen. Leaders may be heads, subject coordinators or subject leaders and others with a leadership role; in short, those with the power and resources to sanction and make such provision operational and to provide a mechanism to scaffold sustainability. Along with leadership guru Peter Senge, we define leaders as people who 'lead through developing new skills, capabilities and understandings. And they come from many places in the organisation' (Senge 1990: 15).

The 'leadership factor' has been shaped considerably by, for example, the observation and dissemination of practice that was developed over the years by the former influential Centre for Information on Language Teaching (CILT). Although it is no longer in existence, the legacy of this leading organisation endures in much of the established or developing primary languages practice in schools today, and good practice is still strongly pioneered by Scottish CILT and Northern Ireland CILT. Snapshots of leadership in primary languages that have been taken for this book show 'practice that works' and we explore the context of such practice, demonstrating the power of such leadership in working to ensure status for primary languages on a par with 'core subjects'.

The power of leadership

> Our children's development is poor in English. Learning a foreign language does not help this factor and adds to the learning failure of some children.

> We are striving to raise academic achievement in the core subject areas and our timetable reflects this. We would find it difficult to accommodate yet another subject area without compromising existing provision.

> The pressures on staff to deliver an ever-changing curriculum mean that there is little energy to develop foreign language learning unless there is consistent long-term support.

Teachers with experiences of previous, but not always satisfactory, early language-learning experiments have expressed concerns regarding the teaching of primary language learning and its sustainability in light of the pressures cited. Leadership has to attend to views that are similar to those of the three heads quoted above on language development, and set aside the time and energy to innovate. Fortunately, there are many teachers and heads who have offered different, more positive arguments:

> Languages are essential for life. A curriculum is incomplete without languages. I insisted on two languages with Spanish first as a condition of being appointed to the headship.

> We ensure languages are central to all we do. This not only means our traditional French – and some Spanish – but also looking at the backgrounds, cultures and languages of the children we have from many other parts of the world.

In recent years many leaders, with their different yet interlinking primary MFL stakeholders, be they schools or training institutions, for example, have made primary foreign language learning happen and have put it indelibly in the curriculum of many a primary school, as we mentioned in the Introduction. Sharpe (2001: 198), perhaps presciently, argued for 'an overall policy of gradualism rather than a "big bang" approach to making MFL a statutory part of the National Curriculum.' It can be seen that the early language-learning experience has, indeed, been shepherded into the KS2 curriculum on a very gentle temporal gradient, but it is now, at last, in situ.

The central role of the head as a driving force

Leadership and headship should not be seen as synonymous, nor is it true to say that leadership is a prerogative of headteachers alone, although the role of the head is essential. When asked about the 'push' factor behind one school's successful venture into early language learning – Spanish in this case – across the school, a languages consultant/adviser we interviewed replied 'Headteacher, headteacher, headteacher!' The headteacher's own perspective is that she empowered others: 'I acted as a catalyst and supported those teachers who were enthusiastic about foreign language teaching. Personally, I hardly know any Spanish!'

Barth (1990) refers to a 'community of leaders' having the potential for shared leadership. A more shared or distributed pattern of leadership can help to secure a measure of sustainability where primary language learning is fragile. Without it, the 'bang' of recent enthusiasm might be in danger of dissipating. In essence, though, nothing happens without the active support of headteachers, who have the 'position power' and the resource power to enable early foreign language learning to become a vital part of their school's curriculum.

The subject leader – manager of the internal and external environments

Effective subject leadership becomes all the more important if headteachers do not have any foreign language capability. The focus on middle management and 'leading from the middle' recognises the importance of the subject leader as a key agent of change as well as for school improvement, and research such as Fullan (1991, 1993) and Harris (2003) has demonstrated unequivocally that leadership is central to achieving these missions. Subject leaders might be considered as lead professionals, with a significant role in helping colleagues to develop subject expertise as well as demonstrating best practice in their subject. This is a much-needed function in primary MFL. A subject leader in one of the schools we visited situated on the south coast had developed her confidence in primary MFL over the years and was clear about how she was now able to offer differentiated support to colleagues:

> Some teachers are still scared of foreign languages and even if they have a certain level of competence themselves they don't want to display their lack of competence in front of children. I suppose it's a bit like singing, some people like to do it, some people don't apart from when they're in a car. Different teachers need different support and they also need different levels of support.

This subject leader defined her role thus: 'to monitor the provision of MFL in the school, to standardise the provision for the children and to ensure progression.' This definition of the role reflects very well the mentoring, managing and monitoring dimensions of a subject leader's role as identified in the research undertaken by Busher and Harris (2000), and reflects the five interlocking processes that, they maintain, are the hallmark of effective planning and help to create an effective subject area. The five processes are:

- working with staff
- establishing baselines; measuring current performance
- having a clear vision of where to go
- creating sensible maps, timetables and ladders to achieve the preferred goals
- devising a means of monitoring progress on the road to achieving the goals (target setting).

The job description for a primary language subject leader will comprise all of these dimensions, with a focus on the concerns of teaching, learning, assessment, staff management and resources in the internal arena of the school as well as connecting to external links such as partner secondary schools, parental contact and the community at large. A new subject leader saw her job very much in these terms, describing her responsibilities as being:

> To plan a French curriculum overview at the start of the year, make term plans with learning objectives, provide an overview of the learning and key vocabulary in French each term for parents to take home, make resources to support learning, mark books, create displays across the school, monitor learners' progress and assessment, write year group reports, attend parents' meetings, plan secondary-school liaison and show the value of French to the whole school. I absolutely love my role in the school and very much enjoy teaching MFL across the years.

Monitoring is the dimension that can cause anxiety. However, as one subject leader argued, where there is planning that includes the class teachers, a simple system of recording pupil progress and peer observation opportunities, the monitoring is in essence all about sharing and dialogue. An experienced London teacher commented on the supportive and instructional function of the subject leader in respect of monitoring:

> In a culture of accountability and increased observation, it is less threatening for teachers to be observed by the languages coordinator who isn't part of the senior leadership team. Teachers are more likely to take risks, which is a good thing as it then opens them up to richer opportunities for learning rather than 'playing it safe', which they may feel they should do if being observed by the SLT [Senior Leadership Team] and especially with a view to performance management.

Having identified the key role of leadership and emphasised the importance of sharing leadership, let us at this point situate the full range of leadership in the context of a school. The following case study is a snapshot in which the headteacher and others with leadership responsibilities for primary MFL learning and teaching demonstrate what leadership looks like in a real-life primary-school context. It provides valuable data for highlighting issues concerning leadership. The school that is spotlighted has a vibrant, continuously evolving and evidently sustainable provision, and is illuminative of key issues that are important in developing and sustaining an effective provision – issues supported by a considerable canon of research (Fullan 1991; Fullan and Hargreaves 1992; Hammersley-Fletcher, 2005; MacBeath 1998; Sergiovanni 2001; Stoll and Fink 1996).

Case study: the 'ancient mariner's' tale

The school is a mixed primary school located in a medium-sized town where unemployment is high. Of the 200-plus pupils on roll, its register of Additional Support Needs (a term the school used in preference to Special Educational Needs) shows some 40 per cent of children in need of support for learning or behavioural difficulties. The school represents an oasis of learning and calm behaviour for many children with unsettled backgrounds and has invested heavily in literacy support. The current headteacher, who has been in post for some years, is a confirmed Francophile herself; indeed she sets the tone for language learning. As the school is church aided, she begins the day with greetings and prayers in French in whole-school assembly. Pupils respond with their return greeting in French.

A previous head, with great vision and before the primary MFL initiative of the last decades, introduced French to pupils in the late 1960s. This was not due to the national pilot project at the time but was based solely on the head's belief that pupils could benefit from learning and enjoying French in the way that he had done as part of his time in the merchant navy. After the retirement of the charismatic 'ancient mariner', the French experiment remained operational yet unsystematic, although successive heads reacted favourably to sustaining the primary French project.

The current head consolidated the previous patchy provision of language learning for Years 5 and 6 and extended provision to the whole school, including Year 1 pupils. The deputy head, the leader for early years, oversaw this move into KS1 and 2. The provision has grown organically, very much in graduated form, as teachers have developed confidence and have planned an ever-developing scheme of work together. It is a developmental process that we recommend. The primary MFL coordinator has been both a KS1 and KS2 teacher. All teachers, for the most part, teach their own classes, using locally produced course materials supplemented by an array of additional resources bought by the school or made by the teachers themselves. The coordinator has attended external training sessions and all teachers have had some in-house training and support.

Recent appointments to posts at the school have been made in open competition, taking into consideration candidates' qualifications for MFL gained during their school careers and their teacher training. A former chair of governors who was an MFL teacher educator supported the launch of the language-learning enterprise and initially coached the Key Stage 2 teachers. She organised an Easter holiday project connected to some aspect of cultural learning and including some language work, attracting some 80 children's efforts on a project about Belgium, for example, a tradition that has been sustained by other governors. While French is the main language taught, some pupils get bursts of Spanish and German when their teachers have knowledge of these languages, and there is spontaneous enrichment from parents and visitors in the form of, for example, Romanian, Polish, Bulgarian and Dutch. The school's input to training future teachers of primary languages is considerable. In any one year, the school has several trainee teachers on various training routes, as well as trainees from France as part of the reciprocal training arrangements of a local teacher-training institution.

All teachers are enabled, through the support of the subject leader, to make an input of a progressive and cyclical nature; for example, the younger children learn greetings in French just as they practise greetings in English as a social activity in class. Sometimes they do this activity in a circle-time activity as part of their Personal, Social and Health Education (PSHE) programme. Greetings are recycled continuously as children move up the school and are extended to other languages and to more complex varieties of expression. The headteacher is an opportunist. A graduate MFL trainee who is a native speaker was asked to provide a 'lifesaver' of target language commands for all staff. Native-speaking French trainees have been asked to make signs in French for posting around the school. A French-speaking Belgian parent living opposite the school has coached the teachers in pronunciation and simple phrases in after-school sessions. One teacher has some Spanish and another some German, so these languages, rather precariously, have been added to the linguistic menu, 'extra spice' as it were that could, arguably, be left out of the recipe. French predominates for historical reasons and because of the headteacher's active support of French.

Crucially in terms of primary–secondary liaison, an MFL teacher, the head of department from one of the local secondary schools, comes in to work collaboratively with the Key Stage 2 teachers and to teach Year 6 children occasionally. This provides an opportunity to share good practice as well as provide a platform for continuity of provision from Key Stage 2 to Key Stage 3. Leadership is enacted by many members of staff in their different but complementary roles. Nonetheless, the headteacher is pivotal in her central role as project leader, as shown in the web of leadership diagram (Figure 2.1). This is one model of dispersed leadership and there are, of course, many other variations, but the point we are making is that this type of leadership and its scope make language provision resilient.

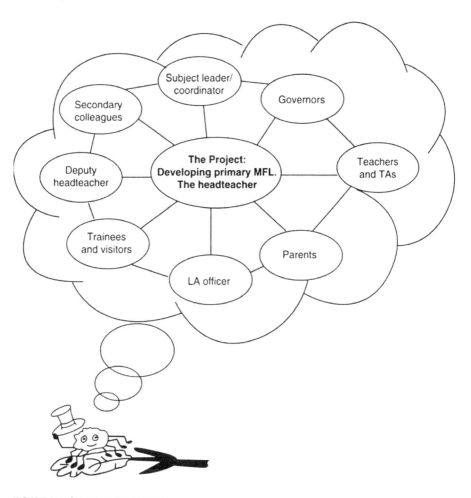

FIGURE 2.1 School leadership web

Let us now elaborate the 'who does what, why and how' in terms of leadership. Table 2.1 shows a breakdown of roles in tabular form.

TABLE 2.1 The who, why and how of leadership in the case-study school

Lead role – who?	Motivation – why?	How leadership is demonstrated
Headteacher	Personal 'crusade' on behalf of all the pupils deriving from own experiences of travel	Whole-school drip-feed approach and international mindset; use of position and resource power
Subject leader/ coordinator	Own enjoyment and belief in value of language learning for pupils	Lead subject teacher and coach to peers; professional development opportunities taken and shared with colleagues, e.g. new ideas and materials obtained and shared with colleagues in staff meetings
Deputy headteacher	Belief in opportunities for early years: commitment to inclusion	Primary MFL developed as part of basic skills and developing bi-literacy
Teachers and teaching assistants	Wish to have ownership of MFL teaching in their own classroom	Developing subject expertise over time with possibility to coach others: support for children with SEN and EAL children
Secondary-school teachers	To ensure coherence across key stages and cross-sector collaboration	Modelling subject expertise, both linguistic and pedagogical; sharing good practice
Governor	Belief in language learning as life opportunity	Provision of materials; support for projects; coaching; monitoring school development plan with regard to foreign language learning
Parents	Wish to be involved in life of school; one uses her foreign language competence to help staff lacking in confidence	Foreign language lessons by one parent for teachers with particular focus on pronunciation; others provide cultural artefacts and share knowledge
Trainee teachers and foreign visitors	Specialist subject provision in class	Class inputs and whole-school tasks such as notices around the school in French and German
Adviser/consultant	Strong belief in early language learning	Wide range of training provision, resources and one-to-one support

Leadership roles

Table 2.1 is not designed as a hierarchical list; it locates the head at the centre on account of her position of power. She also provides instructional leadership and leads by example using French incidentally throughout the school day and awarding foreign language stickers for good work, good effort, improvement, etc. The head works in tandem with the subject leader and with the deputy headteacher, who is responsible for the early years, and has involved children from Year 1 upwards in the project.

While excluding the Reception class children ('They have too much to learn at this stage and it [primary MFL] might bewilder them') Years 1 to 3 have a brief timetabled slot and teachers are asked to make incidental use of French. Since none of the other teachers are language specialists, the support of the subject leader is again essential to the successful teaching of French. The subject leader's role extends to coaching all colleagues at both key stages, teachers and teaching assistants (TAs), who are, in turn, expected to demonstrate dimensions of subject leadership in their classrooms. The contribution of TAs at all levels in supporting the children's language learning needs is invaluable and serves as important professional development for them. The leadership of the subject area at primary level is complemented by that of secondary colleagues who, where they have time and funding to be able to do so, visit the primary school to model and share subject expertise.

Some school governing bodies talk of a 'dream ticket' comprising accountants, lawyers and architects as useful people to have available to dispense 'free' advice. We could also add a governor linguist, or at least someone with a keen interest where primary MFL is concerned, as potentially very useful. However, a governor's role is often transitory and bound to a term of office so does not score over-highly on sustainability grounds, and as a result there is a limit to what governors can do. It would be ideal if the school could create a sustainable structure of governing support with, for example, one governor role attached to primary MFL, another to monitor and support primary–secondary liaison and perhaps a third to support the international dimension of the school. All these roles have an in-built dimension of leadership. In a similar way, the potential for parental leadership contribution will be dependent on the skills and knowledge parents can offer. A school could undertake a kind of 'audit' of the languages parents know actively and, in their quest to involve them in their children's learning of a foreign language, help parents to be able to practise with their children and identify any possible leadership role such as in the case-study school context.

A practical, working example of parents in partnership is that of a French-speaking Belgian parent who was on hand for support in this school over a sustained period of time. The teachers felt very comfortable practising pronunciation with her and she assumed a role in coaching the teachers. As she lives close to the school, this support has continued. The headteacher frequently welcomed visitors to the school, including a considerable number from continental European educational institutions wanting to come on study visits. Where primary MFL is buoyant in a school, the school acts as a magnet to potential visitors. In this case, where they were French- or German-speaking, they were asked to take a lead in certain events – in assembly, in MFL lessons, by designing materials – a good example of reciprocal support. Trainee teachers with an MFL specialism have also been asked to utilise their specialist knowledge for the benefit of the school and to take a 'bottom-up' lead.

The DfES (2004) research found conclusively that those local authorities with primary language coordinators or advisers had the most extensive and potentially sustainable practice. This was due to the wide range of resources they made available, the expert coaching and professional development on offer, the networking opportunities and the exuberance of colleagues in primary MFL leadership roles. Similarly, Wade and Marshall's research reported an 'increase in external support for language learning . . . with support from LAs and local networks having increased substantially' (2009: 31). Nowadays, this networking and support role is something that is being incorporated into academy conglomerations and learning trusts.

The leadership vision

What, then, can be inferred from this case study about ways in which leadership permeates and sustains the language-learning enterprise? How does leadership manifest itself with respect to primary MFL? How exactly does it support primary language learning? A key issue is the personal engagement of the headteacher and their leadership vision based on a strong personal commitment. When asked where her personal commitment came from, the subject coordinator of this school replied, 'Well, it's partly because I like France so much.' She continued: 'I think it is very restricting when people think they can get on in life just by speaking English. It's arrogant and it doesn't do much for a person's ability to communicate with other people.' A headteacher of a London school who taught Spanish to infants said: 'Languages are essential for life. There is more than one language, one culture. In this school we have many children from other cultures already speaking other languages.'

In Chapter 1, we looked at factors in favour of an early language-learning opportunity. These positions have been more than adequately debated over the years and a measure of consensus has been achieved as to the value of the enterprise: positive attitudes towards foreign language learning and towards other cultures, linguistic sensitivity, cultural awareness and enjoyment in learning. What is striking in the testimonies of the case-study headteacher is the 'bigger picture' vision for the learners: 'Learning French opens horizons. The world is theirs. Learning a language enables them to have greater opportunities.' The desire to introduce children to the joys of foreign language learning derives in part from a personal successful and enjoyable voyage into 'otherness' by those involved in leading the project. As the headteacher said, echoing the feelings of her subject leader:

> I didn't enjoy learning French at school and couldn't see the point, but then we started to spend our holidays in France and we have friends who live there and I think it is rude not to know something of the language and the culture.

Here we have a Francophile headteacher who now enjoys learning the language herself and visiting France, as does the school's subject leader. It is clear from this example and from what we know about the importance of directive, visionary leadership that the personal drive of the head is a key motivating factor in successfully embedding MFL into the fabric of a school. MFL provision might also be influenced by an opera-loving Italophile or indeed a person with no specific predilection for a particular country and language but simply – and this is the essential ingredient – a desire to broaden the cultural and linguistic horizons of the school, its pupils and staff.

While joyous and inspiring, visions need to be made concrete and operational. As Trethowan (1991: 3) wrote: 'There must be absolute clarity in the leader's mind about what constitutes the key features of the vision. The vision has to be hard, well thought out, practical . . . related to time and place.' The leaders have to take decisions about who will teach, how they will teach, what they will teach, which language and what time allocation will be given. Furthermore, leaders need to decide what they will use to support their teaching and how to monitor and assess teaching and learning. They also need to take into consideration means to ensure progression and how they will interpret the KS2 NC (2014) in a way that matches the needs and resources of the school, and be quite clear about the value of the enterprise. Schools have adopted different ways of incorporating primary languages provision into the curriculum, but at the heart of the model there needs to be a clear delineation of learning purpose and systematic arrangements for supporting and assessing the learning, leadership and a shared learning culture. On a recent round of visits for this third edition of the book, it was found that every school had its own unique arrangements, all of them very idiosyncratic but essentially in harmony with their own particular culture.

The school culture – a culture of learning together

Each school is unique and creates, based on its own way of organising itself, its individual culture. A school culture at its simplest is, as Nias *et al.* (1989: 181) wrote: 'influenced by particular sets of circumstances (for example buildings, personnel, organizational arrangements) and expressed in special ways (for example through language, rituals and symbols)' or quite simply: 'the way we do it here' (ibid: 15).

The case-study school has an identifiable culture of learning together and specifically one that celebrates language learning. The research of Jennifer Nias and colleagues in primary schools emphasised the importance of a 'warm' culture in which to innovate and create, for it is not so much the bearing of the individual headteacher but rather the creation of a culture that promotes development and innovation. Sometimes elements of a school culture that are stable and resistant to change can be positive factors, as with the upholding of the tradition of teaching French initiated some 50 years ago in the case-study school. Sometimes this stability can be problematic, in that many individuals prefer to stay within their 'comfort zone' and will resist innovation and change, especially if they are not convinced that it will be of benefit or if they do not have ownership of the change. Other aspects of the school culture, such as planned curriculum development, policy construction and professional development, are manageable and more susceptible to change, especially where the critical mass of staff is involved in the development from the early stages of planning. A top-down management approach never really works in any circumstances, but then a solely 'bottom-up' approach is not without its difficulties either, as is known from cases where teachers were enthusiastic about foreign language teaching but the headteacher remained sceptical.

It has long been recognised that leaders create cultures, and that creating a culture for learning is crucial. A primary language-learning scenario is likely to be a learning experience for many of the teachers and others involved in terms of linguistic and pedagogical competence, for enthusiasm alone takes one only so far and cannot be a sound basis for sustainable learning. However, teachers who are motivated by the experience of their own learning are likely to excite their pupils in turn. Such enthusiasm is tangible in the subject leader and the headteacher in the case-study school. A learning-centred head will give strong messages about learning and professional development and will seek to develop what Sergiovanni (2001) calls 'leadership density' and Continuous Professional Learning (CPL) opportunities to build capacity for leadership of learning. The research of Earley and Weindling (2004) included ten case studies of highly effective heads which showed without exception that headteachers paid great attention to the development of leadership capacity throughout the school. Middle managers or coordinators, for example, gained confidence and shaped the rest of the staff's perceptions of them as experts in their fields. Leadership can thus be defined as 'that part of a manager's work concerned with helping people to tackle prescribed tasks to the optimum of their ability' (Day *et al.* 1998: 41).

The case-study school subject leader has risen to the challenge and, having been encouraged and empowered by the headteacher, now feels able to coach her colleagues in their classrooms and assume the role of leader of learning.

To summarise, features of a school culture conducive to developing sustainable primary MFL provision include:

- receptivity to experimentation on the part of the teachers;

- active encouragement by, and involvement of, the headteacher;

- a 'slowly but surely' approach where all can engage with innovation at their own pace;

- collaborative learning at an organisational level coupled with differentiated provision as needed;

- empowering staff through the development of leadership skills and opportunities to share leadership;

- creating a network of support, both within the school and beyond, by engaging with higher education institutions (HEI), other schools and the school community;

- a deep-seated wish to provide opportunities to 'expand horizons' and to move beyond the parochial.

An international mindset and valuing diversity

The notion of 'expanding horizons', though well-intentioned and sincere, can be a very nebulous concept and yet the intercultural dimension, or what can be called the 'international mindset', in accordance with Paige and Meisterhauser (1999), has, arguably, never been so important in primary schools. As the headteacher of the case-study school commented, never before have children been forced to be so politically aware or to begin to understand their developing role as active citizens in a European and global context.

This head and the subject leader travel extensively and enjoy other cultures and, with their colleagues, capitalise on the cultural diversity of the school, the increasing diversity of language and cultures incoming children bring and the many visitors from abroad who enrich the school's cultural fabric and language-learning environment. Such a 'border-free leadership' perspective implies that, in the cosmopolitan school, school leaders will have to engage creatively with international issues, not just local ones, and develop an 'international mindset', articulating a vision that meets the needs of learners from all over the world. In this one small primary school, there are such learners: 'We have children from across the world . . . Italy, France, and bilingual families from North Africa . . . Dutch, Japanese, Romanian, Bulgarian, children from all sorts of cultural backgrounds.'

As Cable *et al.* (2010) assert, the promotion of primary MFL in itself is a way to explicitly value diversity. While the children's languages, cultures and heritages are already welcomed and celebrated, and the parents invited as much as possible into the school, part of this school's international project is to consider how to exploit further the languages that the children have as part of a language-learning project that goes beyond the teaching of French. When school leaders actively develop an international mindset they 'walk their talk'. They enjoy and encourage travel, real or virtual, and provide opportunities for the learners to experience such enjoyment, with trips and exchanges, e-links and participation in Comenius projects (now Erasmus+), other EU-funded actions, or town-twinning links. As such, leaders and teachers can relate the project to the cultures and languages of the children in the school community. In so doing, school leaders become part of the international community of leadership.

Where projects are concerned, schools need to fully exploit international networking to develop their own skills and strengthen provision in their own schools. One teacher commented on how this is not automatic:

> We have peripatetic teachers coming into school to do the languages teaching, the head insists on this. But we have lots of our teachers involved in Comenius projects and travel all over Europe meeting other teachers but even so the teachers haven't really embraced language learning. The teachers themselves need to be actively involved in speaking and teaching the language for the whole-school commitment to MFL to work.

Conclusion

This chapter has sought to underline the importance of leadership in the development of primary MFL, to define and illustrate the concept of shared leadership and to emphasise the importance of planning for sustainability in order to avoid the disappointment of primary MFL remaining on the margin through a lack of key leadership skills. A successful primary MFL project is a whole-school enterprise. Primary MFL has crept into the primary curriculum like an ivy plant and has developed secure roots that are important for sustainability. Sustainability, we are asserting, derives from developing leadership skills and sharing leadership to create a kind of leadership web that provides different levels of support and expertise, for as DuFour and Marzano (2011: 2) write: 'No single person has the knowledge, skills and talents . . . to meet all the needs of all the children.'

All schools will have some, if not all, of the human resources available as in the case study. Some dimensions of shared leadership form a solid resource basis for the important decision-making about primary MFL policy and the implementation of policy and provision.

Some schools' arrangements are fragile because of a lack of secure leadership, especially subject leadership scaffolding, which may mean that the metaphorical ivy could easily lose its grip. This has happened in many a secondary school where second and/or third languages (usually languages other than French) in particular have disappeared. This is especially true in cases where all the subject expertise was invested in one person. Sustainability needs to be considered from the very start of the project and become part of the school, staff and governor development/improvement/learning plan. Being involved in teacher training and ensuring primary languages teachers' subject knowledge is a huge step in future sustainability.

As with any new subject or project, leadership is necessary not just to maintain but also to sustain, enhance and develop the project. Some heads and other leaders prioritise the development of primary MFL as a performance objective and/or as part of their leadership training. In so doing, they illustrate the concept of leadership as learning and establish themselves as lead learners in their primary MFL learning community.

Questions on which to reflect

- What are the key factors in planning for sustainable effective primary MFL provision?
- Look at a particular school with which you are associated and identify the leadership web. Who are the leaders and what do they lead on? Where is leadership lacking, or where could it be improved?
- How can leadership skills and capability be developed to undertake the roles needed to support a strong web?

Planning and use of resources: doing the groundwork

In this chapter we will consider how to approach planning MFL teaching and learning. Planning issues that we discuss are those of setting achievable targets – learning intentions or objectives – and using resources effectively. We will suggest ways in which teachers can improvise and adapt material from different sources, not forgetting that the greatest resources available are the teacher and the pupils themselves. We use the metaphor of the Russian doll to emphasise the interconnected nature of micro- and macro-planning and we include examples of lesson plans and schemes of work to illustrate the mesh between learning objectives and the integrated use of resources within short-, medium- and longer-term planning.

Key issues

- ■ MFL is most effectively delivered when teaching is embedded within a longer-term view to ensure cohesion and progression.

- ■ As with other subjects, it is important that teachers are sympathetic with the aims and objectives that constitute the scheme of work and that these are meaningfully conveyed to pupils.

- ■ Resources are overwhelmingly identified by primary teachers as the most important factor in enabling them to teach MFL in primary schools (DfES Report 572, 2004; Wade and Marshall 2009).

- ■ The single most important resource in MFL teaching is the teacher and the quality of the teacher–pupil relationship.

- ■ As teachers' confidence in MFL teaching grows they become less dependent on following prepared material and can instigate activities and adapt materials more freely.

- ■ Primary teachers' expertise in using age-appropriate techniques and adapting resources for cross-curricular purposes means they are especially well placed to adapt MFL material to suit the particular needs of pupils.

Introduction

In recent years a plethora of MFL materials has become available on the market, especially via the internet (see Chapter 8 for more on this and other applications of technology). Many resources offer familiar learning trajectories but familiar characters and storylines are dusted down and revamped or completely rewritten for the twenty-first century. For example, instead of the classic French 'prototype' family, *Les Dupont*, that many of us were familiar with from our textbooks of the 1960s and 1970s, children today are more likely to be presented with the daily routines, likes and dislikes of *La famille Simpson* or footballers and pop singers presented in colourful moving images. Despite these changes and many developments in our understanding of child learning, however, the pedagogic rationale underlying many of the MFL materials available has not changed fundamentally and many activities that can be seen today in a primary MFL lesson might have been seen 30 or 40 years ago. Does the abundance of good-quality materials blind us to what the learning objectives really are in primary MFL? In this chapter we will look at ways of approaching planning that include setting achievable targets, considerations affecting which new language to present, how to present a new language, how to encourage pupil participation in a way that maximises ownership of the new language, and the use of different resources that contribute to whole-child skills development for early learners.

Defining resources

A broad definition of resources includes all support material that is used to help teachers plan and coordinate pupil learning within and away from the classroom. We are including here the syllabus or scheme of work that the teacher has been asked or has chosen to follow, or that they have created themselves. The terms 'resources' and 'materials' are often used interchangeably to refer to any of the 'props' that might be used in the MFL class, such as picture cards, posters, clothes, toys, cue cards, worksheets, books, display items, songs, videoclips, etc. (Internet resources and activities will be dealt with separately in Chapter 8.) Resources can be used in the classroom by the teacher, by the whole class, by pairs, groups and individual pupils. When used by the teacher they often function as demonstration props, and we will see later in this chapter how new language might be presented.

The scheme of work is a resource in that it functions as a framework that shapes and guides teachers' planning of *what* is to be taught, *when* (in sequence) and (in a good scheme of work at least) suggestions of *how* it will be included. In our view, the scheme of work is a bank of ideas best used when dipped into and tailored to personal preference and particular pupil needs rather than followed slavishly. The conventional structure of an MFL scheme of work is discussed below and an approach to planning is suggested starting from lessons and building up to medium (termly), long (yearly) and whole-school schemes of work. Although we present the lesson first as a minimum unit of planning, in reality it is the longer-term overarching objectives that will form the starting point when planning MFL learning. The different levels of planning mesh together like a Russian doll. The end product is the classroom teaching and learning but this is encased in broader frames of planning that ensure coherence, variety and balance.

As with any other resource material, the scheme of work is there to provide guidelines and suggestions as a support mechanism. It is a mixed blessing that MFL is not always formally assessed in primary schools, but this does mean that teachers usually have greater autonomy in deciding what, when and how MFL should be taught than, say, maths and English teachers (although there is increasing flexibility in these areas, too). This broader definition of resources was highlighted by the DfES Research Report (2004) into MFL provision at KS2, showing that 'local or in-house schemes of work' are the most popular syllabus plans, used by 34 per cent of respondents. These have often been adapted themselves from existing LA/QCA (later Qualifications and Curriculum Development Agency (QCDA)) or coursebook-based schemes in the light of practitioners' experiences and beliefs as well as other localised circumstances such as material and time constraints. Cable *et al.* (2010) found that teachers and schools were increasingly using the Key Stage 2 Framework objectives and QCA Schemes of Work (2007, 2009) to structure planning, and our own more recent investigations show that existing schemes of work have been adapted over the years to accommodate the stipulations of the KS2 NC. Many teachers have adapted schemes of work and resources from popular websites.

FIGURE 3.1 Russian doll

Among the resources used in teaching MFL in the classroom, audio material was the most popular, used by over half of respondents. Audio resources (on DVDs, sound files or streamed through the internet) are often used for songs, but also to provide non-specialist classroom teachers with an authentic source of native-speaker quality target language that they can then use with the children as a listening activity, ensuring that pronunciation is accurate.

This use of audio material also highlights another valuable use for foreign language resources, which is the teacher's own linguistic development, away from pupils. Many teachers use pedagogic material to familiarise themselves with the language they are going to teach rather than use the resource with the children. In this way, the resource is an excellent teacher support (and means of professional development) and the children have the benefit of the language being presented 'live' by their teacher, which may help them feel more secure with new input in the early stages. Later, of course, exposure to a variety of new voices, including native-speaker voices, will greatly enhance phonic awareness and add a cultural dimension to the learning.

Resource dependency

Teachers will depend on resources in MFL teaching to differing degrees and will naturally adapt them to their own personal styles. As well as being a time issue, heavy resource dependency can be the result of teachers' lack of confidence. The teachers we spoke to when researching this book who used MFL-specific (commercially produced) resources the least were those who were either most confident in their use of the foreign language (often having studied it to degree level or to A-level) or, more importantly, those who had gained confidence through experience of teaching MFL and were now able to instigate activities more spontaneously using either materials not specific to MFL or by exploiting links to other subjects. These teachers had, over time, developed a repertoire of skills enabling them to use the patterns of language they were familiar with confidently and, with minimal or no resources, they were able to organise activities to encourage pupil engagement with the foreign language. This might be something as simple as spontaneously giving an instruction or counting heads in the foreign language, a last-minute game of hangman (*le pendu*) on the whiteboard at the end of the day or longer activities in the MFL slot such as role playing or singing without scripts.

The 'value added' of using resources in MFL

Since the 'fuzzy felt' of the 1960s and the audio-lingual approaches of the 1970s, MFL has often led the way in terms of innovative resources, and electronic resources now offer more support opportunities than ever, combining both sound and image. Nonetheless, the most essential resource by far is the teacher – their relationship with the children and their imagination in delivering MFL.

The teacher: the greatest resource of all

Primary MFL is now an expanding commercial market and there is an abundance of new resources available, some excellent and some not so good. While we recommend the use of good resources, it is essential that they are not seen as an end in themselves. Indeed, slick resources are, in our view, the *least* crucial element in the learning procedure. Before the level of resources, we would rank as important the various constituents that determine pupil motivation, chiefly the interpersonal quality of the pupil–teacher relationship, but also other variables such as teaching time (frequency of input), the value attributed to the subject (status within the school) and links to the whole-school experience (as discussed in Chapter 5). We cannot emphasise enough that the teacher is the greatest resource of all and that pupils themselves are resources for each other (see Chapter 7 on assessment). Nonetheless, attractive resources are, of course, intrinsically motivating and serve the needs of teachers. More importantly, curriculum planning must incorporate a range of activity types that will encourage both inclusion and real progression.

Planning

MFL provision, where provision is indeed *planned* to fit within a sequence of learning objectives rather than being random snippets added at the whim of an enthusiastic teacher, is often presented according to the topic. This fits in with the dominant theory in language teaching, which emphasises communicative language teaching (discussed in Chapter 5) and suggests that a 'logical' syllabus design reflects the following intersection: topic → language needed. The learning objectives thereby combine the functional outcomes of the topic (what the children *do* with the language) with the language perceived as facilitating this goal. The 'language needed' is often broken down into *key vocabulary* and *structure* (or grammar) and these can then be layered to form differentiated objectives. Learning objectives, of course, go beyond functional communicative needs and most programmes now recognise the importance of broader educational aims such as developing learning skills and intercultural awareness as well as dovetailing with cross-curricular learning.

The QCDA Schemes of Work for KS2 and the following Key Stage 2 Framework both proposed a 'curriculum design' around learning objectives that are skill-based rather than topic-based, and this focus on skills development has continued to drive the goals of the KS2 NC:

> By the end of each key stage, pupils are expected to know, apply and understand the matters, skills and processes specified in the relevant programme of study.
> (DfE, *Languages Programmes of Study: Key Stage 2*, 2014)

In the initial learning stages, language is often presented as single words alongside short formulaic phrases or chunks (greetings/introducing oneself/saying where one lives), and so the question of whether or not to 'teach' grammar (in the traditional sense of rules that are learnt and applied) does not arise. Most language phrases are therefore treated as 'vocabulary' in the sense of discrete lexical items. However, there remain questions around how much grammar should be taught explicitly and what type of grammar is relevant to primary MFL as this becomes increasingly linked to goals in the English curriculum, in particular how foreign language teaching maps onto the SPaG (Spelling, Punctuation and Grammar) objectives, especially with older children. With the holistic view of learning and curriculum development encouraging greater overlap and harmony both horizontally (across the primary curriculum) and vertically (across programmes of study for different key stages), it is useful to consider how explanations about language should be included. We use the term 'grammar' for this, a term that has now made a bold reappearance in the latest English and MFL programmes of study.

Planning: the issue of grammar

The question surrounding the teaching of grammar – i.e. how explicit it should be – is, like many such questions, something of a red herring. We do not advocate teaching mechanistic drills in MFL that have no contextually bound meaning (that is, beyond the context of children doing what they are told to as a classroom activity). However, we do believe that it is appropriate to explain to children how the language works if such an explanation is called for. In the same way as literacy teaching seeks to provide a basic toolkit for raising language awareness in English, so teaching 'language awareness' in MFL further reinforces this aim.

The word 'grammar' tends to have negative associations for many of us who remember feeling bewildered by abstract explanations of case and gender declensions – among other seemingly impenetrable concepts – yet the problem may have been that these concepts were often divorced from context and without immediate opportunity for real practice. Within any communicative approach to language teaching, the distinction between teaching 'grammar' and teaching 'language' or 'communication' becomes nonsensical as grammar is simply part-and-parcel of what a language is. Even if we wish to focus on the socio-functional aspects of the language we are teaching, it would be unrealistic to do this without ever referring to the rules that have been formulated to help explain which words go where and why.

The catchword is 'emphasis'. For example, if pupils have learnt to say 'I play football', 'I play basketball', etc. in Spanish, a logical next step might be, when discussing what the children did at the weekend, 'I played . . .' If we want to teach *jugué* (I played), children do not need to overtly learn rules about forming the preterite, radical-changing verbs, adding a *u* to keep the *g* 'hard' before an *e,* including the accent to conserve the syllabic stress in regular preterite verbs, etc. Clearly, such grammatical description is inappropriate in the early phases. To encourage the use of *jugué* we must convey a sense of 'pastness' to encourage pupils to use the word appropriately. One way to do this is to teach the words for today (*hoy*) and yesterday (*ayer*) and then miming and repeating:

> *Hoy juego al fútbol*
> *Ayer jugué al baloncesto.*

As pupils practise *juego* versus *jugué* they can be prompted by the words *hoy/ayer,* teacher hand movements suggesting now/in the past, pictures, dates on a calendar, etc. In this way pupils will arrive at their own translation of *jugué* without being confused and demotivated by cumbersome metalanguage, and, as they use the different forms more often, will naturally spot emerging patterns in the language they use. When this happens, some pupils may ask for explicit explanations: at such a time it is appropriate to help clarify rules explicitly for those pupils who wish to know them. Pupils themselves will start to identify patterns and should be encouraged to formulate rules when ready. This is what is meant by *inductive* grammar teaching. Since the first edition of this book, and especially since the implementation of SPaG in 2014, we have seen teachers use 'grammar words' such as noun, verb, and even 'agreement' with growing confidence as children's awareness of grammar develops in English.

Planning: what to include

As a starting point for planning, let us now turn to a simplified system of approach that incorporates the *topic–language–resources* trichotomy. This could be a first lesson and/or constitute a first section of a scheme of work. Taking the classic beginners' first topic 'greetings' in Spanish, Table 3.1 is an initial draft of what might be included.

These rubrics may need further breaking down. We have stated the overall topic, but what exactly do we want pupils to be able to *do* at the end of the learning sequence: i.e. what are the learning intentions? How long should the learning sequence be? How are we going to get them there? How do we know they have reached the set target? In other words, objectives need to be more precise. There is now a train of thought that would insist that primary MFL does not need to be so objectives-driven and that the overarching objective is to engender in pupils a positive attitude to language learning and an openness to language learning that will pave the way for later learning. We agree with this belief but would also argue that in order for progression to be assured and for MFL to be systematically embedded in the primary curriculum, language learning requires as much pedagogic planning as any other subject.

The objectives implicit in the topic used as an example here might be:

Pupils are able to do the following in Spanish:

- ■ Say hello;
- ■ Ask 'How are you?' in two different ways;
- ■ Respond appropriately using a range of adjectives to express fine/great/terrific/not too bad/not great!

TABLE 3.1 The topic–language–resources trichotomy

Topic	Language needed	Resources
Greetings	*¡Hola!*	Video clips showing Spanish people greeting each other.
	Buenos días *¿Qué tal?*	Smiley/grumpy/neutral faces to generate different answers.
	¿Cómo estás? Bien, gracias / muy bien / *fenomenal / bastante bien / fatal. ¿Y tú?*	

Inherent in these objectives lie other sets of expectations about the degree of accuracy in pronunciation, how quickly we expect pupils to be able to memorise the language and how soon we expect them to be able to produce the new language spontaneously. It is unlikely that all of the expressions given in the example could be covered in one lesson, even for older beginners. A first lesson for younger KS1 children might just focus on *¡Hola!* and *Buenos días* and practise these thoroughly before moving on.

Another objective to be added, especially for KS2 children, is the exploitation of the written form (receptively in reading or productively in writing), a contentious issue discussed in the next chapter. Similarly, it might be a good idea to introduce at the outset the more formal *¿Cómo está usted?* to sensitise pupils to different forms of address in other languages. This encourages sociolinguistic awareness, which is the foundation for adapting language 'for different purposes and audiences' (DfE, *Languages Programmes of Study: Key Stage 2*, 2014).

The decisions surrounding these objectives may be taken by regular class teachers, but unless they are also MFL specialists they will usually seek the guidance of the MFL coordinator and a scheme of work. As teachers' confidence and experience grow they will naturally adapt their objectives to the pupils they know and what they understand to be manageable and useful. In other words, teachers develop an intuition for MFL pedagogy.

As well as topic, we would expect to find that the scheme of work or syllabus would explicitly list the core language to be taught, e.g.:

> Topic: Greetings
> Learning outcomes: Pupils can understand and say 'Hello' in Spanish
> Language needed: *¡Hola!*

Let us move on to *how* these objectives can be achieved, bearing in mind that planning is circular and that methods and resources can be negotiated and modified as objectives become fine-tuned or reoriented once personal preferences, as well as logistics, come into play. In the example above we have listed a couple of resources that might be used for this simple interactional language but, of course, none is necessary! The language can be presented by a teacher and practised by pupils without any other resources. The QCDA Scheme of Work (2007), for example, suggested simply moving around the class and shaking hands with pupils to introduce 'Hello' in the foreign language. Pupils then greet each other using the new words. This is a useful suggestion and reminds us that, in terms of resources, simplicity is often the cornerstone. In the lesson plan exemplar given below, children use finger puppets to practise saying *Guten Morgen* to each other. Similarly, exaggerated facial expressions, intonation patterns and thumbs-up/down gestures can be used to convey *bien, muy bien, fatal,* etc. as effectively as pictures, to convey meaning and to gauge the level of understanding (see Chapter 7 on assessment issues).

Examples of lesson plans and a scheme of work

At the level of lesson plans, we need to consider how much is appropriate for the pupils' level. Let us look at some examples of how the broad-brush objectives mentioned above can be broken down and built into lesson plans, which then fit into a medium-term (one school term) scheme of work and then into a whole-school plan. These thoughtful examples were borrowed from a primary teacher (MFL specialist) in the north of England. Firstly, we see how she has planned two initial 20-minute lessons for Year 1 beginners in German (Table 3.2). We are then able to see how these two lesson plans fit into a medium-term plan or scheme of work (corresponding with seven 20-minute lessons or one school half-term) (Table 3.3). A London teacher finds the model of a four-part lesson the most effective, as described here:

> Using the target language all the time, I start with a warm-up revision activity to link to the previous lesson. I then organise table group games to practise those points. Next I do the new input, for about seven minutes; new vocabulary is always in sentences. Next the children do a task in their books and they know presentation is very important. I typically finish the lesson with a song.

As we can see, less is more in primary MFL in terms of the content objectives. These remain modest, certainly in the early stages, but are such that they ensure maximum interactional value in the foreign language; for example greetings, dialogues, class instructions, numbers and colours, all of which can be used authentically almost from the start. We can also see how differentiation has been built into the pupil learning outcomes. A long-term (whole-school) plan might appear as in Table 3.4.

The long-term plan shows revision as well as clear progression. The plan is not set in stone but retains some flexibility. It shows how certain topics are determined by the time of the year and cross-cultural opportunities that can be exploited (more on this in Chapter 9). For Spanish, it would be appropriate to introduce *el turrón* as a Christmas treat or maybe to celebrate any of the many regional feast days (for example San Isidro, San Ponç), when covering dates and the calendar (and for French *le poisson d'avril* and *le quatorze juillet*, etc.). In italics, we have shown the key story texts that can be covered, one each year starting from Year 2, and we discuss the use of stories in MFL in the next chapter on teaching language skills.

Conclusion

In this chapter we have suggested an approach to planning MFL using the *topic–language–resources* trichotomy, which then needs to be further broken down into specific learning intentions and lesson objectives. We have emphasised the circular nature of planning, with localised circumstances (pupils, resources, capacity) shaping our learning goals. Furthermore, pupil performance will feed into and direct our ongoing planning, as it must within the constructivist framework of formative assessment (discussed in Chapter 7). Short- and long-term planning, fitting together like a Russian doll, are essential in MFL, as with other areas of the curriculum, to ensure variety of resources, balance of activity, clear and focused direction and pupil progression.

TABLE 3.2 German lesson plan

GREETINGS AND INTRODUCTIONS (1)

Lesson plans for Y1 German beginners. Two 20-minute lessons.

Week	Key objectives	Key structures and vocabulary	Teaching activities (20 minutes)	Resources	Expected outcomes	Links
1	■ Know that Germans often shake hands when greeting people. ■ Be able to say *Guten Morgen* with good pronunciation. ■ Look forward with confidence to next German lesson.	*Guten Morgen!* *Ganz still bitte!*	1 Greet individually with handshake, *GM* and a smile. 2 Shake hands. 3 Echo my *GM* in lots of different voices, and sing to tune of *Alleluja*, which emphasises syllables. 4 Teach children how to respond to *Ganz still bitte*. 5 Hand out puppets to each child for them to say *GM* with a partner. 6 Choose volunteers to show their role play to the class.	A finger puppet for each child.	Children will be able to use a finger puppet to say *GM* to a partner. Some children will show this to their class.	Cultural awareness of hand-shaking.
2	■ Be able to pick out the words *GM* from among the other words of a song.	*Guten Morgen!*	1 Class echo my *GM*, using different voices. 2 Children say *GM* and shake hands of people nearby. 3 Listen to Detlev Jöcker's *GM* song from CD. Encourage children to count number of times they hear *GM*. Repeat as necessary. 4 Listen to song again and join in with the *GM*s. 5 Invite individuals to say *GM* to me. 6 Pass round teddies. Children say *GM* to each one before they pass it on. 7 Play Jöcker song again. 8 CD can be left with class teacher to be played at other opportunities before next lesson.	CD player and 'Start German with a Song' CD by Detlev Jöcker, track 1, 'Guten Morgen'. Selection of friendly teddies.	Children will be able to join in singing the *GM* parts of the song. Some children will be confident enough to greet me individually in front of the class. Leave CD with class teacher for 'passive' listening opportunities before next lesson.	Turn-taking. Pair work.

TABLE 3.3 Medium-term plan

GREETINGS AND INTRODUCTIONS (1)

Medium-term plans for Y1 German beginners. Thirteen 20-minute lessons. Part 1, Lessons 1 to 7: Greetings

Week	Key objectives	Key structures and vocabulary	Teaching activities (20 minutes)	Resources	Expected outcomes	Links
1	▪ Know Germans often shake hands when greeting people. ▪ Be able to say *Guten Morgen* with good pronunciation. ▪ Look forward with confidence to next German lesson.	***Guten Morgen!*** ***Ganz still bitte!***	1 Greet individually with handshake, *GM* and a smile. 2 Shake hands. 3 Echo my *GM* in lots of different voices, and sing to tune of *Alleluja*, which emphasises syllables. 4 Teach children how to respond to *Ganz still bitte*. 5 Hand out puppets to each child for them to say *GM* with a partner. 6 Choose volunteers to show their role play to the class.	A finger puppet for each child.	Children will be able to use a finger puppet to say *GM* to a partner. Some children will show this to their class.	Cultural awareness of hand-shaking.
2	▪ Be able to pick out the words *GM* from among the other words of a song.	***Guten Morgen!***	1 Class echo my *GM*, using different voices. 2 Children say *GM* and shake hands of people nearby. 3 Listen to Detlev Jöcker's *GM* song from CD. Encourage children to count number of times they hear *GM*. Repeat as necessary. 4 Listen to song again and join in with the *GM*s. 5 Invite individuals to say *GM* to me. 6 Pass round teddies. Children say *GM* to each one before they pass it on.	CD player and 'Start German with a Song' CD by Detlev Jöcker, track 1, '*Guten Morgen*'. Selection of friendly teddies.	Children will be able to join in singing the *GM* parts of the song. Some children will be confident enough to greet me individually in front of the class. Leave CD with class teacher for 'passive' listening opportunities before next lesson.	Turn-taking. Pair work.

continued . . .

TABLE 3.3 *Continued*

Week	Key objectives	Key structures and vocabulary	Teaching activities (20 minutes)	Resources	Expected outcomes	Links
			7 Play Jöcker song again. 8 CD can be left with class teacher to be played at other opportunities before next lesson.			
3	■ Know *GM* is suitable only for the morning. ■ Know there are other greetings, which can be used according to the time of day. ■ Begin to join in with parts of the Jöcker song other than *GM*.	***Guten Morgen!*** ***Guten Tag!*** ***Guten Abend!*** ***Gute Nacht!*** ***Hier ist 'Grüne Spinne'!***	1 Greet the children with *GM* and soft spider toy *Grüne Spinne*, whose leg they can shake as they pass him round and greet him! 2 Discuss what if it were a different time of day. Consider English greetings we could use. (Be aware that children may not be fully familiar with all English formal greetings.) 3 Use pictures to represent morning, afternoon, evening and night. Check children are very clear about which picture is for which. 4 Children echo my *GM, GT, GA, GN* in a variety of voices, showing appropriate picture. 5 Finish with *GM* song from CD. Children join in what they can, by listening to CD and watching my mouth shapes as sing along.	Soft toy with arms or legs to shake. Pictures representing morning, afternoon, evening and night. Jöcker CD and player.	Children will confidently shake hands and say *GM* to the new soft toy. Children will know English and be aware of German expressions for greetings at different times of day. Children will begin to imitate all words in the *GM* song, without necessarily understanding them yet.	Literacy links with knowledge about formal aspects of their own language. Links in CD to *Wie geht's* part of topic Lesson 8 onwards.

38

	Learning objectives	Key language	Activities	Resources	Expected outcomes	
4	▪ Pronounce *GM, GT, GA, GN* with clarity and good pronunciation. ▪ Learn new song. ▪ Know how to order greetings according to time of day.	*GM!* *GT!* *GA!* *GN!* *Ganz still bitte!*	1 Greet with *GM* or *GT*, as appropriate. 2 Teach new song *GM, GT, GA, GN* to tune of *Frère Jacques*, with children filling in the echoed parts. 3 Look at pictures from last session and order according to time of day, asking children to name clues in picture that help us know which is which. 4 Sing new song, pointing to picture which corresponds to words as they are sung. 5 Remind children how to respond to *Ganz still bitte!* 6 Hand out finger puppets. Children work with a partner to get their finger puppets to greet each other at four different times of day. 7 Confident pairs show their role plays.	Pictures. One finger puppet per child.	Children will be able to join in with the echoed parts of the new song. Children will be keen to do a finger puppet role play, and some children will be confident enough to show it to the class. Pictures and some puppets can be left in a *Deutsche Ecke* in the classroom for further informal opportunities for practice before next lesson.	Order pics according to times of day.
5	▪ Begin to sing *GM, GT, GA, GN* song independently. ▪ Learn a new game, *Sprich oder schweig*. ▪ As individuals, say the four greetings with confidence and accuracy.	*GM!* *GT!* *GA!* *GN!* *Noch mal! Jetzt wollen wir 'Sprich oder schweig' spielen!*	1 Sing *GM, GT, GA, GN* song to *Frère Jacques* tune and move towards children now singing both parts, not just echoes. Repeat, varying volume. 2 Explain the rules of 'Only repeat if it's true', where fingers are put on lips if it's not true. Say this game is called *Sprich oder schweig* in German. Play it 'gently', using the pictures, acting as though the untrue statements are your genuine mistakes!	Pictures. Microphone (e.g. faulty toy echo mike). Jöcker CD and player.	Children will soon realise how to respond to *Noch mar.* Children will enjoy and be able to spot the teacher's 'mistakes' in *Sprich oder schweig*. Some children will need support in following through the pattern.	Patterning.

continued . . .

TABLE 3.3 *Continued*

Week	Key objectives	Key structures and vocabulary	Teaching activities (20 minutes)	Resources	Expected outcomes	Links
			3 Pass round microphone. Children speak their favourite greeting into it. 4 Establish a pattern (e.g. *GM, GT, GM, GT*) and pass round microphone, children saying the greeting that fits. 5 Enjoy the Jöcker CD song again.			
6	■ Get the gist of unfamiliar spoken German where gestures are used to support meaning. ■ Be confident as individuals to say the greeting that matches the missing picture card. ■ Respond appropriately to target language phrases to play 'Was fehlt?' game.	*GM!* *GT!* *GA!* *GN!* *Ich teile euch in 2 Gruppen.* *Ihr beginnt.* *Was fehlt?* *Stimmt das?* *Ja/Nein.* *Mach(t) die Augen zu/ auf!*	1 Sing *GM, GT, GA, GN* song together, pointing to appropriate picture cards as it is sung. 2 Divide class into two, using target language and lots of body language. One half leads the song, the other follows, then swap. Point to appropriate picture cards as the children sing. 3 Quickly play *Sprich oder schweig* with the pictures. 4 Explain they're going to play a game entirely in German, and they need to know *Was fehlt?, Stimmt das?* and *Ja/Nein* (lots of facial gestures, etc., to help, and echo in different voices). 5 Say *Mach(t) die Augen zu!/Mach(t) die Augen auf!* accompanied by exaggerated gestures. Ask children to do this a few times till all respond	Picture cards.	Children now comfortable enough with German to cope with some target language instructions, where these involve an activity the children are already familiar with (here, splitting into two groups), and where gestures and cognates ('*beginnt*' rather than '*fangt an*') are used. Children will quickly respond to new phrases like *Was fehlt?* and *Stimmt das?* because of context within which they are used, intonation and gestures.	Thinking skills involved in working out what's missing.

40

	Learning objectives	Target language	Activities	Resources	Learning outcomes
			confidently. Ask remainder, *Stimmt das?* to encourage *Ja/Nein* response. 6 Lay out pictures in order. Use correct greeting for each one, then say *Augen zu!* When all children have complied, remove one of the pictures. *Mach die Augen auf! Was fehlt?* 7 Choose a child to repeat, maybe removing more than one or all of the pictures. 8 End lesson by waving and saying *Auf Wiedersehen* as you depart.		The plural or the singular forms of the imperative can be used. Plural is logical because of the number of children, but in reality many German primary teachers use the singular form so each child feels personally addressed.
7	■ Children will use gesture clues to work out meanings of unfamiliar words. ■ Children will use all four greetings learned so far, plus two alternative 'goodbyes' in a finger puppet role play.	*GM!* *GT!* *GA!* *GN!* *Was fehlt?* *Stimmt das.* *Ja/Nein.* *Auf Wiedersehen!* *Tschüss!*	1 Greet everyone in a variety of voices, and quickly play *Was fehlt?* using pictures. 2 Invite confident individuals to come to the front to take charge of game, using target language instructions to their classmates. 3 Pretend to leave, saying *Auf Wiedersehen!* (formal) and *Tschüse* (less formal). Return to discuss what they could mean. Practise echoing me with different voices. 4 End task: Use finger puppets to greet someone. Children choose the situation (e.g. time of day, and formal or informal goodbye) in their role play. 5 Children perform.	Pictures. A finger puppet for each child.	Children will have the confidence and understanding to design a role play with a partner, making appropriate use of words learned so far.

TABLE 3.4 Long-term plan

Year	Autumn term	Spring term	Summer term
Y1	Greetings (hello, goodbye) About me (who, and how, I am) Taste *Lebkuchen* and say 'Merry Christmas'	Numbers to 10 (+ use Y6 to teach Y1s some of this) Colours/rainbows Easter rhyme and egg hunt	Breakfast foods Action songs and *Fingerspiele*
Y2	Classroom language (includes greetings – revision from Y1) Starting school Christmas as Y1 (or try *Spekulatius* or *Stollen?*) Easter rhyme and egg hunt	Toys (genders) (+*Gute Nacht zusammen*) Farm animals (or swap to *Im Zoo*?/musical instruments?)	*Dornröschen* Numbers to 12 (with plus/minus, and odds and evens and *Es gibt 12 im Bett* performance)
Y3	*Wo ich wohne* (+ places in Germany/countries where German is spoken) *Sankt Martins Tag* Weather/seasons *Sankt Nikolaus*	Brothers and sisters (to introduce some plurals and revision of numbers to 12) Easter rhyme and egg hunt	Colours (Y1 revision and extension) *Brauner Bär* story (colours, genders)
Y4	Numbers to 31 (and number magic) Minimonster verbs/days of week *Adventskranz*	Skills *(ich kann nicht und/ aber ich kann nicht)* *Fasching*? Clothes	Foods (*Papperlappap* song) (+ *Die kleine Raupe Nimmersatt*) Alphabet?
Y5	School activities *Ich . . . (nicht) (gern)* (+ Leisure – more verbs with *gern*) *Ein Apfel für den Weihnachtsmann*	School equipment *Ich brauche ein/e/n . . .* + *Ich kann/nicht* (from Y4) Busy families (intro. to 3rd person + revision/ extension of Y3 *Geschwister*)	Birthdays (cardinal/ordinal numbers, months)
Y6	Journeys (+ places, days, families) Christmas carols Discussion on stereotypes of Germany/Germans and racism	Time (and add in all journey skills, using 1st, 2nd and 3rd person to say who, when, how, where to, etc.) Describing people (+*Jeder Mensch ist anders*)	Bodies and health (Possible extras: *Eiscafé*, Shopping, Prices, *Rotkäppchen*, Sport, *Freizeit und Hobbys*, *Bremer Stadtmusikanten*, Holidays, Around town (*Rinteln*, directions), *Rattenfänger von Hameln*, *Tagesablauf*)

Questions on which to reflect

- Look at an MFL scheme of work that you use. In what ways is it compatible with the KS2 NC?

- Do you see real opportunities for progression built into your MFL scheme of work? And how do the skills develop through the years?

- Taking one of the learning objectives from the KS2 NC, think about how this could be reached through an appropriate activity that would be meaningful and enjoyable for your pupils.

Teaching the four skills: practical ideas and activities

This chapter leads on from the previous 'groundwork' chapter on planning to focus more specifically on the classroom reality of teaching and learning. We suggest ways of presenting and practising language and how to engage pupils' interest through the practical use of resources and stimulating activities. While we acknowledge that listening and speaking skills are naturally given priority in primary MFL, we argue for blending, that is integration, at the appropriate stage of reading and writing to support aural and oral development in MFL as well as to reinforce generic conceptual skills, especially as these relate to their wider language development.

Key issues

- Planning must incorporate development of all four language skills (listening, speaking, reading, writing) as they reinforce one another in the foreign language and support first-language cognitive development.

- Different skills should be emphasised at different developmental phases with the written form introduced last, in line with first-language progression.

- Despite some resistance (now much reduced since the introduction of the KS2 NC) to the inclusion of writing in primary MFL, the written form (both for pupil reading and for pupil writing) can play an important role in reinforcing oral and aural skills in MFL.

- Where skills are treated as transferable in MFL and cross-curricular links are made explicit, these, among other skills, contribute to developing phonic awareness in first-language development.

Introduction

The secondary national curriculum for MFL has always segmented the four skills (listening, speaking, reading and writing), although we acknowledge that the four skills are not taught in equal distribution. This skills division is of course somewhat arbitrary as most acts of communication are the result of combined competence, but it remains true that different activities privilege different skills and, for parity of opportunity across the range of different pupil learning styles as much as anything, it is beneficial to include a range of aural, visual and oral activities. The Key Stage 2 Framework moved away from the four-skill model, using the neologism 'oracy' to cover the strand of 'listening, speaking and spoken interaction' – a grouping that emphasises the interdependence of the skills – but the new KS2 NC has gone back to using plain terms like 'speaking' and 'listening'. In fact, while a major development in the KS2 NC is the renewed focus on reading and writing, there is also an emphasis on exploring 'the patterns and sounds of language . . . (and linking) the spelling, sound and meaning of words' (DfE, *Languages Programmes of Study: Key Stage 2*, 2014), an approach which we have always advocated.

When deciding on how to plan stages in a lesson and in longer-term sequences, it may be useful to follow the sequence of *presentation* → *practice* → *production* (the 'three Ps'), in other words the principle of moving from presentation of new items then reducing support to shift the focus from teacher input to pupil output. Of course, this process needs to be broken down into stages where pupil participation is 'scaffolded' – including through peer teaching – to become increasingly autonomous. The 'three Ps' sequence (presenting → practising → producing) has long served as a useful frame for introducing new language and for planning use of resources. The framework is not without critics, whose arguments centre particularly around the artificial nature of dividing language into neat stages, stating that this does not reflect the messiness of real interaction. We do of course agree with this claim. However, we think that the three-stage sequence provides a useful pedagogic frame, notwithstanding the benefit of varying approaches at different times and the need to revisit language items as well as skills in new, increasingly challenging contexts. We begin this chapter with a discussion of these stages.

Presenting, practising and producing new language

The first planning stage is deciding what is to be taught. The teacher might be guided here by the scheme of work or by the course they are following. Modelling language clearly and unambiguously is important in order for children to understand what is expected of them. Levels of perceived difficulty will depend on pedagogic decisions (the *form* of the lesson) but also on decisions about the language to be included (the *content*), for example the degree of lexical inter-comprehension and the degree of personal and cultural resonance attached to the content. The following are some general considerations that may guide teachers' decisions about which new language to present and in which form, in the context of introducing 'food vocabulary' in French:

- The number of items (this will depend on age and prior learning but could range from one to ten items of new vocabulary).

- Is the language to reflect the world of the children – the sort of food they might eat at home – for example *samosa*? Or will the new words aim specifically at increasing cultural awareness by using more 'typical' French or Spanish foods? (This is a key question that we will consider further in Chapter 9.)

- How many of the words are cognates (*le chocolat*), direct French borrowings from English (*le hamburger*), direct English borrowings from French (*la quiche*) or 'false friends' (*les chips*)? Many words may already be familiar to pupils, in which case the French pronunciation becomes the key focus.

■ It is often useful at the outset to think about how the vocabulary will be used in context because this may affect the form in which it is initially presented. For example, if the words *j'aime/je n'aime pas (les champignons, le poisson)*, etc. are used, then it is appropriate to introduce the language with the gendered and numbered definite article (*le, la, les*), but if pupils are going to follow up with *je mange, je bois, je prends (du thé, des frites)*, then it would be useful to present the language with the partitive article (*du, de la, des*) in the first instance. While such decisions inform teacher planning, there is, of course, no need to make this point overtly grammatical for pupils.

Once we have decided on number of vocabulary items and their associated grammatical elements, we can think about how we will present the language by means of a task. Here it is useful to think about what the context of production might be (e.g. a shopping list, ordering food in a café, saying what you had for breakfast) and tie in the educational benefits of what the children are learning, e.g. learning strategies, transferrable knowledge about language.

Traditionally, items are drilled with pictures that can be on flashcards or electronic images. If using a course with video, then the language can often be presented in a naturalistic context right from the beginning. Lexical domains such as food, as well as clothes, colours, etc., lend themselves perfectly to the use of authentic props (called 'realia'). But again, elaborate props are not a prerequisite. Simple drawings on a whiteboard can suffice or, especially for action topics like sports and hobbies, mime is effective (often with song) and involves the pupils in multisensory learning.

The important aspect is that the language is clearly modelled by the teacher repeating several times before inviting pupils to repeat. Primary teachers are generally expert at this style of clear, unambiguous presentation. As the pupils repeat with the teacher and move on to answering simple questions, this is the *practice* stage, during which pupils are led to use the language in response to controlled visual and/or spoken cues. Here the teacher can vary the tone of voice and speed of delivery (loud and soft, slow and fast) to help pupils stay attentive. After drilling, many teachers then follow a sequence of three-stage questioning that operates on the principle of gradually withdrawing support, leading to less teacher-led practice – first with the whole class and then focusing on individual pupils:

■ (*Ne répondez pas si je me trompe*) *C'est du lait* [Pupils only repeat if the teacher's phrase matches the card s/he is holding or showing on the board].

■ *C'est du pain ou de la viande?* [Multiple choice: pupils say which of the two they see].

■ *Qu'est-ce que c'est?*

The time spent on practising in this manner depends on the teacher's confidence that pupils have 'got' it. The trick is to revisit vocabulary frequently and to change styles of presentation to avoid monotony. Teachers will know when pupils have assimilated items at this stage by eliciting individualised responses to cues, which can be oral or otherwise (e.g. pointing to pictures), or by asking for simple translations or explanations from pupils.

Although we have included the 'What is it?' question here (*Qu'est-ce que c'est?*), we suggest that, beyond presentation drills, questioning should be more open to maximise inclusiveness through greater participation and to increase cognitive activity within the group by encouraging children to think of a range of possibilities. For example, if pupils have been learning classroom objects in Spanish, a teacher following the traditional question–answer format might then point to a chair and ask *¿Qué es?* Some pupils will be able to remember and will answer correctly *una silla*, but if the question is phrased more openly as a cue – *¿Qué ves en el aula?* (What can you see in the room?) – followed by a demonstration of some possible responses, e.g. *veo papel, veo la puerta*, many more pupils will go on to give 'right' answers and still more pupils will be trying to think of more words. The more able pupils will pick up the cue first but all pupils will be included; even if they repeat previous responses they are still practising the language. With food items, the cue might be *Qu'est-ce que tu manges au petit déjeuner?* or *Quel est ton plat préféré?* and so forth.

When pupils are able to respond appropriately to cues, they are ready to use the language items more autonomously in the *production* stage. In reality, they will still need guidance and support, but this is the stage at which they are able to appropriate the language into their repertoire, taking ownership by applying the language to a context. In the next chapter we look at some ways in which this can be done by embedding the language across the curriculum. Using our example of French words for food items, pupils can be asked to describe what they ate for dinner the previous evening (Year 6); enact a simple restaurant sketch; describe their favourite meal; and, once the written form has been included, write a menu (see p. 118), a shopping list, a recipe, etc. All of these can be done in collaboration with other children in pairs and groups leading to cookery, display work, and acting out a sketch, as well as drawing and labelling. One activity we have seen KS1 learners enjoy and which links to speaking practice is drawing the food on a paper plate. The possibilities are endless, but it is important to remember that the final expected range of outcomes (the 'learning intentions' discussed in the previous chapter) will shape initial decisions about the language we wish to cover in the sequence.

Teaching the four skills: resources and planning

Listening

Although it seems common sense to assume that children need to hear the new language before being expected to speak it, the way in which new language is presented is often underplayed. We talk of '*speaking* German or French' and seldom attribute equal value to *understanding*. Similarly, while we now allow children to hear words several times in the foreign language before asking them to reproduce them (following our understanding of first language acquisition), the time allowed between listening and reproducing often remains very limited and totally disproportionate to the vast input young children have in their mother tongue before being expected to produce an utterance. This period of receptive silence is Krashen's 'silent period', during which children are exposed to a vast amount of input without being under pressure to (re)produce language. Far from being a time of passive receptivity, language is actively assimilated at this stage through ongoing cognitive processing.

The process of 'parrot-fashion' reproduction of language is rooted in the behaviourist tradition whereby pupils will accurately repeat the modelled sounds through a drill of listening and repeating. While we would agree that this style of learning has an important role to play in memorising new vocabulary and provides an entry of sorts to the production phase that is helpful in the short term, we would also emphasise that the quality and style of the input is important in developing phonic awareness and listening skills. In other words, understanding elements of a foreign language is as important as being able to speak in the language. Although younger children, arguably, do have greater powers of mimicry, the behaviourist listen–repeat paradigm is not sufficient in itself (children actually not being parrots!) if the input is not scaffolded in some way to aid assimilation.

'Scaffolding' strategies in developing listening skills include visual support, speaking at different speeds, adopting exaggerated intonation, even using hand and body language (like an orchestral conductor) to stress salient informational elements or to draw attention to certain phonic features. There is much debate about using the written word as a support in aural comprehension. Some teachers we spoke to in researching teachers' views for this book believe that this can lead pupils to mispronounce words because they apply English phonic patterns. However, we are convinced of the usefulness of the written word as a *support* – that is, not the sole means of presenting new language – and believe that it paves the way to developing literacy in MFL. We have seen many cases such as the one cited by Alison Hurrell (1999: 71): her pupils were unable to understand the word *dangereux* despite her repeating it several times, saying it slowly, dividing up the syllables, etc. As soon as she started to write it on the board (d-a-n-g-e . . .) the pupils understood immediately what she had been saying in French. Using the written word may also avoid pupils improvising (wrongly) when they cannot understand what they are saying/singing, as illustrated by our example cited in the next chapter of singing 'sunny semolina' instead of *sonnez la matine* in *Frère Jacques.*

It is also worth remembering that when pupils *do* mispronounce written words in a foreign language this is no more than they do when developing literacy in English, where the patterns of written forms need to be learnt even though children are able to say the words, as for example when early readers pronounce the 'k' in 'know'.

The time between initial input and pupil production of target language varies according to age, language content and, especially, individual preference. While most children will join in choral drilling within the safety of numbers, many are reluctant to speak in the foreign language when they are not used to it. It is not helpful to rush or force this process as the different pupil modes of participation are highly individual; for example, if some do not wish to speak the new language (yet), this reticence should be respected. Hurrell (1999: 71), borrowing Krashen and Terrell's (1983) legal metaphor, calls this the children's 'right to silence'. One scaffolding activity we have seen work – also used in English phonics development – is silently mouthing the words with exaggerated facial movements for pupils. We cite an example further on in this chapter of 'silent mouthing' as pairwork. This strategy helps to increase confidence and to prepare pupils for when they are ready to speak. Pupils enjoy replicating the movements – in one school called 'mouth dancing' – and it raises phonic awareness of different mouth shapes in different languages.

Another strategy to familiarise pupils with foreign language sounds is for the teacher to use target language without necessarily requiring pupils to respond in the foreign language. This type of cross-linguistic dialogue is quite usual in bilingual families and still serves the purpose of normalising foreign language use and getting pupils used to different sounds. It is also a good way of checking pupils' comprehension.

While all use of the foreign language in the school will help develop listening/comprehension skills, focused skill-specific activities can include listening to taped native speakers giving information or engaged in dialogue. As pupils are being asked to listen to specific information they can be asked to complete a grid or circle a picture on a worksheet, such as in the example below, to focus their attention. Indeed, Lotto (Bingo), upon which this activity is based, is only a fun form of a listening exercise presented as a game, and so eternally popular.

Listening activity to practise food and drink vocabulary

The visual on the board (Figure 4.1) helps to set the scene, and the teacher can point to each of the three characters as s/he reads their turn. The script (Figure 4.2) can be read a few times. This activity lends itself to potential links to speaking practice as the pupils could be asked to give their answers in French and (older) children might even read the script. Audio transcripts can be used in different ways, and can be a useful support to pupils with SEN. The internet now provides limitless source texts, but most need to be modified to be accessible to English primary-school children.

FIGURE 4.1 Picture of café scene

Each child is given the following activity sheet (Figure 4.2):

FIGURE 4.2 Nine fruit and drink pictures

Script (read by teacher):
'*Vous désirez?*' *demande le serveur.*
'*Moi, un hamburger avec des frites, s'il vous plaît*' *répond Emilie.*
'*Très bien. Et pour Monsieur?*'
'*Un sandwich au jambon, s'il vous plaît*' *dit Loïc.*
'*Et comme boisson?*'
'*De l'eau, s'il vous plait*' *ils répondent.*

Coche les plats et les boissons que tu entends (Cross out the food and drink that you hear).

With the food items in this activity we can see how pupils are helped by the choice of cognates. Furthermore, pupils might be told that there are four items (three food items and one drink). The concept of drink can be conveyed by the teacher miming as s/he reads *Et comme boisson?* Although *de l'eau* may be difficult to grasp, some pupils will be able to deduce by a process of elimination (*ce n'est pas Coca-cola!*).

Although not actually language, music and 'sound', in a broader sense, constitute a valuable resource in evoking certain emotions and images, which can be expressed through the target language; for example, *Ce morceau de musique te fait penser à quelle couleur?* In a similar way to the visual conceptualising described below, 'Foley score' sounds (involving props to make certain noises such as those heard in radio plays) can be great fun for storytelling (e.g. slow footsteps and a scream or a quickening horse gallop in the rain) and evoking images; for example, *C'est quel animal? Il est comment?* The key here is to enjoy different sounds, which is effectively what we are asking children to do with the foreign language, and to encourage creativity.

In one school we visited recently, a German teacher told us how she emphasised the *sounds* and *shapes* of words to great effect:

- With Year 2, we learn the story of Sleeping Beauty (Dornröschen) through the song. The children love the word *böse*, as in '*die böse Fee*', the wicked fairy, who casts the terrible spell on Dornröschen. It can be said in a very nasty way, and a lot of fun can be had with one half of the class chanting '*Die böse Fee!*' while the other half responds '*Die gute Fee*', with a totally different expression.

- Some of the words I introduce with the Year 4 food topic include *lecker* and *igittigitt*, which mean 'yummy' and 'yuck' and can be great fun to play with in class. The children love the sounds.

- Sometimes we play with silent words too! *Hör zu!* looks gorgeous when you're lipreading! When we have learnt *hör zu, schau her, steh auf, dreh' dich um* and *setz dich*, we form them on our lips for partners to read and respond to! If I ask the children how they know which one I was saying, they can describe the lip shape for it.

Speaking

Speaking and other means of communication

Oral competence in the foreign language is often seen as the ultimate goal of foreign language learning: to be able to *speak* 'fluently'; yet it is also the aspect of engagement with the foreign language that strikes the greatest terror into the hearts of many teachers and (especially secondary-level) pupils alike. This may be because speech production is, by its nature, *spontaneous* (we have less time to prepare what we want to say than when writing) and *interactive* (we speak *to* someone and they respond, so failure to exchange spoken turns successfully leads to *immediate* communication breakdown). These same characteristics apply equally, of course, when we are communicating in our first language. The key difference is that we feel confident enough to be able to deal with communication breakdown or to manage the course of interaction towards a successful outcome because we are instinctively satisfied with the range of extralinguistic communicative strategies at our disposal (rephrasing, repeating, changing intonation, body language, etc.). This repertoire of extralinguistic strategies is gradually acquired in first-language development through exposure and trial and error. Likewise, they are important skills in foreign language learning and should form an integral part of developing competence in speaking skills both through exposure (listening) and through explicit 'learning' or discussion of the characteristics of communicative competence in the foreign language. It is often surprising how much foreign language learners of all ages can successfully communicate with little strictly linguistic competence in the foreign language when driven by the momentum of real motivation to convey meaning. This can be a great motivator for less confident or SEN pupils as they realise that they can convey meaning creatively through gesture and sounds. The desire to communicate using the target language and other communicative strategies without having recourse to English is to be promoted from the start to encourage good communicative habits in early learners for progression and, later, for secondary school.

Children often like to use a 'foreign' character when they are practising dialogues or presenting phrases to the class. This can be themselves with a foreign language pseudonym, or might take the form of a puppet or a cuddly toy which becomes a foreign language 'friend' or alter ego. Simple finger puppets are easy to make using card wrapped around the finger and decorated, or a ping-pong ball with a hole cut in it large enough for the finger. Sock puppets, simple glove puppets or even a spoon puppet (a face on the back of a wooden spoon with hair stuck on) are all easy and cheap to make. Figure 4.3 shows ingenious use of a flannel wash-glove. The puppet is given a name, usually a name in the target language such as Stefan, Etienne or Juanita, and the children, who can become quite attached to their puppets, use the character of the puppet to express themselves in the target language or to explain things to. Obviously, the puppets do not 'speak' English!

This stage of removal from their English-language reality makes an enormous difference to the 'affective filter' of the pupils (this is Krashen's (1982) term for the screen of emotional and contextual factors that cause embarrassment or awkwardness and so can inhibit participation in language-learning activities). A more sophisticated yet highly

FIGURE 4.3 Wash-glove puppets

enjoyable version of the puppet can be created as an electronic avatar, through websites such as Voki (https://voki.com/). We have found that the use of avatars is especially popular with children who have communication difficulties.

Using the target language

It is important that pupils are encouraged to use the target language in real contexts around the school and around the classroom, but for this to happen they must feel safe and supported – to know that it's OK to make mistakes, to repeat words, to mispronounce, etc., as that is in the nature of all communication. Furthermore, pupils will be more encouraged to use the foreign language unselfconsciously if they see that it is being used around them by teachers (and other members of staff) for natural communication and in different contexts. We return therefore to our insistence on the need to have MFL embedded throughout the curriculum and the life of the school, starting if possible from KS1. Schools in the twenty-first century should be developing international – and that includes multilingual – perspectives. If foreign language communication is exclusively experienced within the realm of the specialist teacher it is, by definition, perceived as segmented and detached from the real business of day-to-day classroom life – the so-called 'Spanish and vanish' problem inherent in depending solely on peripatetic specialists, however good. Some schools have a 'French corner' in each classroom, whereas others have prominent displays in the entrance corridor to send a clear message that languages matter in their school.

We are not suggesting here that teachers interact all day in German or French. Many would not wish to do so and/or would not feel able to do so. What we are suggesting is that the drip-feeding model of MFL provision that is already in place in many schools (in the form of greetings, register calling, etc.) is expanded to some teacher–teacher interaction and to some MFL delivery in new places (different areas of the curriculum, the lunch menu, assembly singing, etc.). Even young children often perceive *speaking* a foreign language as difficult, and express negative ideas such as 'French is hard to pronounce' (said to the authors by a seven-year-old London pupil). But we are convinced that these ideas are often, albeit subliminally, 'learnt', given that we have also seen many examples of early learners adapting successfully to accurate phonic production of new sounds. Perceived 'difficulty', we would therefore argue, is a socially produced attitude. (We discuss issues surrounding the *choice* of one MFL over another in more detail in Chapter 1.)

One useful way to increase MFL for daily interactional purposes is to teach (and for teachers to use) key interactional phrases, for example, (in Spanish) *sí, no, vale, de acuerdo, ¿Qué significa?, ¿Cómo se dice . . .?, no sé, no entiendo, necesito . . ., bueno, bien.* This can constitute appropriate targets for class teachers' own continuing professional development (see Chapter 11).

Using images to create meaning

Images are used extensively in MFL. Throughout the book we cite many examples of images, labelling pictures, drawing pictures from a text, video clips and so forth. The value of images is in the creation of new linguistic links in the target language. These new connections do not *replace* but build on and reconfigure existing associations. The use of young learners' creative imaginations in the production and expression of mental images is already well established in the primary curriculum and can be tapped into to encourage the construction of new meanings through MFL. The type of activity described next draws on the pupils' own imaginations, and while teacher resources and preparation are minimal, the activity is a rich, dynamic and creative process.

Pupils are asked to 'imagine' a monster and to describe it mentally in the target language: How many heads does it have? What colour is it? What is it called? Where does it live? etc. As pupils envisage their own fantastic monster they can be led to answer certain questions, but it is more interesting if they are left to describe freely as the association will be highly original. Pupils then share their mental images, maybe making comparative statements about their own and others' monsters using their own initial descriptions as an *aide-mémoire*. This activity allows pupils the time and space to plan what they will say and to seek help as they need it.

Another activity that helps sentence development as well as being creative and fun is to give pupils a simple sentence such as 'A man gets out of his car. . .' (*Un hombre baja . . . de su coche*) and ask them to insert an adverb or to add another phrase or to describe the man and the car, again using language that has been learnt or, indeed, asking for a new word. This type of text expansion is used a lot in first-language literacy (creation of 'super sentences') and so meshes well with, but adds a further dimension to, the foreign language as it increases awareness of difference in word order and may reveal more about language-specific conceptual imaging, given that bilinguals often associate different images with the 'same' words in different languages. (The intercultural implications here are discussed further in Chapter 9.) This activity type is also flexible and allows for a range of differentiated outcomes; that is, there is no 'right' answer.

Speaking beyond word level

Within the context of the specific development of MFL-speaking as a skill, there are many games, songs and role plays that help proficiency and familiarise pupils with certain words and phrases. As with listening, these require some visual or aural support, which may come from pictures, realia, a verbal description, etc. Examples of these resources are given throughout the book. One key issue that we would like to raise again here, though, is the importance of progression. New language is often presented in the form of lists of lexical items, yet at some stage pupils need to move beyond word level to produce more complex phrases and to link these to make sentences. We suggest that pupils can go straight to sentence level, avoiding the usual vocabulary lists that tend not to get used in context if not learnt within meaningful phrases. This stage of progression should not wait until secondary school. Primary teachers are expert at developing this awareness of sentence- and discourse-level sophistication in English so can easily apply it in MFL. In fact, the approaches used in literacy can be applied equally in MFL; for example, adding adjectives to qualify nouns, then using connectives to add subordinate clauses, then building up to linking phrases with conjunctions used either causally (*puisque, comme*) or temporally (*quand, alors*). These can be introduced orally in drill form with musical rhythm as in the examples here:

Quand il fait beau je joue au foot (dans le parc).
Quand il fait du soleil je fais une promenade.
Quand il pleut je regarde la télé.

J'ai sommeil	*alors*	*je vais au lit.*
J'ai faim	*alors*	*je mange un sandwich.*
J'ai chaud	*alors*	*j'enlève mon pull.*
J'ai soif	*alors*	*je bois de l'eau.*

These activities use picture prompts (or mime) to piece together recently learnt phrases, but this type of sentence-level development is often best supported, at least in part, by the written form. This brings us to the discussion of developing reading and writing skills in MFL.

Reading

Dispelling the myth

Some primary teachers still believe that MFL provision for early learners should focus exclusively on listening and speaking and that using written foreign language leads to:

- mispronunciation (pupils mispronounce as they read while they reproduce accurately without written support);
- confusion with developing literacy in English (hindering first-language development);
- demotivation (reading and writing are associated with 'boring schoolwork').

We have found no evidence to support these myths. On the contrary, we suggest that reading and writing skills support and reinforce speaking and listening skills. In most schools the written word (in foreign languages) is clearly in evidence around the school anyway, so we cannot assume that pupils will just make sense of it without structured guidance. We have seen many examples of skilful teaching using all four skills successfully. While pupils will inevitably mispronounce some new words as they see them (as they do in English), recognising different systems of phonic patterns will eventually raise awareness of sound links and will improve pronunciation. The KS2 NC also makes explicit the mutually reinforcing link between developing language awareness in the MFL alongside language awareness in English: '[Pupils understand] key features and patterns of the language; how to apply these, for instance, to build sentences; and how these differ from or are similar to English' (DfE, *Languages Programmes of Study: Key Stage 2*, 2014).

Awareness of phonics in MFL

Here we cite Hurrell's suggested 'phonic clouds' concept (1999: 81) as one nice way of approaching reading from a phoneme-script perspective – i.e. linking 'the spelling, sound and meaning of words' (DfE, *Languages Programmes of Study: Key Stage 2*, 2014). Particular phonic groupings (which may be written as single letters or clusters) are suspended from the classroom ceiling in the form of a hanging mobile. Each time pupils encounter a new word with that sound in they can add a new 'cloud' (see Figure 4.4). In the illustrated example we look at how this can be done with the pronunciation of the Spanish phoneme /x/, written as *j* or as a soft *g* (when preceding *i* or *e*).

The phonic cloud can be used with phonemes that are always spelt the same as in the example, or with phonemes that are spelt differently (homophones). In French this can be especially useful because of the irregularity of the phoneme–script correspondence; for example, /ɛ/ is found in *la tête, le verre, le crayon, le lait, la haie*. Homophones can also make for challenging, fun learning and surprising match-up games.

Just as children learning to read English learn to appreciate that some letters in certain words are silent and others are pronounced differently in different contexts, pupils learning a foreign language can make the same distinctions. The pronunciation of –*ough* is a classic example of this (having at least seven possible pronunciations, as in through, thorough, though, bough, cough, tough, bought) and is particularly difficult for children having English as an additional language. This is another example of where MFL provides greater equity of opportunity among pupils of different home languages, as all pupils will be confronted with the challenges of new phoneme-script associations, some making inferences from English and others drawing on different first-language repertoires.

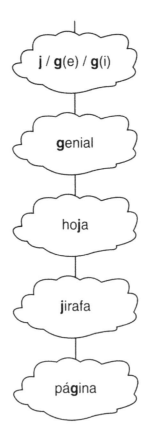

FIGURE 4.4 Phonic clouds

Getting started with reading

Almost all primary schools that have any engagement with MFL provision have used labelling as a minimal form of developing reading skills through familiarity with foreign language words. These are often posted around the school as laminated words (*la sala de profesores, la cantina, et vestibulo*, etc.) and in the classroom (*el ordenador, la mesa, la pizarra,* etc.). This is a good starting point (and pupils will enjoy creating such resources themselves as they start to take their first steps in writing in MFL), though the words risk becoming invisible if they are not used regularly in interaction. Similarly, the foreign language can be used (alone or with English) to label tasks that younger pupils are doing, such as colouring in (see Figure 4.5).

In the classroom, books are an obvious reading resource. There is now a wonderful range of MFL books available for early learners and these will suit all needs levels, although using text on the board can be a cheaper way of working from text as a class. Other alternatives are 'big books' for all to enjoy (an English big book can be adapted by covering English text with the foreign language text) and home-made story cards made, for example, by trainee teachers or even older pupils. (We have seen laminated A4-size story cards that function as mini-readers of just three or four pages with pictures and very simple sentences.) Making resources can be exploited as a valuable, collaborative activity that pupils enjoy and that gives them a stake in the process of their learning (see the section below on exploiting narrative in MFL).

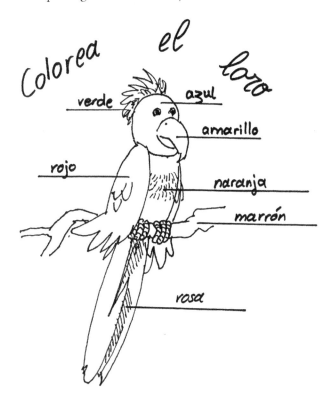

FIGURE 4.5 *Colorea el loro*

Text on the board can be used in many ways to support other skills, from reading a dialogue to text comprehension. We recently saw Year 3 beginners in Spanish using the following dialogue written on the board to consolidate what they had learnt orally. After a few lessons they were able to reel off the dialogue without the written support:

A *Hola*
B *Hola*

A *¿Cómo estás?*
B *Muy bien, gracias*

A *¿Cómo te llamas?*
B *Mi nombre es . . .*

A *Adiós*
B *Adiós*

Simple texts can be retold orally in English (as a checking device) or interpreted pictorially. For example, KS2 pupils will enjoy illustrating the following text, which consolidates language recently covered, and they will be keen to focus on the detail:

> *Monsieur et Madame Viret habitent dans une maison rouge avec une grande porte jaune. Ils ont un beau jardin avec des fleurs et un pommier. M et Mme Viret ont deux enfants, Jeanne et Michel. Jeanne a dix ans et elle porte des lunettes. Michel est plus petit et il a les cheveux noirs et frisés. M Viret est gros mais sa femme est grande et mince. La famille a un gros chien qui s'appelle Minou. Minou est blanc avec des taches brunes sur le dos. Il a de petites jambes et une longue queue.*
>
> *Aujourd'hui il fait du soleil alors M Viret porte des lunettes de soleil et Mme Viret porte un joli chapeau de paille.*

The text could go on to describe more clothes, the car, nearby buildings, etc. This illustration activity works best if it is timed, because pupils then focus on understanding and using as many linguistic clues as possible rather than the detail of the drawing itself. Simpler descriptions would be appropriate for younger pupils; for example, physical descriptions and clothes also work well when children are asked to draw an identikit picture from the description given by a crime witness. The 'wanted' posters (see Figure 4.6) can then be displayed with the descriptions.

An alternative reading skills task is to draw a simple picture on the board (such as that in Figure 4.7) and write some sentences next to it that pupils identify as true or false (*verdad o mentira*). These can be presented in multiple-choice pairs as in the example, or not, depending on the level of support and easiness the teacher wants to allow for. Discussion of how pupils arrive at their decisions is a challenging and extremely rewarding activity that supports their knowledge about language.

As well as being a valuable end in its own right, reading in the target language is also extremely useful for facilitating the development of other skills, as in listening (for example responding to questions in the target language or circling the right picture) or speaking (for example reading target language cue cards or other prompts). Being able

SE BUSCA

VIVO O MUERTO

FIGURE 4.6 *Se busca: Vivo o muerto*

El chico está triste.
El chico está contento.
Hace frío.
Hace sol.
Come un helado.
Come un bocadillo.
Tiene su gato con él.
Tiene su perro con él.
Lieva gafas de sol.
Lieva un sombrero.

FIGURE 4.7 Boy eating ice-cream with a dog

to spell in the foreign language is a useful skill as pupils begin to write, and it establishes good habits by maximising use of the target language. However, learning the whole foreign alphabet might seem a little daunting at first (having only just learnt the alphabet in English) so it is a good idea to start by spelling out certain words as they are learnt (or by spelling out learnt words as they are revisited in their written form).

MFL linked to whole-language development

David Wood (2004) reminds us of the importance of developing reading skills in the form of phoneme–script correspondence as a means of developing awareness of the very nature of language:

> When we help children to learn to read, we are doing more than teaching a new and neutral 'code' for representing what they already do with and know about speech. Rather, we are introducing them to radically new ways of thinking about language itself.
>
> (Wood 2004: 203)

If reading is ignored or sidelined in MFL, then the understanding of language as more than a code is inevitably limited to appreciation of first-language conventions only. We see literacy development as a holistic, evolving process that includes appreciation of different media and supports as well as different levels of language used in different contexts. Developing MFL literacy forms a vital part of this process. To deny pupils access to MFL in its written form is to deny access to a rich source of literacy development and a valuable learning support as well as a new world of (inter)cultural signs. Reading and writing in MFL, with appropriate age-sensitive material, also provide extension and differentiation opportunities.

Writing

As familiarity with reading the foreign language increases, most children, who will already have writing skills in English, can be guided to progress to writing in the target language. For instance, one London teacher introduces writing to KS1 children by enabling them to write the day and date in Spanish every Spanish lesson, and increases their writing output exponentially as the pupils progress. Many of the conventional objections to writing in primary MFL are similar to those used to argue against developing reading skills in the foreign language: the claim is that creating an unfair divergence between the more able and the less able will inhibit the less able pupils' motivation. As a result they will be more likely to struggle and develop negative attitudes to MFL, and will treat it as yet another subject where difficulty in reading and writing is keeping them behind (see Sharpe 2001: 86–7). However, while we are sympathetic with this view, we believe that reading and writing in the MFL can provide valuable support for speaking and listening in terms of phonic awareness, as we have seen above, not least of all enabling children to separate words by knowing where they start and end. In this respect, reading and writing are a support, not a hindrance. Wade and Marshall's (2009) research has shown that reading and writing in MFL tend to be the preserve of Years 5 and 6, while another study found that:

> most literacy activity involved reading rather than writing, which was frequently presented as a homework activity for the older children. The shortness of lessons and the relatively limited confidence and expertise among some staff appeared to constrain the amount of time spent on literacy activities, with implications for timetabling and staff development.
>
> (Cable *et al.* 2010: 6)

Of course, we are not suggesting extensive writing tasks, nor that writing should have priority in MFL lessons. Each teacher will have their own view about how much writing is appropriate for their pupils and when it is appropriate to introduce this skill. Pupils who struggle with literacy will only be disaffected if they feel out of their depth with writing in an MFL, so there is much potential for differentiation here. Indeed, if MFL is to be taken seriously as an integral part of the curriculum, it would be artificial to exclude any written forms of the language in a school environment. Here we discuss a few ways that can lead pupils to begin writing in the foreign language.

Many primary MFL teachers do provide some kind of exercise book or folder in which children keep worksheets, puzzles and personal information in the target language, and that exposure to the written word is in fact considerable. Some colleagues make extensive use of such books with older pupils and encourage the children to make mind maps of new input, for example, and to make their own notes and drawings about their learning as a kind of personal reflection so as to help them learn in their own way.

A good introduction to writing is to exploit those words that pupils are most familiar with, for example colours and classroom items that are labelled. Gapping out letters, which is a good way to focus attention in reading, can lead on to pupils writing in the missing letter. For example, once pupils are familiar with the following dialogue, having practised it a lot orally and having read it several times over an extended period, many will be able to fill the gaps. In this example, the same letter is missing, but different letters could also be omitted, or even letters that make up a different word of their own, depending on the level of support desired:

> *¿Falta qué letra? ¡Escribela!*
> *Buen_s días. Me llam_ Alejandr_. Y tú ¿C_m_ te llamas?*

In the first instance, writing may be limited to copying text down, for example for simple vocabulary or for labelling – though this may not be the easiest start to writing in the foreign language (see Hurrell 1999: 83–4 for a discussion of the pitfalls of copying text down) – but it is important that there is progression that allows pupils some degree of autonomy and creativity in writing, as much as in other skills. Here we can move the principle of 'gapping out' to sentence then text level. The eventual goal, for older children, will be having the confidence to produce written work in the foreign language autonomously. Again, we are not suggesting extensive writing tasks, but short dialogues, menus, brief descriptions, etc. Teachers' knowledge of their pupils and their abilities remains the ultimate guide.

In the section below we suggest a line of progression in writing. Each level represents a more complex, less supported stage of skill development than the previous level. The stages are in no way prescriptive (indeed, many will contend that there is no such natural order) so the stages are naturally recurring and multi-directional, and any tried-and-tested approaches can be revisited. We emphasise that pupils will already be familiar with the language. It is important that words are first presented orally to early learners, and then only exploited in their written form once they have been fully assimilated into pupils' repertoire. This helps to overcome the potential problem with mispronouncing the written form.

Progression in developing writing skills

Copy words – e.g. colours (as in the parrot colouring activity in Figure 4.5), or making labels for school furniture;

Gap-fill letters into words – e.g. completing learnt phrases (example on p. 61), or completing partially completed crossword puzzles or wordsearches;

Copy short phrases – e.g. short dialogues or Christmas card greetings;

Gap-fill words into short phrases – e.g. completing learnt songs with words gapped out, or copy sentences – e.g. from the board or in dictation (traditional but can be fun!);

Gap-fill short phrases into sentences – e.g. description of topics such as daily routine, ordering food, or talking about a hobby;

Produce words (using reference material such as a glossary and the teacher as necessary) – e.g. labelling, or writing topic lists in games;

Produce short phrases – e.g. answering questions in a listening activity, describing pictures, gap-filling phrases in a dialogue, or finishing off sentences;

Produce sentences – e.g. answering questions about something (a text, a video or a picture), writing a fuller description, or translating English sentences.

Exploiting narrative in MFL

In the long-term scheme of work in the previous chapter we showed key story texts that can be covered, one each year starting from Year 2. This taps into a principle that cuts across all of the four skills but which can be built up as skills competence progresses: namely that of listening to, recounting and inventing stories. Children enjoy stories in a foreign language in the same way that they enjoy stories in English (and other mother tongues). Stories appeal to a basic cognitive style of making sense of the world through narrative. They are an excellent way to familiarise children with the sounds and rhythms of a foreign language and to encourage reading. Stories with which children are familiar may be better, at least to begin with. Detailed comprehension of the language is not as important as the children's enjoyment of the sounds of the language and, with the support of pictures, exaggerated tone of voice or gesture, they will concentrate to understand the storyline. As Cheater and Farren write: '[the children will be] captivated by the structure and shape of the tale, the sound of the voices, the rhythm and repetition of little-understood phrases' (2001: 51) in much the same way as in their first language. Stories naturally include many elements of repetition (think of the 'Who's been sleeping in my bed?' and 'Why, what big . . . you have?' routines) and this will help to reinforce the sound patterns to pupils, who will more than likely want to join in when they know the phrase that is coming. There are many traditional tales, such as those cited in our German scheme of work, which are available in many languages or even in bilingual editions. We have seen that wonderful stories like Rosen and Oxenbury's *We're Going on a Bear Hunt* are enjoyed as much in French (*La chasse à l'ours*) because the story is known but also because of the rhythm and the onomatopoeia. Similarly, Ed Emberley's successful stories such as *Go Away, Big Green Monster!* have been widely translated (in French to *Va-t-en grand monstre vert*) and have been recommended by several primary specialists we spoke to. Creative writing in foreign languages, modelled beautifully by Storybirds (http://mfl-storybirds.wikispaces.com/), sends a powerful message about the joys of language learning for pleasure and aesthetic appreciation of language, not simply for routine transactional purposes.

Conclusion

While 'fun and games' are an important part of MFL and play a major role in motivating pupils, early learners also need to be challenged and to have their learning guided through clear stages of progression if initial motivation is to be maintained. We have suggested in this chapter that whole-child development through MFL means the integration of multisensory learning through different resources and activities and also through integration of all four language skills. This chapter features many practical suggestions for using resources and setting up activities to this end.

We do not believe that writing should be emphasised over speaking and listening in MFL – or even that it needs to be introduced in the very early KS1 years – but nor do we advocate steadfastly ignoring the written word. Such hardline positions are not helpful. More important are an open mind and a willingness to use whatever support proves effective in helping pupils make meaning through MFL.

Similarly, while we recognise that some activities in MFL will be teacher-led 'transmission'-type activities, for example repeating together phonetic drills and singing, we also urge teachers to ensure that pupils are encouraged at the production phase to use the new language to create and construct their own meanings (mistakes and all).

Questions on which to reflect

- Other than the activities suggested in this chapter, can you think of whole-language development strategies from English lessons that might be integrated into your MFL teaching?

- Are there opportunities for reinforcing MFL learning through labelling classroom objects or having useful 'chunks' of language visible in the room or elsewhere in the school?

■ Can you identify problems (of pronunciation, spelling, etc.) specific to your MFL that might need extra attention? Which helping strategies might be appropriate; for example, use of cognates, phonetic drilling through rhyme?

5

Teaching approaches: differentiation, motivation and learning across the curriculum

The enormous developmental changes that define primary teaching and learning necessitate a wide repertoire of age-sensitive teaching approaches, and one that will mesh effectively with later learning. This chapter will look at key issues in secondary-language learning that primary teachers need to be aware of, and will then go on to discuss different ways in which primary pupils can be involved in active MFL through content-based learning tasks using drama, games and a host of other activities that support whole-curriculum learning.

Key issues

- Developments in primary MFL need to mesh with developments in secondary MFL, and so an awareness of the KS3 MFL curriculum is needed.

- Activities need to be challenging, with scope for differentiation, to take into account different age-related motivations and particular learning styles.

- MFL has the potential to support and reinforce other areas of the primary curriculum. It is best seen as part of curriculum-wide language and literacy development.

- In order for MFL to be embedded successfully across the curriculum it must be seen as more than a discrete, skill-based subject. We advocate forms of 'content-based' language learning, which ensure new language is used meaningfully.

Introduction

The primary teacher is in a unique position to deliver MFL as a cross-curricular experience. Unlike colleagues in secondary school, the primary teacher is already an expert in delivering whole-curriculum learning and has privileged access to a complete overview of pupils' experience of school and their social and academic progress. These are major assets in the process of successfully embedding MFL across the curriculum. Of course, as with all innovation, support is needed for necessary basic skills and awareness of how to expand existing practice in new directions. This chapter aims to contribute to such support by first looking at the aims underpinning MFL pedagogy in the secondary school – aims which earlier-stage teachers need to be aware of – and then considering how MFL is most effectively embedded in the curriculum by linking to other curriculum areas, as well as constituting its own specialist subject status. We will justify this position on the grounds of increased pupil motivation and meaningful use of language in context and will suggest several practical ways in which cross-curricular learning can be implemented.

MFL in the secondary school

MFL teachers in the secondary sector, like other secondary subject specialists, are sometimes reproached for lack of awareness of the child's experience of school prior to Year 7. Various initiatives are now in place that seek to redress this limitation in order to improve pupils' smooth progression, socially and pedagogically, between the two very different environments of primary and secondary. (This transition is discussed further in Chapter 10.) Similarly, it is essential that primary MFL teachers take into account curricular frameworks beyond KS2 in order to ensure continuity, and so in this chapter we will consider some of the key changes that have affected secondary MFL teaching and learning in recent times and the impact of these on children learning primary MFL, for while primary teaching has its own distinctive characteristics, in many ways the delivery of MFL also shares many features in both primary and secondary. What, therefore, are these differences, and how could they mesh?

Since the introduction of the National Curriculum (1988), secondary curriculum subjects have been characterised by increasing uniformity of content and style as national frameworks define pupils' progression through commonly scripted attainment level descriptors and a common Programme of Study. The current KS2 NC offers a useful framework to complement the KS3 NC, though neither prescribe methods or content. They espouse increasingly shared positions about what constitutes good practice, including encouraging greater pupil autonomy and reflexivity through key trends such as assessment for learning and strategy training.

The secondary MFL curriculum for England and Wales was implemented in its original form in 1990 and was revised in 2000, 2008, and most recently in 2014. Its current incarnation requires that:

Pupils should be taught to:

Grammar and vocabulary

- identify and use tenses or other structures which convey the present, past and future as appropriate to the language being studied;

- use and manipulate a variety of key grammatical structures and patterns, including voices and moods, as appropriate;

- develop and use a wide-ranging and deepening vocabulary that goes beyond their immediate needs and interests, allowing them to give and justify opinions and take part in discussion about wider issues;

- use accurate grammar, spelling and punctuation.

Linguistic competence

- listen to a variety of forms of spoken language to obtain information and respond appropriately;

- transcribe words and short sentences that they hear with increasing accuracy;

- initiate and develop conversations, coping with unfamiliar language and unexpected responses, making use of important social conventions such as formal modes of address;

- express and develop ideas clearly and with increasing accuracy, both orally and in writing;

- speak coherently and confidently, with increasingly accurate pronunciation and intonation;

- read and show comprehension of original and adapted materials from a range of different sources, understanding the purpose, important ideas and details, and provide an accurate English translation of short, suitable material;

- read literary texts in the language [such as stories, songs, poems and letters], to stimulate ideas, develop creative expression and expand understanding of the language and culture;

- write prose using an increasingly wide range of grammar and vocabulary, write creatively to express their own ideas and opinions, and translate short written text accurately into the foreign language.

(Languages programmes of study, Key Stage 3, National Curriculum in England, 2014)

These aims mesh more or less with the KS2 NC for Languages and Rachel Hawkes, a language specialist teacher and trainer, has kindly shared her work comparing the two curricula across the four skills (see, for instance, http://www.rachelhawkes.com/PandT/ 2014_Curriculum/Handout_1_Curriculum14_Overview.pdf)

At Key Stages 4 and 5, there are, in England, only three main examination boards offering MFL GCSE and AS/A-levels (OCR, Edexcel and AQA) and there remains little difference in format and content between the different boards' examination papers, so an increasingly uniform picture has emerged about what children need to learn in MFL and how this can be achieved. Furthermore, since the move to entitlement status in 2004, MFL, while still compulsory at KS3, is no longer a core-curriculum subject at KS4 (although there is a current shift in favour of KS4 languages through initiatives such as the EBacc). This has effectively meant that secondary schools that have a strong track record in MFL have kept it compulsory and other schools whose achievement in MFL is low and whose pupils often feel disaffected with MFL have removed the compulsion and, in some cases, have seen the MFL take-up at options plummet, with consequent effects on staffing numbers, staff morale and the status of MFL within the school. Wingate (2016) feels that the curriculum content and pedagogical approaches may be, at least in part, at the root of this disaffection.

Focus on communicative language teaching

The KS2 NC was designed to lead into the current secondary Languages curriculum. In terms of language content (development of intercultural competence is dealt with in Chapter 9), both the current secondary Languages curriculum and the KS2 NC reflect current thinking on communicative language teaching. But what does this really mean? To answer this question we need to consider the aims of the National Curriculum in terms of the communicative competence it sets out to equip pupils with. Although content is not prescribed in the NC for the secondary stage, the topics that still drive curriculum content could be said to combine the following two aims:

- achieving functional competence (being able to do things – perform certain functions – with language);
- ability to use and apply grammar through knowledge and practice of linguistic features (sequenced according to a traditional hierarchy of 'difficulty', often starting with nouns and articles; then progressing to adjectives; then on to present-tense, usually regular, verbs).

Let us look more closely at these aims. First, what is meant by functional (communicative) competence? What are the functions we expect children to be able to perform with the language they learn? The secondary NC's interpretation of communicative functional competence broadly aims to prepare pupils to:

- talk about themselves/their own world (self, hobbies, family, pets, food, holidays, school, town, likes, dislikes);
- get by in the target-language culture (ordering food and drink, asking for directions, buying things).

On a linguistic level, in order to be able to meet these communicative aims, children are taught words (including spelling, pronunciation and gender), then phrases and sentences (using given verbs), then texts (suggesting appropriate types of phrasal and sequential sequencing with connectives and adverbial markers). There is some difficulty with the mesh between these communicative and linguistic aims, however. Consider the following points:

- Many functions can be acceptably achieved with non-standard or minimal language. Compare these sets of desired 'model' responses (bracketed) with alternatives (marked ★):

A   *Quel âge as-tu?*
B   *★Dix, et tu? (J'ai dix ans – et toi?)*

A   *Qu'est-ce que tu prends?*
B   *★Une coca-cola. (Un coca-cola.)*

A   *Où habites-tu?*
B   *★Je habite with mon familie in un maison dans Redhill, à Surrey.*
     (J'habite avec ma famille dans une maison à Redhill, dans le Surrey.)

We can see that the alternative phrases (★), though incorrect grammatically to differing degrees, achieve the communicative (information-conveying) function and would probably not cause comprehension difficulties to our legendary 'sympathetic native speaker'.

■ Many of the 'getting-by' functions in some texts and secondary schemes of work (booking accommodation, going to the doctor unescorted or hiring a car) are ill-suited to the real communicative needs of children and so are projected on to some imagined future of the child as an adult tourist. These situations are the legacy of an understanding of communicative needs (for adults) identified through the Council of Europe's seminal work on establishing 'threshold levels' of competence in the 1970s.

■ Many functions require a more sophisticated linguistic repertoire than will have so far been provided. A classic example is when discussing jobs:

A   *Qu'est-ce qu'il fait dans la vie, ton père?*
B   *Il est . . . Miss, how do you say stock portfolio manager?*

In this case, a quick-witted teacher might respond *Il est financier* or may have pre-empted the problem by only including a finite number of options. For example, rather than asking this question, the teacher may point to a picture of a man working in an office and ask for the image to be matched to the previously taught item *employé de bureau*. Nevertheless, there will inevitably be other occasions when pupils will be frustrated as they attempt to produce free language that is beyond their linguistic means, and the teacher will need to juggle the planned learning objectives with the child's enthusiasm for wanting to express their 'truth' – that is, to be genuinely communicative. The traditional 'ladder' of linguistic progression, then, only loosely, and somewhat artificially, corresponds to the communicative function being taught. It is important, therefore, to establish the link to and fro between new language being taught and the communicative context in which it is used: in other words, to make the use of the language meaningful.

When the Key Stage 2 Framework for Languages was being rolled out in 2006 it was an eagerly awaited support framework, and research since that date has shown that most schools that have implemented MFL have used the framework as guidance. Many are using the QCA schemes of work as a core reference but adapting them to suit their context, to complement other areas of the curriculum in their school day and to match their own choices about materials, suitability and usefulness. In our view, this is exactly how a framework should be used. The implementation of the statutory KS2 NC has led to further amendments, in particular more extended inclusion of reading and writing and a greater focus on grammatical awareness.

In the same way that there is much common ground between the ways in which English is taught and the possibilities for teaching MFL in the classroom – indeed, here we are arguing the case for mutual reinforcement – there is also some neat dovetailing that can be done across the key stages, and this is discussed more in Chapter 10. The following is an example of a lesson we saw recently combining explicit teaching of first language (English) literacy with MFL.

A Year 6 English lesson with MFL

The teacher asked pupils to describe what a verb is. Most were able to answer that it was a 'doing word' or that it 'describes an action' and to give an example and to identify the verbs in sentences, first in present tense, then in different tenses, then in compound forms. The teacher had prepared some sentences on PowerPoint that had gaps for the children to fill in with different verbs. Some sentences offered limited possibilities, e.g.:

Last night I _____ a football match on television. (watched)

while others could be gap-filled with different choices:

I _____ an ice-cream on the beach. (ate/bought/dropped/had/fancied etc.)

Pupils were also able to do some gap-fills in this way with Spanish sentences, though these were more restrictive in regard to possible choices, like the first English sentence cited above. Some pupils understood the sentence but had forgotten the Spanish vocabulary and said the word in English: e.g. 'play' instead of *juego* in

(Yo) _____ al fútbol todos los días.

Pupils were asked to describe the difference between a regular and irregular verb in English (*-ed* endings and irregular endings) and then to give certain verb paradigms, e.g. sing-sang-sung, eat-ate-eaten. Some pupils, though a small number, were able to give past participles in Spanish, too, and explain regular endings *-ado* and *-ido*.

Later, children were asked to go through the six persons of an English verb (I sing, you sing, he/she/it sings, we sing, you sing, they sing) and were able to say that all forms were the same except for the third person singular, which takes an 's'. Then they chanted some Spanish verb tables. This in itself is not of 'high value' (Heafford 1990: 88) but we were impressed that pupils were then able to answer, 'OK, so what's the third person plural of *comer*?' While some pupils struggled, they were asked to explain their answers and show on a verb table (arranged in two columns for singular and plural), for instance, that third person is the third one down and that 'singular is one person and plural is more than one.'

	🧍 Singular	🧍🧍🧍 Plural
1st person	I, *yo*	we, *nosotros*
2nd person	you, *tu*	you, *vosotros*
3rd person	he/she/it, *él/ella*	they, *ellos/ellas*

At another school where literacy is also a central focus of the MFL provision, that is, knowledge *about* language is seen as a principal benefit of language learning, rather than aiming for linguistic competence in a given language (knowledge *of* a language), we saw in the pupils' exercise books several written 'rules' in boxes on verb conjugations, possessive adjectives and spellings. For example:

word endings –sion in English	=	*–sione* in Italian
word endings –tion in English	=	*–zione* in Italian

Other examples of how MFL can be taught in the style of existing curriculum delivery include the following.

A Year 4 maths lesson with MFL

Numbers have always been one of the first things taught in MFL and many adults can still count automatically to 20 in at least one foreign language, even without being able to say much more. Numbers in the foreign language can be practised in many enjoyable ways and can then lead on to reinforce simple maths.

Pupils counted numbers to 30 together in French, first following the teacher's prompts, then chanting all together in time with the teacher, then individually around the room so that each pupil represented a number (to 24). As each pupil called out their number, they stood up then sat down again. Afterwards, all odd numbers went to one end of the room (*les impairs, allez à côté de la porte*) and the even numbers next to the carpet area (*les pairs, à côté de la moquette*). The teacher then called out some simple arithmetic sums and the pupils arranged themselves in lines of three accordingly, repeating their numbers, e.g. *trois plus cinq égalent huit; vingt-quatre moins dix égalent quatorze*. Pupils helped each other find the answers and thoroughly enjoyed the activity, which lasted about ten minutes in total. The high level of involvement and physical interactivity leads this type of activity on to a higher level of 'value' from that of choral chanting.

In another lesson we saw numbers in French practised with sets of dominoes. On the carpet, small groups of Year 2 children were asked *Trouvez-moi les dominos avec un total de sept*. The children looked for combinations such as 5+2 and 3+4, and were asked to speak out the numbers that they had found (*cinq plus deux*, etc.). Then pupils were asked *Trouvez-moi deux* (then later *trois*) *dominos avec un total de vingt*, and the procedure was repeated with more numbers on two and three dominoes as children made sums such as 12+8=20 (*douze plus huit font vingt*).

Examples of songs as a cross-curricular link to music based on Years 4, 5 and 6 lesson observations

Singing is a tried-and-tested way to familiarise pupils with the foreign language. Teachers who may not have a high level of proficiency feel 'safe' with the contained nature of the language in a song text and the rhythm and repetition help reinforce vocabulary, structure and phonic awareness.

We have seen many lessons using foreign language songs, especially French classics like *Frère Jacques, Sur le Pont d'Avignon* and *L'Alouette*. Songs like *L'Alouette* lend themselves naturally to specific areas of vocabulary so, unsurprisingly, we saw children pointing to their heads (tails and beaks!) while singing it. In the same school we saw the tune of *Frère Jacques* used to practise other phrases like *Quel âge as-tu? Quel âge as-tu? J'ai huit ans, J'ai huit ans*, and the tune of *She'll Be Coming Round the Mountain* to practise animals and phrases of liking/disliking like *J'adore les serpents, oui, c'est vrai*. YouTube provides many modern as well as traditional songs, some in karaoke format. We also saw the theme tune of *EastEnders* used to chant phrases of daily routine while pupils mimed actions:

> *Je me suis levé à sept heures;*
> *Je me suis lavé,*
> *Je me suis habillé.*
> *Puis j'ai pris mon p'tit déjeuner;*
> *Et je suis parti,*
> *Pour aller à l'école.*

Songs worked best where there was some support in the written form in the early stages, but this remains a contentious issue. With very young children reading ability may be too low to offer any support, but this need not be a problem. In one London school we saw Reception children finish their lesson by dancing in a conga line while chanting a Spanish song! The words were written on the screen but they were familiar with them and had learnt through repetition. One Year 4 class teacher on the south coast told us she was reluctant to introduce the written form because she wanted the focus on oral practice, and that seeing the words would confuse the children. However, without having some preparatory focus on pronunciation, many of the songs were confusing to some pupils and involvement was largely symbolic. Who else remembers learning *Frère Jacques* as a child but not really understanding what it was about? Both the authors confess to not having had a clue – 'Instead of *Sonnez la matine* we both used to sing "sunny semolina"!'

These examples demonstrate how MFL can be integrated across the curriculum rather than, though preferably as well as, being treated as a separate, discrete subject. There are valid arguments for both approaches: subject-specific MFL sessions enable focused foreign language work for its own sake and thereby give MFL a certain status in the school and in the child's (and parents' and teachers') perception of MFL learning. It may also be argued that certain pedagogic approaches lend themselves specifically to MFL learning, for example comparative grammar work; as we have seen with the examples above, this also feeds into and reinforces literacy. MFL is often seen as a special, 'distinctive' subject – possibly because the class teacher may be nervous about teaching it or because it may not be taught by the regular teacher – and often gets tagged on at different times as a 'bit of fun' or 'light relief' in the form of songs or a game. This distinctive status is a double-edged sword. In the short term, the 'gamey', 'something extra' attitude to MFL delivery may offer very positive associations with the subject (as fun or light relief from the 'serious' business of learning), but in the longer term, there is a danger that if it is only seen as a special 'appendage' to the main business of core-subject learning, it can too easily be detached and eventually dropped without having any perceptual negative impact on 'normal' curricular development.

Different motivations

The rationale for introducing MFL to younger children, discussed in Chapter 1, also takes into account the different motivations for different age-specific teaching and learning approaches. As Keith Sharpe acknowledges:

> while it may be difficult to show clearly that young children are more efficient learners of foreign languages, it is perhaps less difficult to argue that on the whole they are easier for teachers to motivate . . . Primary teachers tend to be skilled motivators, and the material they are working with is more plastic than if they were teaching older pupils.
>
> (Sharpe 2001: 35)

Primary-school children also tend to be less self-conscious when presented with a new mode of communication. In Piagetian terms, they are less rigid in their perceptual understanding of the world than secondary-age pupils, and this, coupled with more holistic curriculum delivery by the same class teacher, makes it an ideal time to embed foreign language awareness in their thinking. By age-appropriate motivation we are referring to such initiatives as the following: children in KS1 in one school learning Spanish are given a teddy by the teacher to look after when they have made a good effort. The child looks after the bear for a week, taking it home and bringing it to class. As well as making a diary with pictures and sentences about the bear's week, the teacher takes the opportunity to incorporate the bear into the content and activities of the Spanish lessons. The children love this and find it very motivating.

It is broadly recognised by secondary-school teachers of MFL that Year 7 pupils still enjoy 'child-like' activities such as singing, chanting and acting out, and that they will participate in these with few inhibitions. They are still very playful and often seek to 'please' the teacher in a way familiar to primary teachers (this may, of course, be said of older pupils as well but the adolescence threshold discourages overt approval-seeking). By Year 9, often considered a difficult 'in-between' year, pupils are growing out of the activity types they enjoyed in Year 7, yet the linguistic resources available to them for free discursive language production remain inadequate at KS4. This means that communication in MFL lessons can be restricted to highly structured mechanistic exchanges (such as scripted role plays) and this leads to frustration and low motivation.

Although the underlying motivating factors may be universal (competitiveness, positive feedback, fun) and apply equally to the secondary context, the primary teacher is able to capitalise on younger children's relative lack of inhibition and greater focus on pre-puberty physicality through games and drama activities.

The benefits of integrating games in MFL learning seem evident:

■ The enjoyment factor is paramount. If children are motivated they will focus their energy into the learning process and give the activity their whole attention. In an already heavily burdened curriculum, pupils are positively disposed towards a subject that entails fun and games.

■ Pupils understand the principles of games and will usually be familiar with the English format of the game to be played in the target language. Time is therefore not wasted on learning the 'form' of pedagogic conventions and pupils instinctively focus on the language being used.

■ The routine and repetition element of games both allows the teacher to feel comfortable if they are not very secure with using a new target language and, more importantly, lends itself to reinforcing specific target-language phrases and vocabulary without seeming to pupils like a boring drill.

■ As the pupils are focused on the outcome of the game, this is real 'task-based' learning, which leads to increased fluency and confidence in the target language.

There are hundreds of these types of activities listed in publications new and old, but here are a few to give a flavour:

Fête déguisée: To familiarise children with clothes vocabulary, colours and sizes. Children dress up from a fancy-dress box, or this can be done on a non-uniform day. Children are given a couple of minutes to look carefully at what classmates are wearing, then they stand back to back (or blindfolded) and try to remember what their partner (or another pupil chosen by name) is wearing:

> *Tu portes un chapeau rouge.*
> *Tu portes une casquette bleue et blanche.*

A handout with labelled pictures and a colour chart would provide support at the beginning if required.

Un défilé de mode: On the same theme, older children can plan a fashion show with catwalk commentaries in the target language. This can be great fun for assemblies.

Numbers: Old favourites that familiarise pupils with numbers are the games of *Lotto* (on improvised bingo cards) and *Ring the Number*, where two children from the different teams stand on a mark then rush to circle the number on the board called out by the teacher. Teams can have different-coloured marker pens (*les Bleus, les Verts*) and this can now be done on an interactive whiteboard.

Directions: Pupils 'guide' a blindfolded classmate around the room or hall by giving directions in the target language.

Tongue-twisters: Although some writers have said that they find these needlessly confusing for language learners (e.g. Lee 1971), we think pupils find them amusing and they can aid pronunciation and phonic awareness when the phonemes being practised are referred to at other times. As with other figurative expressions they can be written on the wall, and children will enjoy illustrating them: e.g. *Le chasseur sachant chasser chasse sans son chien!*

Mime: Pupils guess what the teacher or a classmate is doing: e.g. *estás comiendo; estás jugando al fútbol.* The action can also be done in slow motion (*a cámara lenta*).

Find a partner: Any variation on the idea of pupils moving around with cue cards looking for someone whose cue card has the matching birth month, star sign, telephone number, sport, etc. will offer opportunities for maximum participation in speaking practice.

While these activities are fun and effectively consolidate new lexical and structural input, they are not an end in themselves. It is important to ensure that pupils are *stretched* in the foreign language and that progression is built in. For instance, the phrases practised in the mime game can then be used in a circular story, orally, with other elements brought in (for example adjectives and other vocabulary), and this might culminate in a piece of writing in the target language for older KS2 children (from pictures or a gapped writing frame). In this way, language practised through games, drama and physical activities feeds into other areas of the curriculum. Although this seems ambitious – maybe even controversial – such a process of 'embedding' is a key feature of a cross–curricular model of MFL and, indeed, offers many potential possibilities for differentiation. We do not suggest too much needs to be made of differentiation by task for early learners (rather, this will be by outcome), but simple measures, such as those in one urban school, where KS1 children are given worksheets to practise and revise language items that have colour coded differentiated learning objectives at the top of the sheet. The children tick the colour level they wish to start with, complete the relevant activity, then return to undertake activities at another colour level.

Focus on content versus skill

Where MFL is given its own regular slot in the timetable, the question arises about the nature of the content as well as how much time should be allocated. The traditional view in the secondary school of MFL teaching as developing a technical *skill* rather than focusing on the *content* of what is actually taught has sometimes resulted in a narrow definition of what MFL is for. As discussed above, the skills-focused communicative function has led to disaffection among older secondary pupils who often feel that the level of content is undemanding (or childish) whereas the subject is 'technically' difficult, requiring application of complex rules, memorisation of lists of words and grasping new grammatical concepts. This reported discrepancy looms large in the research of Lee *et al.*

(1998) which underpinned the KS3 Strategy for MFL with its renewed focus on making the technical language work interesting and achievable. In the same vein, many pupils complain that the MFL work they do in the secondary school is less fun or more difficult than what they did at primary school, where memories of foreign language learning are of playing games, singing songs, acting out scenes and drawing displays. One Year 7 secondary pupil in London told us: 'It [MFL] was more fun at [primary school] with Miss [primary teacher]. We used to get to sing and do clapping and that. With Miss [secondary teacher] we do more writing and it's more difficult.'

It is difficult to know whether pupils like the one quoted here would indeed truly enjoy the same style of teaching they remember enjoying at primary school, or if they are simply expressing a cosy nostalgia for a memory of their former lives as younger children. Indeed Lee *et al.*'s (1998) research, and a more recent study by Wingate (2016), showed that a more likely source of disaffection is that the content of the secondary MFL curriculum is too undemanding (while, at the same time, still perceived as 'technically' difficult). It is hoped that once MFL has been taught to all primary children, the secondary curriculum can shift up a gear in terms of content, given that all children will have a command of the basics by Year 7, thereby paving the way for more challenging age-appropriate content at Key Stages 3 and 4. It could be argued that this would present a case against diversification (away from French predominance) but, as we state elsewhere in the book, the gains made by language learning at primary do not constitute measurable stocks of knowledge specific to a given language – a lexico-phrasal bank – so much as an openness to different modes of communication through developing a repertoire of effective language-learning strategies (pattern recognition, phonic awareness) and positive attitudes to the experience.

The imbalance between content and skills learning in MFL needs to be addressed in both secondary and primary schools if MFL learning is to be seen as a vibrant, meaningful and *integrated* part of the curriculum. In many other countries – such as with the *sections européennes* in French secondary schools – the drive to increase foreign language proficiency and to develop a wider, pragmatic awareness beyond purely linguistic skills has led to the foreign language serving as a medium to teach other areas of the curriculum: that is to use the foreign language to learn content, rather than consciously practising it as a skill. This 'immersion' method is the extreme end of what content-based language learning can mean.

Foreign-language-medium teaching has existed since the advent of compulsory education in the form of fee-paying schools aimed at expatriate, mother-tongue children or children from 'international' families, all of which are factors that weigh heavily in favour of linguistic diversity and openness to language learning. More recently, mainstream state education has used the idea of foreign-language-medium education to develop a variety of projects to encourage the use of foreign languages across the curriculum. Content and Language Integrated Learning (CLIL) describes the teaching of different subjects through the medium of a foreign language. CLIL is increasingly present in mainland Europe but remains limited to a few case schools in England, especially recently established bilingual free schools (for further information on CLIL see the excellent work by Coyle *et al.* (2010) and Hood and Tobutt (2009)). We are not suggesting here that pupils should be immersed in MFL across the curriculum and that other subjects should be taught exclusively in a foreign language, but that MFL should be seen as an integrated element of the mainstream curriculum. Instead of focusing on foreign language competence as a discrete skill, the most effective way of cultivating this skill is recognised as using a foreign language as a means of *developing* (i.e. extending) the content learning of different subjects. In this light, the focus shifts from the *means* to the *end* and foreign language becomes a vehicle for learning about the world. This places the emphasis on the content (the substance of what is being learnt) rather than the form (the lexico-grammatical structure) that is used to convey the meaning.

The ways in which this has been achieved are diverse and depend largely on institutional and practical limitations as well as scepticism about the broader benefits, particularly in relation to fears of hindering first-language development (after all, national exams in 'content subjects' are still taken exclusively in first language). However, to reiterate, we are not suggesting that the MFL replaces English as the medium for most classroom teaching (even if there were staffing and resources available), but that adapted forms of content-based language learning both reinforce MFL learning and the English-medium learning of different subjects.

Let us look briefly at which forms adapted content-based learning may take.

Integrating content-based language learning into the curriculum

No one doubts that elements of foreign language learning in its traditional guise (the skills-oriented language lesson) still has a place. On the contrary, content-based learning, if anything, brings into focus a specific set of objectives that need the same degree of planned lexical and structural 'scaffolding' (progressively and recursively planned exploitation) that the communicative approach in the MFL lesson espouses. The difference with the integration of content-based learning is that communicative outcomes are tied to immediate learning needs, enabling students to realise these needs to achieve short-term completion of tasks and to gain knowledge accepted as part of intellectual development in the school context. It should be noted, though, that conventional, skills-oriented (functional) language teaching, with its aim to equip students for foreign travel through linguistic and intercultural preparation for anticipated encounters with the other, remains as valid as ever. Content-based learning does not aim to replace this type of learning but to extend it and imbue the learning process with more direct meaning-making. As the curriculum becomes increasingly joined up, MFL offers a privileged lens through which first-language literacy and language awareness can be examined within an integrated framework of learning new content.

One of the main obstacles to implementing content-based learning in its 'strong' form is, of course, the lack of truly effective bilinguals (or native speakers) working in our schools, yet these are not necessarily the best language teachers in any case. Added to this are concerns that pressures to meet curriculum requirements and to adapt English-language materials will only obstruct delivery of the National Curriculum. However, content-based language learning can also be applied in a 'weaker' form whereby different elements of other subjects are delivered in the foreign language. This is a manageable aim that can both add richness to the whole curriculum and also reinforce the vitality of the language-learning process. In this way, MFL is embedded across the curriculum.

The primary-school environment lends itself perfectly to this style of language teaching as, unlike in the secondary school, the primary teacher has a profound understanding of the whole curriculum and how the different disciplines mesh together. The primary-school teacher can therefore either integrate the foreign language into an area of the curriculum that suits their own skills and linguistic comfort zone or, where they are working with an MFL specialist, they can work together with the MFL teacher to plan cross-curricular input.

The following two examples illustrate how MFL can be taught in this way. The first looks at how another area of the curriculum can be taught by the regular class teacher using MFL and the second at how the regular class teacher can work in collaboration with the MFL specialist to ensure delivery of meaningful, content-based language learning.

Example of the regular class teacher using MFL to link to art and literacy

After completing a story book in literacy and having exploited this in English in the usual way (e.g. comprehension questions, storyboarding, creative writing), pupils then imagined a follow-up scene from the story for a 'what happened next' scenario and designed an illustration using paint and other craft materials, some for a poster and others for a 3D display. These scenes were then labelled in the foreign language and speech bubbles were filled in with some simple foreign language dialogue.

Increasing numbers of children's books are translated into different languages so, although it may not be desirable to use the unabridged foreign language text with the pupils, the teacher may use it to find phrases and vocabulary specific to the story. Like many of the suggestions in this book, this works even better when there is a link to another school in the target language country so that the children's efforts can be appreciated by native speakers of their age. (See Chapters 8 and 9 for more about school links.)

Example of cooperation with an MFL specialist to link MFL to geography and art

The following work module was planned between a Year 5 class teacher and a peripatetic MFL specialist (though anybody else with foreign language capacity connected to the school could help, possibly a native-speaker parent or assistant who is able to bring a confidence with the language as well as cultural knowledge that may be beyond the scope of the regular class teacher). The specialist talked to the pupils in simplified French about a town in France that she knew quite well. (She had spent a year there as a student, but a native speaker could equally describe their town or region of origin.) The specialist used props (a map, posters, postcards and a website of the town's castle) to explain aspects of the town's geography and history. Using simple questions and encouraged by the regular class teacher, the specialist began to ask pupils questions about their own town or region; for example:

> *A Nantes, il y a un grand château célèbre. Voici une image de ce château. Il est beau, non? Est-ce qu'il y a un château aussi à Bristol?*
>
> For some questions, the specialist and the class teacher had prepared dialogue (though the preparation was unknown to pupils) and this encouraged children and also provided them with some information they did not know, e.g.:
>
> *A Nantes, il y a environ deux cent mille habitants* [writing the number on the board]. *Et ici, à Bristol, il y a combien d'habitants?*
>
> [class teacher replies] *Il y a trois cent cinquante mille habitants à Bristol, Madame.*
>
> After plenty of supported oral practice in this way, the pupils were able to use French to prepare a display and a presentation about their own town or region. Working together with the specialist allowed the regular teacher to focus on the organisational aspects of setting up the project work and the specialist was able to give spontaneous linguistic support to both pupils and the class teacher.

The key benefit in adopting this style of approach is that it stretches the pupils in their MFL learning and lifts MFL to a position of real communication where pupils are actually making meaning and developing concepts in the target language. The language-learning and practice strategies entailed in the preparation of materials and the presentation aspect of the project chime with many of those suggested in the KS2 NC, and such an approach represents a simple and effective assessment opportunity.

Conclusion

In this chapter, we have seen how the communicative approach adopted in most secondary schools and endorsed by the National Curriculum could be more motivating if preliminary work covered at primary stages enabled older children to engage with more age-appropriate content-based material. We have highlighted the increasing uniformity of national learning frameworks across the curriculum and throughout the various key stages, a uniformity that aims at cohesion and a holistic learning experience. We have argued the case for MFL being embedded across the curriculum through links with other subject areas. The primary teacher, as a naturally skilled motivator and whole-curriculum expert, is in an excellent position to oversee this type of innovation, and we have given some snapshot examples, based on our research in schools, of how this may be achieved effectively.

Questions on which to reflect

■ In your school, or a school you know, which activities in MFL seem to most motivate pupils of different ages?

■ If your pupils do have an allocated MFL slot, how naturally cross-curricular are the activities? For example, are there links to music, PE, English, citizenship, maths? How might you enhance pupil learning during these activities?

■ Do you think that the activities your pupils do in MFL are progressively challenging in terms of content?

Learner strategies: helping to overcome the 'tricky bits'

Language learning is generally allocated a limited amount of time in primary schools. We will show in this chapter how interaction taking place in the classroom can potentially be enhanced to develop greater autonomy in view of the time constraint.

Time constraints pose a twofold challenge for teachers: in order to maximise the given time for primary MFL, teachers need to focus first on the learning process and second on the most effective learning and learner strategies. In addition, pupils often know instinctively how they best learn, and develop their preferred learning styles. They are also aware of what they themselves find difficult to learn in primary MFL, and what they describe as 'tricky bits'. Dialogue between teachers and pupils in the primary MFL classroom about learning and, when appropriate, on learning strategies, can lay the foundation for pupils to find and develop their own learning solutions and thus enhance the pupils' 'learning to learn' capability.

Key issues

- Given limited class time, MFL learning can be optimised through developing learner strategies.

- Time on task and wait time are mutually reinforcing and crucial to effective MFL learning.

- Pupils need to be involved fully in the primary MFL learning process; when invited to articulate their thoughts, pupils can develop, apply and extend their range of learning strategies.

- Strategy training, readily built in to MFL lessons, can help pupils extend their repertoire of strategies.

- Knowing how to learn a foreign language can help children to become more effective strategy users and, ultimately, lifelong language learners.

Introduction – all about learning in the primary MFL classroom

It is useful for primary MFL teachers to be aware of relevant learning and language-learning theories. Extensive literature on these topics exists and it is not the purpose of this chapter to pick over this terrain in detail. However, we will briefly refer to some of the more pertinent learning theories and apply them to primary MFL.

Piaget's well-known and influential educational theory of cognitive development (Piaget and Inhelder 1972; see also Woolfolk *et al.* 2007) suggests that this development is supported by child-centred pedagogy and initiated by experimentation on the child's surroundings, often termed 'discovery learning'. Piaget also introduced a scale of cognitive development, according to which all children pass through four stages at different ages. Pupils at Key Stage 2 (aged 7 to 11) are deemed to be at the stage of concrete operations; younger pupils at Foundation Level and Key Stage 1 are in the pre-operational stage. These categories imply that all teachers need to plan an appropriate type of learning experience and also formulate strategies enabling pupils to transition to a higher cognitive level.

The rigid age allocation or pigeonholing of cognitive thinking has been criticised by many, as has the neglect of factors such as the influence of the teacher and other social factors. The lack of a social dimension has been particularly challenged. Other aspects of this approach, such as sensitivity to the age allocation as a starting point when considering learning experiences and planning for progression, have been incorporated into the more recent theory of social constructivism. One of the prime initiators of this school of thinking was the Russian psychologist Lev Vygotsky (Vygotsky 1986; see also Woolfolk *et al.* 2007) who developed the concept of the zone of proximal development (ZPD), which distinguishes between what learners can achieve when working alone and what they can achieve when guided by a more proficient other. This concept has gained considerable popularity among educationalists, not least because it reflects the basic model of the teacher–pupil relationship and the intended result of their cooperation in a learning outcome. It emphasises that the intellectual level at which a learning experience is to be pitched has to be within the grasp of the learner. That way, teachers can ensure that there is what Piaget called 'cognitive matching', and can set an appropriate level of learning for pupils to progress to and enable them to feel challenged. The ZPD also describes the value of collaborating in a dialogue between participants with potentially different levels of knowledge/understanding.

Primary MFL teachers, in particular, should not set the intellectual level of a learning experience too low, as disinterest may result. We have seen this in the case of some Year 6 classes where the MFL input was scarcely any different from that which the pupils had covered in earlier years, including at Key Stage 1. This could also be observed in Year 7 at secondary school, where the input often covers the same ground. As one Year 7 pupil observed: 'I couldn't believe it when our French teacher started doing numbers one to ten with us as we had done up to a hundred at primary school.'

When the concept of the ZPD is applied to a learning situation, learning can be accelerated through teacher scaffolding of pupil learning. The concept of scaffolding, a metaphor coined by Jerome Bruner (1960; see also Woolfolk *et al.* 2007) to describe Vygotsky's teacher intervention, is achieved through verbal advice or support activities to help pupils to facilitate their understanding, and by cutting out any potential 'waste' time. The ZPD embraces wholeheartedly the factors that affect learning and justifies the crucial role of the teacher as the main but not exclusive scaffolder, a role that can also be undertaken by pupils themselves as they work collaboratively to challenge and support each other. Within a social constructivist frame, learning is understood to be a social act, taking place not just within the individual but as a direct result of social interaction. Social constructivism highlights the internalisation of speech and language, as Light and Littleton (1999: 92) point out: 'This view of cognition challenges our traditional conceptions of development and learning. It invites us to reject a conception of the developmental process as the creation of the autonomous thinker . . . in its place is a view of learning as intersubjective and dialogical.'

On the basis of the social constructivist approach, Lave and Wenger (1991) developed their Situated Cognition theory, and they, similarly, define learning as a social process that cannot be decontextualised from a real-life environment whereby learners are connected by what they call joint participation in a community of practice. The pupils are, according to this theory, members of several communities: at school, at home, with friends and at various extracurricular clubs or groups. The MFL classroom, with its rituals and routines, is one such community, and it is a concept we find useful as a foundation on which to base ongoing primary MFL pedagogical developments. A 'classroom community', a term used by Behrman (2002), is established when the teacher sets appropriate tasks to ensure contextualised learning. Learning can then be understood as an interactive process taking place between pupils that is facilitated by teachers as they 'scaffold' pupils' learning. Scaffolding support is lessened as time passes, thus encouraging greater pupil autonomy and asserting effective primary MFL teaching and learning as interactive in the classroom. This perspective also fits into a formative and constructive assessment framework (see Chapter 7), which provides pupils with a scaffolded way to improve and progress – an approach that is a key to learning socially and collaboratively in the classroom community. This is of particular importance for the inclusion of children with special educational needs who need to be included in the learning and social space as well as being physically in the classroom (Jones 2013). Cable *et al.* (2010) found that children with special educational needs appeared more self-assured and had greater self-esteem in such inclusive environments.

Language teaching is not restricted to the interaction in the classroom, as Macaro (2001: 1) points out: 'language learning involves much more than teachers and learners simply interacting.' Teachers should seek ways, Macaro goes on to say, to offer practical suggestions as to how pupils can learn better. In the following sections we discuss how learners of primary MFL can develop strategies enabling them to be as successful as possible, for it is those learners with the widest range of strategies who are certainly the most effective. Since strategy is a broad term used in various fields and areas, we will define its specific use within the context of education, and more specifically in primary MFL.

Strategies, strategies, strategies

In general, a learning strategy can be seen, according to O'Malley and Chamot (1990: 1), as 'the special thoughts or behaviours that individuals use to help them comprehend, learn, or retain new information.' Once these skills are acquired, the learner can, as Oxford (1990: 8) states, improve and vary them, and also apply them to new learning contexts: 'specific actions taken by the learner to make learning easier, faster, more enjoyable, more self-directed, more effective, and more transferable to new situations.' Learning strategies thus defined can be understood as techniques enabling the individual to absorb, organise and retain information: that is, as a set of skills that can be transferred to other areas. With reference to language learning, Grenfell and Harris (1999: 22) stress the habitual and individual nature of the learning process when they define the learning strategy quite simply as 'a set of habits or practices which learners may adopt in approaching the learning of a second language.'

Learning strategies have been further subdivided in the following way with, at the macro level, general learning strategies comprising all techniques required for all kinds of learning, such as metacognitive strategies (planning and self-evaluation) and some cognitive strategies such as resourcing, rehearsal or repeating. At the meso level, language-learning strategies are said to relate to all strategies used to cope with language learning generally. At the micro level, there is a further subdivision concerned with second and/or foreign language learning. These levels should not be seen as hierarchical but as operating on a zigzag basis. O'Malley and Chamot (1990) also introduce the dimension of social and affective strategies. Oxford (1990, 2011) suggests many practical ways to develop learner strategies, many of which will be of particular use in supporting children with special educational needs.

Strategy training helps us to see our young learners as self-reflective agents with some measure of control and insight into their own learning processes (there are examples of this later in this chapter), although the role of the teacher is essential in helping to orientate and harness the strategies to promote greater learning efficiency.

In the literature, the terms 'learner strategy' and 'learning strategy' are sometimes used interchangeably. Macaro (2001: 19–20) particularly emphasises the fact that the term 'learner strategies' captures more effectively the learner as active participant in the learning process. This interpretation of the term 'learner strategies' resonates more with our view of the foreign language learner as an active participant in the learning process.

With limited contact time for MFL learning, an enthusiastic and joyous learner response to the teaching context is not sufficient: pupils need to be involved in their own learning. The resurgence of interest in learner/learning strategies is reflected in current discourses on MFL teaching and learning and the popularity of the 'learning to learn' (L2L) agenda that refers to meta-awareness. The personalisation of learning is also important for primary MFL as part of effective differentiated provision, particularly when time for teaching and learning MFL comes at such a premium. It is also about pupil ownership, as Knowles (2009: 94) writes with regard to personalised learning for children, defining this as 'a partnership . . . rather than something that is done to them.'

Wait time and waiting time

One of the obstacles when incorporating the learning of a foreign language into the primary curriculum has been the lack of space in the primary curriculum, which is 'already full to bursting' (Jones 2005: 4) – a sentiment echoed by many headteachers in recent years. It is desirable that children learn as effectively as possible and that good use of optimised learning time is made in all subjects.

From a review of the available research into educational effectiveness, Edelenbos and Johnstone (1997: 79–80) identified five characteristics that they believe determine effective teaching. The first of these, relevant to our discussion here, is the distinction between 'time for learning', in the sense of opportunities for learning, and 'time on task', meaning maximising such opportunities. MFL has been susceptible to being squeezed out when there are other curriculum pressures. The 'time on task' is, as Edelenbos and Johnstone assert, a variable of key importance yet that is difficult to measure since 'what really counts is [the] unobservable mental activity rather than [the] observable physical activity.' In a similar vein, Cullingford (1995: 16) defines 'time on task' as 'those moments when children are actually engaged with the work, rather than getting up to find a pen, talking to a neighbour, dreaming, playing with a pencil, or just waiting for the teacher to give an instruction. This latter time can be described as "waiting".'

'Waiting time' should in no way be confused with the concept of 'wait time' (see Chapter 7 on assessment), which refers to the extended time teachers are advised to wait to allow pupils to think about a response. In such a scenario pupils are in fact on task. Cullingford refers to research studies indicating that children spent a disturbingly high proportion of time – sometimes as much as 75 per cent – in the school day on 'waiting time'. Our observations of primary MFL lessons would indicate a considerable amount of activity: indeed the pace of lessons, generally, is energetic, if not at times frenetic, although activity in itself is not synonymous with learning.

A typical, well-paced language lesson includes a high amount of task-oriented use of the foreign language, such as asking for and going to find a pencil. Simple instructions like this in the target language should be part of the foreign language lesson and can then become part of the whole-school drip-feed approach at any point in any lesson.

Pupils are faced with a considerable amount of new input that they need to absorb in the short time span of a primary MFL lesson and it is helpful if they develop strategies to help them process and, hopefully, retain their new learning, given the considerable load on memory. The question arising from this is: How do young learners cope and what are the possible implications for teaching techniques? At this stage, we will present the results of discussions undertaken by teachers with pupils about their learning styles and consider the implications on teaching.

Learner strategies and 'tricky bits'

In the first part of our survey, teachers we were working with invited pupils to describe aspects of their MFL learning that they found difficult and, if possible, to give reasons. They then asked the pupils to identify and explain what they considered easy aspects of learning a foreign language. The pupils were invited to express, in their own terms, strategies they used to learn, after the teachers had explained to them the authors' interest in knowing about how they coped with, as one pupil memorably put it, the 'tricky bits'. It became evident that the pupils, like the teaching staff taking part in the survey, were aware of the time constraint on their learning time. This applies also to schools where primary MFL learning was guaranteed a weekly slot in the curriculum, and yet pupils felt it still contrasted with other subjects that appear more regularly. In the inimitable style of youngsters, some Year 6 pupils expressed their concern about this constraint and impact on their learning:

> Because when we go out to play we forget our German and we have to remember it for a week.

> It is a lot to take in in one lesson, and then remember for the next lesson – in a week's time.

These two statements are representative of the vast majority of pupils in our sample: nearly all the pupils interviewed commented on the difficulty of *remembering* their MFL input. Myles' research (2016) showed that how often older children hear a word is the single most important factor in word learning: with younger children, how recently they heard the word is a factor. Cable *et al.* (2010) emphasise the need for continuous reinforcement across the curriculum to allow time for revisiting and for consolidation, thus ensuring that the learning input can be processed from short- to long-term memory.

Pupils are able to recognise, and indeed have identified, complicated parts or 'tricky bits' in MFL learning, and we found a remarkable consensus among the children. In Table 6.1 we group the statements pupils made into the following categories: memory, pace and pronunciation.

TABLE 6.1 'Tricky bits' in MFL learning

Difficult aspect	Pupil statement
Memory	
Learning long/really hard words/ lots of words	'Sometimes there are too many words to take in that you can never really remember them.'
A whole sentence	'It overloads your brain.'
Genders	'It is hard to remember which words go in which group.' (The authors noted some imaginative phonetic spellings from pupils such as *maskeling* [for masculine] and *new to* [for neuter].)
Pace	
Having to take in too much	'Once we finish one topic we go straight on to another one and we forget the last topic and then we sometimes get asked about the last topic and we can't remember.'
Pronunciation	
Different and new sounds	'Getting your mouth round pronunciation because it's a sound I have to teach my mouth from scratch'; 'Because the words are complicated and aren't in the English language so we aren't used to them'; 'Letters that look the same as English but are pronounced differently.'

The data in Table 6.1 reflect the importance the pupils interviewed attributed to the act of remembering. It is vital, if the children are to be able to recycle and manipulate language at later stages in their learning, to acquire competence with respect to learning strategies from an early stage onwards. Young learners can and do devise their own means of helping them to remember vocabulary and phrases in the target language, as the descriptions in Table 6.2 show.

TABLE 6.2 Language-learning strategies

Auditory–vocabulary-related techniques

Word association	'If it sounds like another word then use that word to remember it'; 'Good morning, good afternoon and good evening all start with the same word – *buenos días*, *buenas tardes*, *buenas noches*.'
Constant repetition	'It helps if we say them over and over again'; 'Say them over in our heads and out loud and sometimes with actions'; 'We practise saying them over and over again with different voices and we also chant.'
Mnemonics	'Pfeifen-whistle-sounds at the start like you're trying to whistle.' (This is a reference to children being asked to mime and stress through whistling the syllables of words they are learning.)
Visualisation	'I try to remember the pictures and remember how to say the words by closing my eyes'; 'Sometimes seeing the word helps.'
Songs and rhymes	'We make up a rhyme and keep repeating it.'

The written word

Writing it down	'Writing it down helps because then we can look in our exercise books if we can't remember things.'

Modelling on teacher and other pupils

Lip-reading from our teacher	'We lip-read from our teacher to get how she makes the sounds'; 'You can visualise the mouth movements when it is your turn to say it'; 'I try to imitate the accent as well as possible, make it sound funny.'
Reading body language	'We look at the way Miss uses her lips so we can read her lips and look at the actions she uses as she talks.'
Listening and saying/copying	'We pass a microphone [a toy echo mike] round the class so everyone can try and pronounce the words correctly. You hear it over and over again which makes it easier to learn'; 'I try and say the words out loud so I can remember.'

Teamwork and communication skills (social competence)

Working collaboratively	'Say the words with a friend so you both get it into your head' [for mutual reinforcement].

continued . . .

TABLE 6.2 Continued

Word and object association (kinaesthetic)	
Finger puppets and toys as memory joggers by association	'We use finger puppets that help us remember'; 'We like holding objects while saying the words.'

Writing	
Sentence and text construction	'Break down the word for the right spelling'; 'Make small kinds of phrases and build them up'; 'Write a draft and check the teacher's keywords sheet'; 'Write words you're unsure about, spelling it how you think it sounds.'

Psychological	
Feeling relaxed	'Chant the words, practise the pronunciation and enjoy it!'; 'Just listen to the sounds, everything is for a reason, don't be shy, ask questions and if we do well the teacher will be in a good mood and do fun activities.'
Ask for help	'We ask for help if we are struggling with any pronunciation or remembering any words'; 'I say I've forgotten or ask the teacher what it was.'
Go by your intuition	'You've got to feel the language.'

Use of reference material: independent learning (metacognitive strategies)	
Using a dictionary, glossary, word list or the internet	'Google can find a word you do not know'; 'Looking things up on a computer.'

Developing independent learning capability

The statements in Table 6.2 show that pupils can identify how to successfully transfer new input to long-term memory on the basis of repetition, and emphasise the importance of developing listening skills. Without exception, all children at all levels identified language items such as numbers and colours as 'easy to learn' because of constant repetition and practice. As one Year 3 child put it: 'I can always remember how to say hello and goodbye, colours, animals and counting'; and in the colourful language of a Year 5 pupil, 'I remember numbers and colours because the teacher is always yappering about these in French.'

In a relaxed, non-threatening MFL classroom atmosphere, pupils try to develop their strategies by modelling themselves on peers and teachers. In such an environment children will also feel secure enough to seek clarification and to practise 'strange' sounds within the group. It is noticeable that the pupils interviewed were aware of and able to extend their learning, as their statements with respect to means for independent learning show. These, in particular, point to the importance of the ability to ask questions and apply strategies to obtain information. Independent learning depends to some extent on sustaining inquisitiveness and developing research skills. Thus the foundation of research skills can be laid in primary education. A test for independent learning would be to ask pupils to explain their findings in their own words to peers as evidence of understanding.

Teachers can benefit from such knowledge of their pupils' perceptions of their own learner strategies. This can be done by teachers sometimes asking pupils to talk through their work and their thinking in the manner of a 'think aloud protocol' (Macaro 2001). This knowledge can provide the basis for a joint exploration of the subject. The statements are clear reminders for teachers, relating to common-sense pedagogy such as the need to constantly spiral back to structures and vocabulary over the course of learning and to limit the amount of input at any one time to enable the children to 'remember' what they learn.

Enabling pupils to cope with the 'tricky bits'

Talking *about* learning and developing awareness of and knowledge about language provides pupils with an opportunity to acquire a metalanguage in primary MFL and to be able to identify their strengths and weaknesses as part of a formative framework of learning (see Chapter 7 on assessment). 'Think aloud' protocols, where pupils talk through their work giving an account of their thinking and choices, can be useful here. This can be done with individual pupils as a spot-check or in mini–focus groups, for example. Harris (1997: 21) suggests that strategy training can be implemented by establishing the learning needs and areas of concern with the pupils, considering what strategies could be used, deciding how to teach the strategies and drawing up success criteria for strategy learning. This approach could easily be incorporated into regular lesson planning and, crucially, give pupils some ownership of the learning process as they acquire new strategies. Table 6.3 provides examples of support strategies provided by one teacher using target-language German.

The idea of a challenge can be an excellent learning tool and a very powerful motivational strategy (see also Chapter 5), as most children respond to learning challenges. Some Year 3 children in the survey embraced this philosophy when they urged other children learning languages to 'put on your thinking cap and switch on your brain', in terms of thinking of strategies to help them learn. The concept of challenge also resonates with one of the fundamental tenets of the popular Critical Skills approach, which positions itself around a learning approach that is challenge-led and that seeks to engage learners in a collaborative effort, in groups or pairs, to meet those challenges. This strategic learning approach can be incorporated into primary MFL lessons as in the following examples:

> *Focusing on gender:* 'Children some time ago were challenged to learn then recall the correct genders of food items. A week later, they came up with *honig* being masculine because [in their perception] bears like honey and fierce bears are boys.'

> *Focusing on vocabulary by associating word with object:* 'I asked the children to work in groups and to put the vocabulary together from the unit into decorative dodecahedrons that I then hung from the ceiling for them to admire and to use as a kind of reference.'

TABLE 6.3 Auditory–vocabulary-related techniques: comments from teachers

Mnemonics	'I encourage them to use their own meaningful mnemonics, e.g. *lesen* – sounds like lazy and I read when I'm feeling lazy; *basteln* – the start of the word sounds like basket full of handicraft equipment, glue, wool, etc.; *schreiben* – Year 4 made a link with Ancient Egyptian scribes.' '*Schere* was proving difficult with some Year 5s till they suggested it sounded like a shearer, a sheep shearer and they imagine a sheep having a scissor trim.'
Tunes, songs and raps	These are well-known means to support memory and listening skills: 'Tunes are unbelievably powerful. *Hast du Geschwister?* Chanted to a "ner ner-ner ner ner" tune becomes suddenly memorable rather than tricky for Year 3s.' Even a more complex question like *Wie ist das Wetter heute?* can, in the words of one teacher, be 'a doddle even for Year 2 if it is sung.' This teacher states that she puts a lot of things to tunes and uses tunes for individual needs: 'If a child is struggling to recall something, the tune sung quietly to them will often unlock what they are searching for.' Another teacher suggests teaching nouns such as *Orangensaft, Apfelsaft* and *Milch* as a three-part round.
Pronunciation	'I like to show them that German words taste good and some words provoke a kind of tasty reaction among the children. These words include *möchte, Bluse* (the lovely lip-shape here), *Federmäppchen, zwölf, Orangenmarmelade* (the sheer length of it), *Hör zu!* – my Year 2s find they taste lovely together!' 'We came across the word *Leberknödel*, which the children thought sounded delicious, more than what the word actually means (liver dumplings!).' 'In my class we have pronunciation games where the children have to define their own noises and come up with ways to remember pronunciation. One pair suggested they could remember how to say *Erdbeereis* as *Ardbearice* (sic), and "chips" as "ships". Then as a class we came up with a "hot tip" about pronunciation rules. We break down words into smaller bits: *Ra-dier-gum-mi* (pencil rubber), then put them together again, like Humpty Dumpty.' (See Figure 6.1)
Visuals and object associated	'Just put the finger puppet on and away they go.'

To the above, we add 'grammar challenges', given the fundamental importance of grammar in language learning, not least owing to grammar being a central plank of the new KS2 NC 2014 requirements. A teacher in Essex stresses the importance of memorability in helping the learners to understand grammar:

> I try to make the learning memorable, so using cartoons for example to demonstrate a point, or the pupils making up songs and rhymes to hammer home

FIGURE 6.1 'Humpty Dumpty' word-learning strategy

a grammar point or for verbs. I like movement in the classroom so the pupils have to stand up/sit down for masculine/feminine and crouch for neuter. Dictionary work is useful and I always use the terms – what noun can we put here, and using L1 to familiarise [pupils] with the terms.

A London teacher plans grammar input for her French lessons thus:

In every lesson, I always try to implement an element of grammar without the children noticing the complexity of French grammar. Whilst teaching I stop the children and ask the gender of the noun. For example, I say 'Children, you can usually tell me a noun's gender from the article', then I take a bag full of random cards with nouns and articles and they have to pick the correct ones in line with the topic we are learning. With Upper KS2, we start working on sentence building. I decided to make words colour coded – nouns and pronouns red, verbs green, articles blue; for example, *Je* [red] *mange* [green] *un* [blue] *croissant* [blue]. This will help keep the rules and patterns of French sentence structure neat and well-organised in their mind. Basic French sentences are introduced – Subject-Verb-

Object – and I constantly remind the children that they always need two or three elements to make a sentence: *Je* (1) + *mange* (2) or *je* (1) + *mange* (2) + *object* (3).

Such sentences were in evidence in this teacher's classroom on a washing line with mini-pegs so that the children could manipulate the words. This shows how grammar is confronted strategically from the start in a fun way and how language is taught and practised in sentences rather than as vocabulary items: this teacher said 'I never teach isolated words.'

The above examples show how good teachers, as a matter of course, have strategies to teach 'grammar' in age-appropriate ways that reflect the Programme of Study, NC 2014 requirements for pupils to be able to:

> understand basic grammar appropriate to the language being studied, including (where relevant): feminine, masculine and neuter forms and the conjugation of high-frequency verbs; key features and patterns of the language; how to apply these, for instance, to build sentences; and how these differ from or are similar to English.

In response to a question about 'next steps', one Year 6 boy in a London primary school made this related comment on 'grammar': 'We need to know verbs and how they work so we can talk about things and not just know words.' To enable this pupil and his peers to 'talk about things', we would like to stress the usefulness of planning opportunities for active collaborative learning in order to maximise time on task and on pupil interactions. Some primary MFL lessons that we saw would have benefited from less repetition of isolated vocabulary and more of a learning challenge involving more complex language tasks to be worked on collaboratively.

Recognising difference and extending the learner's repertoire

While there is evidence in both pupils' and teachers' comments and observations that listening and speaking are deemed to be the predominant skills, it is important to stress that language-learning activities chosen for lessons should ideally address all skills, since visual, kinaesthetic and auditory learning styles vary between individuals. Indeed, Shaw and Hawes (1998: 61) assert that 'Each person has a learning style as unique as their signature or fingerprint.' It would be impossible to teach a class of pupils on the basis of each individual learning style, but most pupils will respond to an approach where their needs are being met at least some of the time. It may be necessary for those children who have a strong preference in any way, or a special educational need, to pay closer attention to the requirements of their personal learning style and to use materials to match this style in order to optimise their learning. The primary MFL teacher might also take the opportunity to strengthen and build up other learning styles. For example, for children with dyslexia, who rely to a great extent on auditory techniques, it might well be important to encourage development of their writing skills.

EAL children will already have a repertoire of strategies for language learning, and what Anderson (2011: 144) calls 'linguistic and cultural capital'. This capital can be made more explicit and exploited in the primary MFL classroom, both for those children's own learning and for sharing in the learning group. White *et al.* (2007) comment on the usefulness, where possible, of teachers having some knowledge of the specific difficulties of some of the languages represented in a class (different profiles of tenses, for example, such as the fact that Vietnamese does not mark verbs for tense) that might impact the foreign language learning of EAL learners.

In recent years there has been a growing discourse on the gender-specific character of certain learning styles and boys' preference for certain school subjects. The peculiarly British obsession with categorising behaviours and identifying gender-based tendencies in education has sometimes led to over-simplifications about what boys and girls are like as learners. Research findings are contradictory. For example, it is often believed that boys have a preference for a kinaesthetic style of learning and enjoy a lot of interaction and speaking practice, yet other research points to a preference for a more traditional didactic style because of its ordered and routine-based nature (Barton 2002).

The advent of the National Curriculum in the late 1980s obliged both sexes to study an equal range of subjects. Girls generally did well at traditional 'male' subjects such as maths and sciences, yet boys did not do well at traditional 'female' subjects, which included MFL. However, these statistics only tell half the truth. More recent research into boys' 'underachievement', mainly in secondary schools, acknowledges that the term is an over-simplification masking more complex categories of learner than 'boys' and 'girls'.

Much of the gender-divide discussion that centres around learner styles suggests that boys respond best to the following teaching and learning styles:

- clear explanations
- positive and immediate feedback
- fun, dynamic teaching
- knowing where they are going with the task set.

There has been considerable investment in highlighting these preferences in professional development training and in educational literature, yet it is hard to imagine that these elements of 'good practice' do not apply in equal measure to girls. If girls are more conscientious in writing, and prepared to persevere with longer tasks, does this not simply indicate a greater capacity to comply? If so, we believe the differences are more likely to be rooted in social expectation and learnt ways of being rather than reflecting innate biological and cognitive differences. Indeed, differences that are based on assumptions about gender persist in the way teachers interact with pupils, including types of reprimand and the nature of feedback. For example, boys are more frequently reprimanded but the reprimand relates more to inattentiveness and misbehaviour, whereas girls receive more positive feedback, but reprimands to girls, though less frequent, tend to relate to (academic) task performance, and so error is treated more seriously by girls (Wood 2004: 287).

The use of competition, affirmative male role models and inclusion of topics of interest to boys (sport, cars, etc.), which are among the approaches often proposed to engage boys' interests, should surely form part of any balanced, holistic curriculum planning.

We believe the key, especially with early learners where the gender divide has not yet become a self-conscious issue, is to deploy a wide range of styles and to be mindful of individual preferences to avoid stultifying stereotypes – for example that all boys are clamorous and have short attention spans, and that girls are naturally compliant stoics. In fact, when asked which activity types they preferred in MFL, 'more self-confident girls tended to select activities similar to those chosen by the boys' (Barton 2002: 280).

Learning-style preferences

Research into cognitive processes, and short- and long-term memory, have gone hand in hand with exploring different ways of storing and retrieving information. Preferences in regard to information storage and retrieval are often referred to as cognitive styles. In his seminal book *Frames of Mind* (1983), Howard Gardner put forward the theory of the existence of seven non-related forms of intelligence, the combination of which, he claims, releases full human potential. While not necessarily agreeing in any way with this theory nor wishing to reify this approach, we would point out that the theory is embraced and clearly identifiable in PSHE in many primary schools, where each child is encouraged to identify her/his strengths, often in very visible ways with personal 'How am I smart?' posters, for example, on the walls. The children's self-esteem is developed through the assertion and celebration of the fact that each of them is 'smart' in some way.

Teachers, certainly, need to take into account preferences in thinking and learning by developing and providing a range of activities that will appeal to, strengthen and extend preferences. Perhaps unintentionally, many of the 'intelligences' – especially verbal-linguistic, visual, musical and kinaesthetic – are regularly targeted in primary MFL lessons. In Table 6.4 we show how these can be addressed in an MFL lesson, using the example of a Year 6 lesson taught by a specialist primary MFL teacher.

The teacher observed a positive response by the pupils to the variety of activities offered to them: 'I found this method of teaching particularly effective as the variety motivates the children and results in fun and interesting learning.' Although the teacher has described her lesson drawing on multiple intelligences theory, the lesson, we would assert, is effective in that it engenders interactive learning and a variety of activities that respond to pupils' different needs in a fun and relaxed atmosphere. The concept of learning preference and style is useful for teachers in guiding them to plan varied lessons adaptable to the needs of all learners. It is also feasible that the relaxed atmosphere in such a classroom, the 'lowered filter' as Krashen (1982) would term it, makes the various activities appealing to the learners and, with good timing, keeps them on task.

Care must be taken, as with all theories, not to adopt the idea of different cognitive learning styles blindly or to accept these uncritically. The concepts of learning styles and Gardner's Multiple Intelligences (MI) theory have been subject to much recent negative comment by some educationalists. It is also important to note that Gardner himself has expressed 'unease' about the way in which his MI theory, which he said was never intended as a 'blueprint for learning', has been interpreted in classrooms: 'Much of it was a mishmash of practices – left brain and right brain contrasts, sensory learning styles, neuro-linguistic programming and multiple intelligences approaches, all mixed with dazzling promiscuity' (Revell citing Gardner, writing in the *Education Guardian,* 31 May 2005).

TABLE 6.4 MFL applications of Multiple Intelligences in a lesson

Intelligence	MFL applications	Sample lesson
Verbal-linguistic	Brainstorming, listening, speaking, reading, writing, word games	'I began the lesson by asking the class to repeat the words for items of clothing in German after me.'
Intrapersonal	Personalised and differentiated tasks; homework, self-evaluation, building self-esteem	'Pupils can work on individual translation with reference materials.'
Kinaesthetic	Drama, mime, role play, dance, hands-on learning, making and creating things	'Pupils put on the item of clothing I called out.'
Visual and spatial	Artwork, construction, concept maps, flashcards, posters, colour coding	'I asked the class to draw a picture of themselves wearing the items of clothing taught in the lesson, labelling each item in German.'
Musical	Songs, chants, rhymes, rhythms, raps, drills, awareness of sounds	'Music can be a powerful aid to learning and can be used to create an optimal learning state and to boost attention and memory, and so I played a recording of German children's songs while they were doing this.'
Interpersonal	Pair and group work, peer tutoring and assessment, team games, project work	'Teamwork; peer assessment opportunity.'
Logical and mathematical	Pattern identification, hypothesising, experimenting, word play	'Lots of playing with sounds as part of an inductive approach to grammar whereby pupils work out a rule in their own words.'

John White, in a critique of Gardner (2005: 9), opines that 'Putting children into boxes that have not been proved to exist may end up restricting the education they receive, leading teachers to overly rigid views of individual pupils' potentialities, and what is worse, a new type of stereotyping.'

Theories will always need to pass the test of being tried out in a real-life context as it is only when they pass the test in an everyday classroom environment that they can be integrated into lessons. The children's performance will provide evidence of which parts of a theory can be applied successfully, and which aspects need to be challenged or simply discarded. Strategic competence cannot be developed on the basis of a theory alone; rather it relies partially on the teacher's freedom to think and experiment creatively, building on the learners' previously acquired strategies and adapted accordingly. The acquisition of strategic competence can only occur when pupils are offered a variety of activities presented in mixed styles, preferably guided by aspects of the four skills (see Chapter 4), and when the pupils are invited to reflect on their experiences in their role as learners and on their potential. Teachers need to always bear in mind children's potential for mindset growth, as Dweck (2012) asserts, and that intelligences/learner preferences/ different needs, however these are understood and conceptualised, are not fixed but multiple, flexible and extendable.

Conclusion

While it may appear a gargantuan leap from those first ineffably enthusiastic steps of learning a foreign language in the primary school to becoming a strategically competent lifelong language learner, it is at the primary stage of learning that foundation stones are laid. A very good starting point is to understand that what pupils see and hear is understood in terms of what they already know. We found a remarkable synchronicity between the pupils' perceptions about learning and the views of their teachers, and we urge teachers to talk to their pupils about learning on a regular basis in an attempt to demystify it and to make the learning journey a shared and transparent one, for this is the essence of learning to learn. We have emphasised the need to engage pupils fully in their learning and for teachers to encourage independent learning where possible, based on the children's ability and opportunities to learn to self-regulate (see Boekaerts and Corno 2005). In this respect, one Reception teacher commented that she built learning strategies into her lesson plans/schemes of work by answering the question 'How can we learn?' in relation to the learning objective and success criteria. At some point in each lesson, she would ask the children 'How is it going?'

> In this way, the learning strategies often come from the pupils themselves. A child will say, for example in relation to new words, 'it really helps me that the word sounds like it does in English/Spanish/French.' I listen to what they say and adapt if necessary.

Unpublished research into pupils' learner strategies across subjects at KS3 by one of the authors of this book (Jones) with the Assessment Group at King's College London identified 23 themes. Of these, the themes that we think are important for primary MFL and should straddle the KS2 to KS3 MFL learning continuum include:

- setting learning targets and understanding what is needed to achieve these;
- acting on one's own initiative;
- self-assessing one's own learning;
- asking questions and searching for answers;
- looking for patterns;
- making connections between different things;
- building on previous learning;
- remembering what has been learnt;
- working collaboratively in order to learn;
- being able to explain one's own learning;

- having the confidence to persevere with one's own learning;
- taking pleasure in learning.

When added to the cognitive strategies described by teachers themselves, these metacognitive and socio-affective strategies can be powerful drivers of learning, enabling children to make use of their prior knowledge and create new language. Oxford (1990, 2011) suggests dozens of practical examples in her books for embedding strategy in regular language-learning lessons. When children have a range of strategies at their disposal and show an understanding of how they learn best, they can take some ownership of their learning and select different strategies for different purposes. This is a reflection, worded a little differently, of what the children themselves have reported. There are case studies and vignettes of teaching and learning with comments from children and teachers in this chapter – and indeed throughout this book – that provide evidence that this is what happens in metacognitive primary MFL classrooms where a culture of classroom community provides that magic buzz of fun, interaction, enquiry and purposeful learning. In such a learning environment, 'tricky bits' are challenges, not problems, as demonstrated by a little Year 4 boy who wrote that he tried to remember words 'by breaking them down into *cilobols* (sic)', and this from a child who, according to his teacher, could not yet tie up his shoelaces.

Questions on which to reflect

- What would you identify as 'tricky bits' in learning MFL for pupils, and why?
- Which learning styles/preferences/differences have you identified in the MFL classroom and how can these be best catered for and extended to promote mindset growth?

7

Assessment for learning: How am I doing? What have I achieved? How can I progress?

Manageable and sensitive ways of dealing with assessment and the monitoring of progress in primary MFL will be explored in this chapter, bearing in mind the need to respond to the diverse needs of learners, and taking into account statutory requirements and expectations. This chapter reflects on the dilemmas posed by the advent of level-free assessment and the myriad initiatives that have sprung up in response to this dilemma. The main emphasis will be on the framing of all assessment formatively in an Assessment for Learning (AfL) approach. AfL is defined by Black and Wiliam (1998: 2) as 'All activities undertaken by teachers, and by the students themselves, which provide information to be used as feedback to modify the teaching and learning activities in which they are engaged.' This does not dispense with elements of summative assessment, described by Black and Wiliam as 'any assessment made at the end of a period of learning to evaluate the level of understanding or competence.' Assessment will be considered as a support for learning, and for the development of self-learning and pupil autonomy, thereby sowing the seeds of lifelong language-learning capability.

Key issues

- Assessment is an integral part of the learning and teaching loop.
- Useful feedback to help plan for progression is provided by assessment data.
- Since AfL has become well-embedded in the primary school, especially in the core subjects, it is essential to incorporate formative practices into primary MFL.
- All assessment needs to be formative on the roadmap of language learning.
- Teachers need to find ways to monitor and record assessment data in order to have a track record of pupils' progress and as part of the transition dialogue – the dialogue between primary and secondary school.

- Primary MFL assessment needs to be part of the whole-school assessment strategy on an equal basis to other subjects.
- Teachers should devise assessment schemes in a way that meshes not only with the whole-school assessment framework but with their assessment beliefs about how best to promote and gain evidence of the 'substantial progress' required.

Introduction

Assessment is an absolutely integral part of teaching and the learning process in early language learning. Some classes and teachers have met this statement with disquiet, possibly because they immediately think of formal tests, which represent only one aspect of assessment. Tests often cause apprehension and anxiety because of the high stakes involved. Indelible and unchangeable grades and league tables can blot the copybooks of the children, teachers and schools concerned. Indeed, the potentially heavy hand of testing on primary languages has been perceived by some teachers as something that might impact on pupil motivation.

AfL and the benefits it can bring have been strongly promoted over recent years. Indeed, it is well-embedded in primary practice across the board, especially in English, with which primary MFL has profound links. We strongly assert that primary MFL learning should be located within a formative assessment framework that focuses on establishing what the children can do and providing feedback as to the next steps to ensure progression. Progression in learning is a major issue in the establishment of quality and enduring primary MFL provision.

Although Black and Wiliam's seminal 'Black Box' work on formative assessment (Black and Wiliam 1998) takes care to point out that the use of formative assessment is not a 'magic bullet' for education, the improvement it can have on learning in the classroom, as their research proved, is significant and measurable. Jones' ongoing research with the King's College Assessment for Learning Group found classroom practice where teachers really did find that their efforts made a difference. As a Year 6 teacher in the north of England commented: 'It is making a real difference to pupils' learning. They comment on it themselves.'

Many of the techniques offered by Black *et al.* (2003) and elaborated by Jones and Wiliam (2008), specifically for MFL, are simple and easy to incorporate into the classroom and into primary MFL. The aforementioned Year 6 teacher had made sure the children were clear about the learning intentions and success criteria for each German lesson she taught, discussing strategies for learning such as how to get the right pronunciation by thinking about the rules of German pronunciation, giving them time to think and, above all, making the learning worthwhile and important in the eyes of the pupils. Some colleagues are under the erroneous perception that primary MFL is all about throwing soft toys around the classroom. There is a risk that primary MFL itself might be seen – in the memorable words to me personally of Dr Patricia Driscoll, Primary MFL expert – as a 'fluffy bunny' subject, devoid of the rigours of other subjects. In this respect, an appropriate assessment framework is helpful in establishing the necessary rigour.

Pedagogically, we would contend that it is important to evaluate, value and validate what the children have been learning and are able to do in the foreign language. In addition, every other area of the primary curriculum is assessed and well-thought-out assessment gives parity for the children and accentuates the importance of primary MFL. One London headteacher felt strongly about this and commented that 'Languages need to mirror the planning and assessment systems of the core subjects and have a tracking system that can show progression of classes and individuals.' Now that primary MFL is statutory at KS2 and evidence of progression will need to be shown, this will attract an inspection agenda, even more so if primary MFL is proposed by the school as a strength in its self-evaluation. Research by Cable *et al.* (2010) and Wade and Marshall (2009) identified weaknesses in assessment in primary language, but a trawl of recent primary-school inspection reports on MFL are much more positive, as we have seen for ourselves on our recent school visits. The fundamental question really is not *whether* to assess, but *how* to assess.

Primary Languages: a learning-centred perspective on assessment

Teachers have some freedom to develop an assessment system that works for them and that their pupils can adapt and work with; for example, assessment systems created by groups of schools or other existing frameworks. We are asserting that the starting point is the fundamental principles of an assessment approach that focuses on helping pupils to learn how to learn foreign languages as effectively as possible.

Any discussion of assessment is inextricably linked to the process of learning, as Drummond (1993: 15) asserts:

> It is a child's learning that must be the subject of teachers' most energetic care and attention – not their lesson plans or schemes of work, or their rich and stimulating provision – but the learning that results from everything they do (and do not do) in schools and classrooms. The process of assessing children's learning – by looking closely at it and striving to understand it – is the only safeguard against children's failure, the only certain guarantee of children's progress and development.

Indeed, it is important that assessment is seen as an essential part of the whole teaching cycle and that a teacher's assessments should inform teaching plans in a seamless way, and not be perceived as bolt-ons or peripherals. On the contrary, feedback from the learning process through appropriate and sensitive assessment is *an entitlement*. All pupils should have access 'to a coherent, progressive learning experience that develops understanding and skills', as the powerful statement in the former Scottish Guidelines for 5–14 in primary MFL (Learning and Teaching Scotland 2000: 5) expressed it. It is therefore of concern that according to the Recent Language Trends survey (Tinsley and Board 2016), a half of all the primary schools in the survey response did not have a secure assessment system in place to ensure pupil progress.

We agree that pupils have an entitlement to assessment that informs them in a sensitive and systematic way of their ongoing progress from one year to another. Assessment, set in the context of effective learning and teaching and taking account of the five key activities of teaching, planning, recording, reporting and evaluating, will provide vital feedback that will inform subsequent learning and teaching. Such a cohesive approach to learning, teaching and assessment would provide the 'confidence factor' that Alison Hurrell of the University of Aberdeen found lacking in primary MFL teachers and leaders – along with a feeling that 'by assessing the children somehow the essence of what they were doing would be altered, i.e. no more fun!' (Alison Hurrell, personal communication).

The 'fun factor', we are suggesting, will not be hampered by context-sensitive assessment, and teachers should not hesitate to 'junk', redesign or create assessments suitable for their pupils that are in accord with their teaching approach and content of learning. In fact, the 'confidence factor' can help to ensure that the 'fun factor' keeps a prominent place in assessment. Teachers are on a learning curve when it comes to developing teaching and assessment strategies appropriate to primary MFL, an important stage in the continuing development of the community of primary MFL practice. Teachers need to adapt formative practices with which they are increasingly familiar and use them in language teaching, especially given the status of languages as an inclusive subject *par excellence* in the curriculum in which all children can participate and achieve. Jones (2013) comments on how AfL provides a supportive framework to enable children with SEN to progress in a collaborative, inclusive and dialogic language-learning culture. White *et al.* (2007) suggest that a whole-school approach to AfL contributes to effective EAL pedagogy in enabling children to make full use of their bilingual expertise.

Formative and/or summative assessment

The two approaches to assessment – formative and summative – are often contrasted and the latter privileged, somewhat to the detriment of formative assessment. This has probably been, in part, due to the previous dominance of summative assessment and the often negative impact on pupils whose every effort has been graded, not always in a way that provides encouragement, especially for children with special educational needs. However, summative assessments can and should be useful both as part of a formative framework and as part of the learning process. As Black *et al.* write: 'The challenge is to achieve a more positive relationship between the two' (2003: 55–6).

The key issue, then, is to find, select and create worthwhile activities and tasks that will enhance assessment as learning, and that will provide an opportunity for pupils to demonstrate their knowledge. Teachers will need to be clear about the criteria for success and share these with the pupils, just as is the case in literacy and numeracy learning with the now ubiquitous WALT (What we Are Learning Today) and WILF (What I am Looking For) learning intentions and success criteria respectively, anthropomorphised as dogs, owls or other creatures in the primary classroom on wall posters for the pupils to share. This approach has been decried by some educationalists but the use of these formats (popular with the children) is for teachers to decide upon, and the point stands that learning objectives and success criteria need to be clear to the learners.

One primary colleague mentioned that she has a wealth of teaching materials and, in view of a dearth of purpose-designed assessment materials, she simply designates some of them to be used as assessment activities in the lesson: assessment *with* learning. Table 7.1 is designed to give just a flavour of the myriad possibilities available to combine formative and summative assessment. There are many other possible variations on these themes. Most of the techniques are self-explanatory, but we detail below three (*Two stars and a wish, Collecting tokens* and *Traffic-lighting*) which may not be completely obvious to the uninitiated. Each technique focuses on motivating children, getting them to think, establishing a challenge and providing feedback.

Two stars and a wish is a very simple technique that requires the identification of (at least) two aspects of positive feedback, the two stars (what has worked, good effort and so on), when giving feedback. The second part is the identification of a wish, an aspect to develop or something that can be improved in some way. The teacher can give this kind of feedback, and pupils can learn how to do it for themselves and for their peers. It is very important that as well as identifying stars and wishes, the children understand how they might develop their work and know the next steps. It is just as important for children to know the success criteria of the star element so that they can transfer their skills and knowledge on future occasions. Figure 7.1 gives examples of star-and-wish feedback given by three Year 4 pupils to a peer following an oral role-play activity in which the latter had been playing a role. These are good examples of how children can easily learn how to focus and, by giving positive feedback to their peers, help to create a classroom culture of support for their own learning.

Collecting tokens is an activity whereby children attempt to acquire tokens (small pieces of coloured card, for example, or little toys or tiddly-winks) for good responses. This can be done with any of the skills in any combination, and for any defined effort, but is a quick and useful way to assess speaking as a token can be handed out immediately following a response. At the end of a lesson, week or learning cycle, pupils, who keep their own tally of tokens, inform the teacher of how many tokens they have, and (this is very important) for what. They can thus have a very tangible idea of how they are progressing. It can be made into a group competition but it can also be a private, individual activity. Pupils could be encouraged to self-nominate or nominate their peers for a token.

Traffic-lighting, a common practice within the repertoire of activities for assessment for learning, is where pupils assess their own understanding by mimicking the traffic-light system; i.e. no understanding (red), semi-understanding (amber) and full understanding (green). It is a simple and effective procedure that has been in use for some time in core subjects. Our research findings indicate much teacher appropriation and interpretation (which is how it should be).Teachers, for example, use giant traffic lights they have made and ask pupils to respond (e.g. with a thumbs up, across or downwards), or pupils make their own mini–traffic lights or pick a coloured paper cup from a stack of cups on their table. Even more privately, the children can use coloured dots or other shapes in their language diaries or booklets in which they might evaluate aspects of their MFL learning. This gives immediate feedback to the teacher who can then review issues and plan the next learning step. Our research has also indicated that, over time, some teachers have moved to a thumbs up, across, down situation (see Figure 7.2). It has been noticed that some children dislike using the red light, even in a classroom culture that does not penalise 'not knowing' but, on the contrary, seeks to develop the children's confidence in being able to be honest in their self-assessment as a precursor to being able to move forward. Thumbs down or across are perhaps less intimidating and more child-

TABLE 7.1 Examples of assessment techniques

Application of assessment	Practical examples
Peer assessment	One-to-one peer assessment of speaking, writing or drawing in response to a target-language stimulus
	Two stars and a wish
	Group peer review of a spoken effort: e.g. a role play or a walkie-talkie phone
	Conversation between two pupils
	Peer assessment of audio- or video-taped pupil efforts
	Stop and swap work; think, pair and share (TPS)
Self-assessment	Quick recap 'test yourself'
	Self-assessment of taped oral work
	Critical review of written attempt against shared criteria
	Portfolio collection of selected good work or (e.g.) personal DVD folio
	Assessment of progress over time: e.g. tick-lists, comments and targets
	Traffic-lighting to indicate understanding
	Thumbs up, across or down for same purpose
Pupil reflexivity	Extended wait time
	'Stop and think' spots in lessons
	Think, pair and share (TPS)
	Pupil learning diary activities
	Problem-solving skills approach: e.g. setting a language-learning challenge for the lesson
	Class reflection
	Mind mapping/spider diagram techniques
	Traffic-lighting own work: e.g. with coloured pencils, coloured sticky dots, etc.
	Thinking homework/independent learning task
Teacher assessment that is compatible	Two stars and a wish
	Competitions, songs and games with an assessment aim
	Listen and point/mime/tick
	Read and draw
	Hover, check, discuss (HCD)
	Qualitative comments and targets
	Token collection and analysis

Kieran: *You are good at asking the questions*

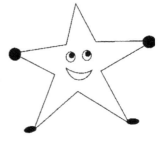

Rebecca: *You had good German and brilliant expression*

Faye: *I wish you had spoken more clearly and a bit louder*

FIGURE 7.1 Three stars and the sentences

friendly than those glaring lights. However, many children dislike showing thumbs down and one teacher suggested 1, 2, 3 fingers as a more private way of signaling. A variation on the theme is used by one teacher who will ask the children to hold up 'can do' cards to show comprehension and to use a small red traffic STOP sign on a lollipop stick that means *J'ai un problème* (cards and sticks are kept in empty, clean chip cartons on the table). The teacher will then discuss the problem and deal with it with the help of the other children. When 'traffic-lighting' of whatever kind is accompanied by use of target language expressions such as the fun Spanish phrases *¡bomba!* (wicked!) and *¡fatal!* (terrible), it can be seen that assessment can easily become a platform for extended target-language use.

Teachers can adapt such techniques and devise many others of their own, as is the case with this London teacher who assesses in collaboration with colleagues:

FIGURE 7.2 Thumbs up, across, down

Another way to assess – although I know this isn't common practice – is to carry out cross-curricular formative assessments. So for example, we used to do a lot of singing in French classes to improve vocabulary, etc. The peripatetic teacher and I did this on a couple of occasions where I assessed the child's singing while she assessed their French vocab. We made it fun for the children and they seemed to really enjoy it. Another thing we did was in handwriting practice, we asked the children to write French words – again they seemed to really like it and the children with SEN were very proud of their efforts.

The important issue is for teachers to be comfortable with such techniques and to use them purposefully for the benefit of progressing children's learning. Pupils also need to feel comfortable with self and peer assessment, for example. They need time to develop confidence in these roles and benefit from rehearsing the techniques and discussing success criteria, as Jones' (2010) research shows.

In the following example, teacher A, an experienced primary MFL teacher who teaches science and maths as well as German throughout the school and who features in the first case study later in this chapter, had been working with her Year 6 pupils on role plays deriving from a topic on school equipment:

The role play recently was based on the idea of expressing 'I can't, I need . . .'

Lesen!
Ich kann nicht lesen! Ich brauche ein Buch!

Prior to the role play, the children had learnt the following verbs relating to the topic of school equipment:

lesen, schreiben, zeichnen, rechnen, malen, turnen, basteln

The children were also familiar with these nouns, based on the school theme:

Bleistift, Spitzer, Malkasten, Pinsel, Füller, Radiergummi, Schultasche, Schere, Buch, Heft, Lineal, Federmäppchen, Turnzeug, Farbstifte, Filzstifte

The teacher's objectives were:

- clear, accurate, German-sounding pronunciation
- good recall of vocabulary learnt
- correct use of *einen, eine, ein*.

She instructed them to play a board game. If a child landed on a 'magic button', the group had to choose a verb they wanted to boss them to do (e.g. *Basteln!*). The child had to reply with *Ich kann nicht basteln. Ich brauche ein(e)(n) . . .*, choosing an appropriate noun.

The children were reasonably familiar with the idea of commenting on each other's work, as their comments show:

Hannah to Robert	You speak with a really good German sound, but sometimes forget to stay in German [he lapsed into English for counting his dice moves!].
Robert to Beth	You remember the words very well, but need to do the 'r' sound better [referring to the guttural German 'r'].
Jack to Keir	I really like your clear pronunciation.
Lisa to Siena	I think you're amazingly quick at learning new words.
Becky to Ellie	You're good at remembering the words. You have good pronunciation. Make sure you say what you mean. [She said one thing, but meant another (noun), on one occasion.]
Alex to Graeme	With your pronunciation, it's hard to tell if you're German or English, but you need to put a bit more effort into your 'r' sound.
Graeme to Alex	What you said made good sense. You say your words very clearly.
Ben to Emily and Robyn	You're very clear.
Ben to Jack	I like the way if you get it wrong, that you go back and correct yourself.
Robyn to Ben	You say your words really clear, and you say 'well done' to others.
Robyn to Jack	You keep forgetting vocabulary. You need to learn 'pencil'.

It is interesting to note how the pupils appear to like 'playing teacher'. Alex's comment to Graeme is a classic in this respect, a perfect take-off of a typical teacher comment! Also noteworthy is the fact that the children find a great many 'star' comments and are able to make criticisms in a non-threatening but direct way in the inimitable style of children. Very young children can learn to give peer feedback in a similarly very effective way.

A headteacher described the prompts she used with infants in their Spanish lessons:

> I ask the children questions such as 'What did you learn from what a friend said?' or 'Do you remember someone who did [the task] really well?' It's part of

the communicative approach and we have lots of dialogue and commentary and feedback.

Whatever peer assessment and other modes of assessment are undertaken in the primary MFL classroom, it needs to be consistent with the whole-school assessment framework. The next section features two case studies of practice that works in two different contexts, the first a primary school in the north of England and the second in Scotland. This underlines the need to plan assessment that is coherent and appropriate to the age range, the primary MFL teaching arrangements and the whole-school assessment ethos.

Case studies: assessment scenarios

Case study 1

In this first case study, the teacher teaches German throughout the school from Year 1 through to Year 6. She describes the whole-school assessment approach herself and points out the main aspects of assessment in the context of her school.

Ongoing assessment

I feel when I am teaching primary MFL I am almost constantly assessing . . . Have they grasped that? . . . Are they ready for the next bit? . . . Do they need more on that? . . . Is child X really confident? . . . Can I partner them in a role-play with child Y? . . . Who needs help? . . . Is that pronunciation as good as it could be? That sort of assessment goes on minute by minute, lesson by lesson. Then at the end of a unit, an end-activity will often be useful to assess them . . . maybe a game, e.g. a card game, or a role play, or some other performance. I'm keen to know if they can recall vocabulary learnt, use structures well, use authentic-sounding pronunciation, be keen, be confident to speak out, etc. Sometimes I just store the information from that in my head – sorry, not very official! – sometimes the class teacher will make written notes. The class teachers are 'in' on all MFL lessons in school, learning alongside the children.

Assessment post-lesson collaboration with colleagues

On one occasion, this teacher sent the following letter to all teachers/TAs:

To all class teachers/TAs:

In the run-up to report writing, may I invite you to use some time during German classes to make some informal written notes on the children in your class?
    Which children:

■   listen attentively?

■   are keen to participate in songs and rhymes?

- are keen to 'show' simple role plays?
- have a good recall of vocabulary?
- pick up new structures easily?
- speak clearly, with a good German accent?
- really enjoy German lessons?

I'll be very interested in the observations you make and I hope they'll make individual report writing for MFL much easier for you, when the time comes!

Attached is a class list but you may of course prefer to use your own class list.

Thank you!

Case study 2

Teacher B, a teaching head who teaches French to her own mixed-age top junior class in a Scottish primary school, identifies many advantages in her practice and many different assessment techniques, and believes that assessment ensures all children are achieving their potential. Free from the severe time constraint that teacher A has, teacher B is able to focus more on the assessment criteria themselves.

Using formative assessment techniques allows the teacher and pupil to see where they are in their learning and where they are aiming to go. Children remain motivated and enthusiastic to learn.

Assessment criteria

With younger pupils, most of the assessment *is* through observation, listening and visual techniques. Our French teaching in the younger classes *is* done purely through talking and listening. Although stories are read and children are exposed to words, we do not assess reading and writing until the last two years of primary school.

We encourage self-assessment in all classes. With young children they can use the traffic-light system to show how well they feel they understand. Older pupils may colour a checklist of vocabulary using the same colours, or simply give themselves a score out of ten for how well they feel they performed in a particular exercise.

Assessing older pupils and the four skills

With the top two classes, we assess all four aspects of learning a foreign language. To assess talking we use recording devices. Children especially enjoy using smart phones for conversations. This encourages them to learn to question as well as respond.

Listening is assessed using tapes giving instructions and directions. We also use story and question sessions and teacher-led questioning and instruction sessions. We use big books for reading and also have sets of the same books in small readers. Children work in groups and pairs to read to each other. Flashcards are used to introduce new reading words after the children have learned to pronounce them.

Writing is usually done as an ongoing assessment of French jotters. Occasionally, we will carry out a writing task for assessment purposes, but these activities are always well supported with flashcards, word walls, posters etc. It's like teaching Primary 1/Reception children to write. You need to provide as many words as they need until they get used to using specific language.

Recording

Pupils like to know how they are doing and are motivated to reach targets. Assessment techniques allow the teacher to see if pupils are retaining key vocabulary and able to use it in the correct context. Teachers can also quickly determine which children have good pronunciation and which need more help. We have a pupil profile for each child and record any key events in their learning. Written assessments can be kept in each pupil's folder to refer back to when necessary. During day-to-day assessment, we discuss learning with the children and also record any problems or successes. These then form the basis for reports to parents and for discussion at parents' nights and help the teacher to plan the next steps required in the French lessons.

As children learn new vocabulary, they are able to participate more and more although it is important to constantly revise topics as children will soon forget vocab that they are not exposed to on a regular basis. Self-assessment checklists for older pupils also let them see how their understanding of French is growing.

Common concerns

The overcrowded primary curriculum tends to leave little time for MFL learning, as we stressed at the beginning of the book, but both teachers in the case studies show in their comments ways to work within this constraint. It can also be seen how aspects of formative and summative assessment blend seamlessly, albeit in different learning and teaching environments. While the first case study deals with time constraints, the second focuses more on means and recording. Feedback for the teacher is paramount and thus assessment provides an opportunity to find out children's difficulties and gives some idea about how effective the lessons are. Primary MFL lessons are a rich source of diagnostic assessment material as evidence can be gathered during any lesson, and observations of pupil work, behaviour and questioning the pupil about what they are doing can be done in a relaxed manner. Areas of strength and weakness can be identified and the information gleaned used for the purposes of differentiation and additional support for those children in need. At appropriate stages, assessment data are used to give information to secondary colleagues ('feed forward') and as feedback for parents.

There is a noticeable concern for the well-being of pupils in the primary MFL classroom. While much emphasis is put on the 'fun factor' by many teachers, MFL learning is potentially intimidating given its strangeness in terms of unfamiliar sounds and spellings and the whole concept of 'otherness', hence the priority that both teachers give to the children feeling comfortable with their learning and assessment.

There are differences of emphasis as to which skills are assessed, reflecting the different teaching programmes and teacher beliefs on these issues. It is a topic to which we now turn for general comment, given its continuing controversial status.

Which skills should be assessed?

While some teachers stick doggedly to their belief that primary MFL learning should be almost exclusively oral and aural, others introduce reading and writing to differing degrees and at various stages. The choice, for the purposes of validity, ought to be mirrored in the choice of assessment activity but this is not always the case, for we noted during our observations more assessment through reading and copying text down, for example, than assessment of oral skills. This is perhaps the moment to mention again the issue of the written word. Rather than 'writing or no writing', the issue is really how the written word is introduced, how much and when, to enable the pupils to make the necessary phoneme–grapheme correspondence without which they will not be able to progress beyond a certain point (see Chapter 4 for further discussion on writing). The inclusion of reading and writing vastly extends the range of assessment opportunities and the possibilities for differentiated learning. A reading assessment involving simple instructions in Spanish on how to make a pizza and drawing the result is a simple and unmuddied test of reading and can have differentiated detail. Designing a holiday poster using as a minimum some previously practised formulaic items becomes both a realistic and collaborative writing activity to which children can make their individual contributions. Learning and assessment activities might include, for example, a 'listen, stop, think and write' task, or a version of *Blockbusters*, requiring children to write text into the game's diamond shapes on the interactive whiteboard (IWB). The skills thus merge in a realistic use of language to make a blended-skills assessment, so that the assessment becomes not of any one skill per se but of the degree of completion of the tasks. This would, in our opinion, enable more valid assessment, enable the assessment to be completely embedded in the learning and offer opportunities for pupil peer and self-assessment as well as teacher assessment. Where collaborative assessment activities are designed, this becomes time-efficient for the teacher and better reflects the dialogic nature of the primary languages classroom. In this way, teaching, learning and assessment blend together seamlessly.

Recording progress and achievement

We have noted some reluctance over the years on the part of primary MFL teachers to record data other than brief summative comments on end-of-year reports. Liz Scott, a former primary teacher and subsequently a professional development officer, working on AfL in MFL in Scotland, commented: 'They have avoided it strenuously for fear of being evaluated on the data.' Henceforth, with the statutory provision, assessment data will be used to evaluate progress. The next step is for teachers to create effective and useful assessment to suit their purposes. Scottish teachers who worked with Liz devised a bank of reporting comments to help them write annual reports, and used a checklist of comments based on level descriptors that referred to criteria such as grammar, oral response, interest level and pronunciation in the case of P6 class-level pupils in Scotland. The collaborative efforts of the teachers also showed imaginative and quite simple ways of recording progress data effectively and reflect the variety of practices that we have found elsewhere that are not time consuming and give ongoing evidence of general progress over time. These include variations on the following:

- lesson logs in pre-printed boxes, in which teachers note down items covered in the lesson with brief comments and notes on any individuals as necessary;
- class lists, one used per lesson, with comments against selected children's names;
- grids that combine pupils' names on one axis and topics covered/skills demonstrated on another; teachers tick or colour-code boxes on the grid;
- comments in pupils' language diaries, notebooks or jotters;
- focus-group observation and monitoring.

In sum, this reflects the suggestion that teachers can collect a range of evidence of learning data during the course of lessons – such as noting oral and written responses, pupils' questions and performance in tasks – all of which provide useful data to evaluate the learning and the teaching.

The ubiquitous annual report is important as it does not differentiate between subjects in regard to reporting and provides a glimpse for parents/carers into what the child has covered and achieved in their foreign language learning. Furthermore, the final report is one that is usually passed on to the secondary school, and along with other details of the primary foreign language-learning provision, needs to contain essential transfer information for secondary colleagues, an issue further discussed in Chapter 10. One Year 6 teacher simply uses the same reporting format used by other subjects, giving a simple descriptive account of each child's achievements and recording the levels attained in each skill. The level descriptors are enclosed for parents to share. The National Assessment Resource (NAR) available on the Education Scotland website has many examples of assessment formats and activities with case studies of individual schools' assessment arrangements, and the social networking platform Twitter, for example, has a great many exemplars.

Portfolio assessment

We have seen little evidence of systematic portfolio recording for primary languages as a method of continuously recording achievement other than in one school discussed later in this chapter, although there is some occasional use of a folder of work, for example, and some schools have used the European Language Portfolio (ELP), part of the Council of Europe's Common European Framework (Council of Europe 2001) on learning, teaching and assessment, Scotland having its own version. This portfolio has a variety of sections for pupils to record what languages they know and how they are progressing, thus providing tangible evidence of achievement as pupils add to it. Other teachers use portfolios of their own creation but based on similar principles. Teachers need to be aware of the dual function of the portfolio: pedagogic and reporting. Kohonen (2004: 5) distinguishes the functions thus:

> The pedagogic function . . . emphasises the process aspect of language learning: helping the students to identify their learning aims, to make action plans, to reflect, monitor and modify the processes and to evaluate the outcomes through self-assessment and reflection. The reporting function . . . on the other hand, is concerned with the product aspect of foreign language learning: providing a record of their language skills and cultural experiences by relating their communicative skills to . . . levels.

These thoughts may seem fairly sophisticated but they are easily adaptable and begin with simple 'can do' lists that are much in use by primary MFL teachers – although not beloved by all as some teachers find 'can do' statements 'too general' and 'restrictive'. MFL can play an important role in the development of metalinguistic awareness and in helping children to be reflective and self-monitoring: the portfolio can be a useful tool for promoting these processes on the route to more learner autonomy (Jones 2012). The recording of achievement is both relatively straightforward for teachers and provides an element of ownership for pupils. Such information provides important feedback about where children are on the 'climbing frame' of foreign language learning.

We are generally in support of portfolio-style assessment (that might include or comprise audio and video recordings) as an umbrella structure for recording progress and as a means suitable for children of all abilities to record 'what they can do'. We would, however, caution against the portfolio used passively and only as a repository of work, a criticism teachers voiced of the ELP – see, for example, Becker, whose research has shown that the ELP has not been 'a sure-fire success' (2015: 272) – and not as a way to engage the learners in thinking about their progress (Jones 2010). Portfolios need to follow the child and identify future learning stepping stones rather than teachers attempting to process children uniformly into a static backward-looking portfolio arrangement.

Issues of progression and continuity

The Languages Ladder Steps to Success™, the national recognition scheme for languages with accredited national certification, was potentially a mode of assessment that offered primary MFL teachers an assessment framework that validated and provided opportunities for 'when you are ready' assessment (opportunities for assessment when a child was deemed ready). This also has not had 'sure-fire success' and is little-used, although the concept of graded learning objectives (the ladder reflecting the graded objectives style of teaching advocated in the 1970s) is crucial to learners' progression. What we can take away from this approach, however, is the general thrust of differentiated rates of progress that meshes well with the personalised learning agenda for all children. The laddering concept is a useful one and also an analogy for the crucial concept of progression being used in some new 'ladder/steps' assessment schemes. This concept has effectively been built into a 'badging' scheme in some areas that have devised bronze, silver and gold standards for children to be assessed against and to work towards (as their own targets). One teacher in Essex explains her particular use of a badging scheme:

> I use these for differentiated testing. I use these medals like Olympic medals so anyone who has trained would be proud to achieve one. It works as motivation for the students. The pupils are able to pick their own test and have a good idea how well they are performing and can compare to previous attempts and between topics. When revising the pupils can choose a topic they did not sit at gold level and try to complete it.

Increasingly, language teachers have been making use of the Common European Framework (Council of Europe 2001) as a frame to guide teaching approaches and to define assessment levels. Regarding assessment, a variety of scales exist, of which the 'breakthrough' level, A1, seems appropriate for young learners in relating 'simple, general tasks . . . that can constitute useful objectives for beginners' (ibid.: 31). It is suggested that at this level, learners can:

- make simple purchases where pointing or other gestures can support the verbal reference;
- ask and tell day, time of day and date;
- use some basic greetings;
- fill in uncomplicated forms with personal details, name, address, nationality;
- write a short, simple postcard.

These would seem to constitute basic pedagogic tasks for early language learners and would put a recognisable level of achievement within the reach of all learners, alongside other, more detailed, qualitative data recorded for each child. Pupils will progress along their 'continuum of learning' as they transition into secondary school (Jones 2005: 3).

There follows an example of levels in use in one London primary school, where there are four levels for each of the four skills. These statements, supplied by the specialist teacher and coordinator, are taken from Speaking level 1 and level 4 of the Network for Languages London Schools Excellence Fund Key Stage 2 Pupil Evaluation sheet in use in this school:

> Level 1
>
> I can repeat words and phrases after the teacher.
>
> I can imitate/copy pronunciation with some success.
>
> I can speak clearly and confidently when reproducing simple words.
>
> I may need some support from spoken or visual clues.

Level 4

I can have simple conversations and give my opinions.

I can put new words or phrases into conversations correctly.

I can use my pronunciation and intonation well when I speak.

I can read or listen to something and re-tell it or discuss the main points.

I can perform to an audience *(recite a short narrative, read aloud, develop a sketch, give a presentation, role play to perform).*

I can describe incidents or my own experiences in a clear voice.

These levels, and all the other levels for speaking and those for the other skills, are followed by a grid: the teacher colours in boxes to track each child's progress, giving an immediate visual picture of the whole class as well as individual progression.

Discussing this framework with the headteacher of another London primary school, she commented that she once used a similar assessment scheme but abandoned it: 'The "can do" statements didn't mirror progression and the children seemed to be stuck at low levels.' What she now uses is a colour-coded tracking system to record the progress of individuals on the basis of a series of learning-objective milestones –'beginning', 'developing', 'achieved' – where the milestones have detailed descriptors of performance. 'It is working very well as a visual formative assessment framework and is also used to discuss success criteria with the children; it gives freedom to repeat topics and greater depth.' The latter point is crucial in recognising the importance of allowing the child time to think about feedback and next steps, as Elliott *et al.*'s recent research on marking and feedback (2016) has shown.

Information on an individual child's progress in language learning is included in a portfolio created by the teacher for each child. This travels to the secondary school, although the headteacher said it is often ignored by the secondary MFL teachers, who 'usually start all over again.' It is dispiriting for primary teachers to discover that their careful attempts at recording and reporting might be ignored by secondary teachers, as assessment data are important not only for primary teachers to record the children's progress, but for secondary teachers to be able to acknowledge and build upon. In particular, there is a need to decide what constitutes, for both primary and secondary teachers, an expected level of achievement on which to build.

Now that teachers have been given what many wished for and level-free assessment is a reality, there is scope – indeed need – for teachers to decide their own levels/criteria/descriptors/tasks. The removal of the AT levels has caused some anxiety. This can be seen, for example, on Twitter, where teachers frequently ask the teaching community about existing assessment schemes. A simple internet search will bring up dozens of schemes that combine a set of levels with descriptors, banks of assessment tasks, ideas for wider data collection and templates for recording. Ultimately, tick-boxing is not enough, as teachers and pupils need to see 'what good looks like' in order to give meaning to the ticking and colouring-in exercise. This means collecting samples of pupil output at various stages to illustrate progression. The sharing of schemes is of course useful in giving teachers ideas, but they really need to take the opportunity to reflect on their own assessment priorities and decide what suits their context, creating assessment opportunities as part of their own planning, teaching and learning cycle.

Naturalistic teacher assessment

In the new 'Life without Levels' assessment territory, some teachers have voiced a concern that the subsequent hive of assessment activity by primary languages teachers has simply led to the replacement of the former AT levels with a plethora of sets of levels. More radical solutions have been suggested that would start with the identification of assessment tasks within a learning unit, tasks that would target the key concepts to be learnt and that would be incorporated into the scheme of work. These tasks would generate pupil exemplar work, spoken and written, and would enable teachers to start from what the pupils produce, to compare, analyse, even rank their outputs and to measure progress in terms of 'start' and 'end' points. This would allow for readjustment of planning, teaching and assessment.

There are simple, non-time-consuming ways of assessing and recording that fit with what teachers already do in other subjects, as has been described in this chapter. Primary teachers are very skilled at what Torrance and Pryor call 'naturalistic teacher assessment – monitoring the performance of the class as a whole, being broadly satisfied that particular groups and individuals are moving at the pace one would expect' (1998: 35). They argue that while this monitoring is useful, assessment 'is more to do with the quality of teacher–pupil interaction and the feedback provided by teachers during the course of such interactions.' This means reacting to children's feedback about their learning and interacting in a way that enhances the dialogical nature of assessment. A London teacher gave an example of good assessment practice in this respect:

> Children can be assessed sometimes in pairs, when delivering a presentation to the whole class on concepts covered that term. They have the opportunity to work on this, in pairs, outside of the MFL lesson with some support from the teacher.

This kind of classroom learning activity fits well with the concept of the 'dialogic classroom' (Alexander 2006) in which pupil dialogue predominates, maximising both children's talk time and time for teachers to listen, monitor and support the learning. In such a classroom, assessment can be a collaborative activity that provides an opportunity for all children, including those with special educational needs (Beltrán *et al.* 2013).

Conclusion

Assessment, when understood and interpreted as a positive, enjoyable and challenging force for learning within a classroom culture that is supportive and provides a stream of constructive feedback and think time, is not in conflict with the MFL teacher's desire to be creative. Much of what teachers and pupils do in the primary MFL classroom can be described as assessment. For example tasks, quizzes, questions, pair- and group-work and homework tasks all prompt learners to demonstrate their knowledge and provide opportunities for the pupils to reflect on their learning. Formative assessment is a good tool for making the shift in the classroom from passive reception by the pupils to metacognition and the development of learning and thinking skills. Primary schools are hives of activity in this respect, acutely attuned to the importance of children's need for thinking time with attention currently focused on the development of thinking skills and critical skills. In languages, wait time gives more pupils more time to 'stop and think' about a suitable response and is a necessary balance to the often frenzied pace of language lessons. Wait time is crucial for our young learners in undertaking thought-processing in the target language. With collaborative activities, pupils can share ideas, as well as support and challenge each other, providing an opportunity for the teacher to move around the MFL classroom while pupils are on task, make observations, and, if necessary, ask questions about what the pupils are doing and why. In this way, pupils can learn, through assessment opportunities, to self-regulate their learning and develop autonomy through supported personalised target-setting (Boekaerts and Corno 2005).

Assessment, we assert, is part of the entitlement to quality interactive primary MFL teaching and learning: assessment *alongside* learning. As one teacher pointed out: 'We need to assess in the broadest sense, otherwise they [the children] may as well learn from a set of TV programmes where the TV delivers, but does not respond to the learning resulting from the delivery!' An assessment framework for primary MFL should, on the contrary, be responsive and serve as a tool flexible enough to cater for different school environments, the learners' needs and teacher preferences. The choice, as they say, is yours.

Questions on which to reflect

- How is progression exemplified in terms of level descriptors and what does 'good work' at each level and in each skill look like?

- How do we find time in MFL lessons for pupils to have 'stop and think' time? What would it be useful for them to think about?

- What are your own assessment beliefs, and how do you reflect these in your practice?

8

Technology and language learning

This chapter will look at ways in which digital technology can support language learning, pupil autonomy, motivation and opportunity to engage with the target language at different levels. We look at recent developments in technology with illustrations of how the interactive whiteboard and the internet can be used to add value to primary MFL learning while enhancing computing skills. Examples of how to fully exploit learning opportunities using technology will be discussed.

Key issues

- ■ Technology can allow for more individualised and differentiated language practice.

- ■ The teacher is the single most important factor in determining the success of technology's contribution to learning in the primary school.

- ■ Technology offers teachers a wide range of possibilities to create a range of multi-media resources that can be tailored to the specific learning needs and preferences of their pupils.

- ■ Technology offers greater flexibility in the creation and exploitation of resources, both for the teacher and for pupils, allowing more varied modes of participation and appealing to a broader range of cognitive processing styles.

Introduction

Today, children in most developed countries grow up familiar with the keyboard and the computer screen in a way that would have been unimaginable a couple of generations ago, and digital technology is just a part of life today for UK children. The ever-evolving hardware of new technologies is a ubiquitous reality in the twenty-first century. The way we retrieve and process information has a dramatic impact on the way we think, the way we communicate with each other and the way we identify ourselves and others. Given that the information revolution is inherently dealing with formative issues of processing information and developing social networks, it is unsurprising that education has been a groundbreaker in the development and application of digital technology.

In schools, the use of technology also represents one of the clearest examples of how cross-curricular learning is achievable, desirable and, given the requirements of our current 'learning society', necessary.

The UK is at the forefront of integrating computing in schools. We were, for example, the first European country to install interactive whiteboards on a massive scale and to have made computing a National Curriculum requirement at both primary and secondary levels. In terms of references to materials and sources of information, given that website addresses are notoriously subject to change, we have not listed many specific websites in this chapter. Our aim here is to discuss pedagogical approaches and ways in which technology can be integrated into individual, group and whole-class work in MFL, rather than to list specific ICT resources, though several are cited that we have seen in practice adding value to primary MFL. A wealth of commercial material does exist, as software and on the internet, both in the form of target-language resources (authentic and adapted) and as 'how to use' guides for teachers. Lists of such websites are easily found by searching the internet or by consulting any one of the many educational IT publications available, some of which are listed in our References section. Most teachers told us that they come across gems by doing searches themselves and also by sharing ideas through social network platforms (Facebook, Twitter and blogs).

Integrating development of technology and MFL skills

Computing and MFL have a lot in common. First, along with music and PE, they are often considered to be skills-based subjects, though, in fact, this label underplays the complexity (and transferability) of the cognitive processes involved. They are also among the subjects that many believe children show an aptitude for (or not!). In other words, they are both subjects that tend to invoke strong reactions from teachers and parents – beliefs that are often passed on subliminally to children – about being either able to 'do' it or not, and, by extension, from the teachers' perspective, being competent to teach the subjects or not. However, we believe that technology, like MFL, is best delivered when it is both embedded across the curriculum (thereby treated as a matter of course by different staff members *and* taught as a separate subject. As a separately taught subject, computing benefits from specialist, focused input that both supports pupils and expands teachers' competence and self-confidence within the context of continuing professional development. As discussed in Chapter 5, this holistic, cross-curricular approach allows both MFL and technology to be used as instrumental means in creating new meanings and new *forms* of knowledge. This represents another major area of common ground between the two subject areas. In the case of MFL, these 'new meanings' are extensions and reconfigurations of linguistically and culturally bound first-language concepts; that is, both in terms of language awareness – such as the links we have highlighted to first-language literacy and other cross-curricular links – and also in terms of broader (inter)cultural understanding (as discussed in Chapter 9). In a similar way, children learn to mediate knowledge as they develop skills in technology. They encounter new sources of information and new ways to manipulate sounds, images, and words, thereby going beyond (and reconciling) the traditional divisions between spoken and written media, verbal and mathematical processing, linear and kinaesthetic learning styles and so on.

The following is an example of how a teacher uses technology to enhance research skills and intercultural learning through MFL:

> For upper KS2 I have used a website (www.the-voyage.com) for an online advent calendar in the run-up to Christmas. For upper KS2, already competent to navigate a website, this is a great way to compare Christmas traditions in Britain and Germany. It's more practical than travelling to Germany (!) and more fun for the children than me just recounting my personal experiences to them. I listed a few items on the board which I wanted them to find out more about (such as *Lebkuchen*, or *Barbaratag*), and then let them explore the site in pairs, finding out about Christmas traditions in a fun way, which they really enjoy. Motivation is high; the quality of the site and quality of its information is high. Afterwards there is a chance to share and discuss what they have discovered, share surprises, and sort out any possible misunderstandings. Many children have internet access at home and took the web address with them so they could continue to open up the days of the advent calendar in the run-up to Christmas, hopefully also teaching their parents some new things!

The role of the teacher

One of the greatest assets of new technologies is their capacity to facilitate more individualised styles and rates of learning. While all primary teachers do instinctively differentiate and adapt their approach to suit individual pupils' needs, there is only one teacher for up to 30 children and so they cannot physically replicate the tireless individual attention given to each child by computers. Of course, this does not undermine in any way the role of the teacher. We believe that good teaching remains paramount, over and above any resource including technology, but that teachers today recognise the importance of using computers as 'electronic assistants', reference banks, and much more.

We have spoken to some teachers who are not yet fully confident with what technology has to offer. One such teacher told us that she feels 'the children know more about computers than I do.' This is a widely held belief but should not deter teachers. While it is true that many children show greater confidence with computers than adults, often using computers at home and at school without inhibition, they often perform very limited functions, such as playing games or looking up particular websites. Our task as teachers is, as it always has been, to teach children a range of skills and ways of seeing the world by using whatever cultural material and resources are available. In the past, these were the spoken word, books, writing, drawing, etc., and these continue, but electronically processed information has been added to the list. If pupils do have greater technical skills, they can be encouraged to take the lead and teachers can learn from them. In this way the learning becomes a two-way process whereby skills and content are brought together. However, even older children continue to need thorough guidance and direction when using computers, so the teacher is not standing on the sidelines but is actively directing, shaping and running the show! Technology also provides welcome opportunities for collaboration with the school's computing coordinator, with other teachers and with teaching assistants.

Extensive research over the last two decades has investigated the implementation and impact of technology in both primary and secondary schools (Beltrán *et al.* 2013; Cox and Webb 2004; Somekh 2007). These studies have consistently confirmed that the role of the teacher is the single most important factor in determining the success of technology's contribution to learning. However, it is clear that teachers will only use technology once they are genuinely persuaded of the benefits. This conviction often emerges from the act of engaging with the technology and experiencing the benefits once the initial phase of discomfort and extra effort has passed. We do not advocate using technology for the sake of it, but where teachers appreciate that it is an enhancement. As one teacher told us:

> I firmly believe there's no point using technology unless it is better than what you're doing already (a fancy projected image of a teddy is not a patch on the real thing, which you can hug when it's your turn!); and teachers need to ensure that the technology skills required by the children in the language-learning situation are well within their capabilities, or the technology learning swamps the language learning.

Next, we outline what we consider to be major current uses and benefits of using technology, but we recognise that it is only through using technology in a safe and supported context that teachers can appropriate the benefits of technology in their own practice.

Whole-class learning

Technology plays an important role, as an additional resource, in engaging pupils in the presentation and practice of language in MFL. The use of presentation software such as PowerPoint need not replace more traditional resources such as realia (i.e. real objects) and flashcards but can be added to the repertoire of bright, attractive visuals. It is obviously convenient for the teacher to use electronic visuals inasmuch as once they have been prepared (either downloaded or created), they do not require storage space, do not wear and can be easily updated and adapted. In the long run, they save teachers time.

As well as pictures, text can be manipulated on the 'big screen' for whole-class participation in any of the ways discussed below. As pupils are introduced to written words and then sentences in MFL, text can be gapped, highlighted and presented in different visual forms, including with motion (moving text) and with sound accompaniment, which all contribute to multisensory processing and will aid memorisation and the construction of meaning by appealing to different cognitive styles.

Any of the activities suggested in the skills sections in Chapter 4 can be developed and given extra depth when presented electronically because of the increased scope for different font characters, sizes and colours as well as mixed media and the capacity to make children's participation with the cues on the screen spontaneously interactive. This is especially true when the whiteboard is electronically interactive. Indeed, the use of the interactive whiteboard goes beyond the transfer of traditional resources to an electronic medium.

The interactive whiteboard

The interactive whiteboard (IWB) is now well established in UK schools. The IWB can be used in real time or to present material that the teacher or pupils might have prepared earlier. One of the most exciting features is the ability to store handwritten thoughts and comments from the pupils and to recall them for a later lesson. In real time, pupils can take a very active part in the lesson by using the IWB to display their work to others or investigate materials on the internet, downloading and saving those materials in conjunction with their own ideas and comments. The IWB has all the features of a stand-alone computer connected to the internet with a large bank of educational software, and it can also display games, texts, graphics and presentations to the whole class. Therefore, whereas individual or group computer work can be very beneficial, the IWB helps teachers to excel in their whole-class teaching skills at the same time as promoting confidence and communication skills among all their pupils.

The following quote shows how a teacher in the south of England uses the IWB and mini-whiteboards to reinforce MFL learning through numeracy:

> During my Year 4 Maths lessons I try to incorporate French where appropriate: an ideal opportunity for this is during the mental starter. To reinforce number bond work I load up the 'Virtual Dice' web page (provided by Birmingham Grid for Learning) on the class SMART board and select the ten-sided dice. By clicking the dice it generates numbers between one and ten randomly. I ask a child to say the generated number out loud in French, e.g. *deux*, and the rest of the class will then write the corresponding number to ten (i.e. eight) on their mini-whiteboards and one child will be chosen to say the word aloud in French. This is really a quick-fire session where the children have to think on their feet to find the number and the French word.

Individualised learning and group work using technology

Working on the computer as play in MFL

Many web-based activities increase levels of interactivity and appeal to different learning styles because they are multisensory, leading the child to follow pictorial, written and/or auditory cues. Many of these practice activities are in the form of competitive games – often giving scores – which children enjoy playing on their own (to beat their own best score) or with partners or in teams. These games appeal to a basic instinct and follow the principles of amusement arcade, home computer and mobile application games.

When the software is attractively designed, the competitive game element of the activities allows fairly mundane drills to pass as fun. These are ideal for practising vocabulary items and, later, word and text gap-filling and arranging in correct order. The computer never gets impatient or tired of repeating the same words and so is ideal for practice drills. There are, of course, many interesting and exciting educational technology games that involve role playing and decision-making based on specific scenarios where children can work in teams to plan strategies. For example, using computer-based modelling, children can sort lexical items into categories and learn about different forms of words such as nouns, adverbs, etc. A program like *Métro* enables children to learn the French terms relating to using the Paris Metro: at each stage of entering the Metro station, buying a ticket, choosing the right line, etc., the pupils have to select the correct French word (from a choice of several) and are rewarded by moving on a station (on a map on the screen) until they reach their destination.

Individual or group work on the computer encourages pupils to take risks in ways that they would be less likely to on paper or orally. Feedback is instant, either from the circulating teacher or from the computer itself. MFL–specific software often has levels of difficulty to choose from and often gives clues upon request. A learner who may be reticent about answering incorrectly in front of the whole class or even to the teacher will not mind being corrected by the computer. When using a Word document, spellcheck can be switched to the target language so that misspellings will be highlighted instantly. The opportunities for unlimited redrafting and improvement change the way a child approaches the task, encouraging experimentation and creativity. An idea for self-assessment is to temporarily store the various stages of redrafting in a separate file so that children can later, retrospectively, analyse the steps they took towards the final outcome (task completion), analysing and tracking their own progress.

Text manipulation

Even at a very simple level of word recognition, computers enable children to manipulate the target language in its written form in a safe, experimental way. This is especially valuable for new writers who are still struggling to form letters on paper, as Dugard and Hewer observe:

> The ability to make changes in computer-generated text without leaving any trace of previous errors or misunderstandings enables learners to:
>
> ■ draft
> ■ evaluate
> ■ revise.
>
> The use of these three skills promotes cognitive activity involving complex linguistic processing that is likely to reinforce grammar, syntax and choice of vocabulary because of the level of cognitive activity engendered.
>
> (Dugard and Hewer 2003: 23)

The advantages of manipulating text on screen rather than on paper are now widely vaunted. For example, writing on a screen appeals to a wider range of learning styles including kinaesthetic; electronic text can be moved around the screen; children can make different word shapes; different fonts for different types of text can be used (e.g. for a menu versus a postcard or even a verb versus a noun). Here, we can see how generic software can be used to full effect in MFL – that is as well as subject-specific software. Colour can be used for describing a colour or to show gender or other word categories. Underlining, bold typeface and boxes can all be used to highlight and differentiate particular words and word groups. Using authoring software, teachers can tailor-make specific exercises to match work recently covered in class, or indeed to match their pupils' learning preferences. These allow vocabulary lists or other sets of words or phrases to be automatically turned into exercises and quizzes. Teachers can also create activities using sound files to accompany word-processed text, for example by inserting hyperlinks to sound files that can be downloaded from the internet.

Children with visual and/or auditory impairments will find manipulating text using technology particularly advantageous because of a myriad of possibilities for extra support, from sound to text enlargement. Even using a non-white background screen to read from can help to reduce the glare and brightness for light-sensitive pupils.

Presentation skills

Children will enjoy using the computer to make MFL displays and as props for presentation to the class. Examples of this we have seen are scanned and digital photos of family and pets that are then labelled (*mi hermana, Lucy, 8 años; mi gato, Bonnie*) and simple menu designs, as shown in Figure 8.1.

The awareness that the computer can be used creatively in this way to produce smart, original presentation styles raises the value of MFL and helps equip pupils with necessary skills for later learning (and, eventually, professional life).

Children's work on presentations and displays provides a clear example of why the teacher's focused planning is important for technology. If clear guidelines are not set,

FIGURE 8.1 Menu layout

pupils may spend disproportionate time and energy on 'form' – for example playing with fonts and page layout – above 'content' (the language focus). It may be a good idea to work on the content while in class and then set the display format as work to do at home or in an art or computing lesson. The point is that computers can do many of the low-value tasks such as copying text down and drawing grids. These activities do, of course, have value while children are learning to draw, write, etc., but in MFL the *focus* should be on using the target language – this is cross-curricular learning at its best – as technology in the MFL lesson is a support medium rather than an end in itself.

Collaborative learning with technology

Computer-produced work (for presentation or other investigative projects that are discussed below) presents a good opportunity for collaborative learning. Pupils enjoy the opportunity to work in a semi-autonomous way and the individual and group work facilitated by computers provides variety in the pace and style of MFL learning, typically an intensively teacher-led subject. Pupils with greater technical skills can be teamed up with pupils who are more able linguistically, and, again, possibly with pupils who particularly enjoy designing or presenting, depending on the task being set. Each pupil then has the opportunity to contribute to the group output and to scaffold each other's learning (learning through Vygotsky's 'zone of proximal development' discussed in Chapter 6) in a valuable and enriching way. Research has long since shown the benefits of such cooperative group work (e.g. Gillespie 2006; Leask and Pachler 2014), and some examples of such collaborative outputs that we have seen in primary schools are:

- using databases for recording survey data in French (*le sondage*) on how classmates come to school, who has pets and which type, the colour of pupils' hair and eyes, etc.;
- downloading images to produce an illustrated class timetable in German;
- using publishing software to prepare a multilingual poster advertising a school event, with individual pupils assigned to specific design tasks.

Creating resources

Teachers creating multimedia resources themselves

For teachers whose technical expertise goes beyond that of regular end-users and who feel comfortable handling relatively easy-to-use software, or for those who have the necessary technical support, it makes sense to create personalised resources, either from scratch or by adapting free resources found on the internet.

An authoring tool like HotPotatoes – which is free to most users – is easy to master, flexible and allows a wide range of activities to be developed, such as multiple-choice and short-answer quizzes, jumbled sentences, matching and gap-fill exercises. An example we have seen at a school in East Anglia is the creation of a multimedia crossword puzzle. The advantage, compared to its traditional paper equivalent, lies in the fact that the definitions can be based on sounds (or images) and not just on writing. The necessary images or sounds were obtained from free educational databases but drawings could also be made by children and then scanned and built in. Sounds can be recorded by an MFL specialist or by a native speaker, for example an assistant or parent, thus avoiding legal problems of copyright. Another great advantage of HotPotatoes is that once the teacher has created the activities they are saved in the form of web pages. No special software is needed to do the exercises as they will run on any web-browser software. Using these sorts of software programs, schools can work collaboratively in a network to create joint websites through which they share resources and software.

Karaoke is now universally popular and offers children the opportunity to practise the target language with elements of performance and written support. We have seen it used to great effect by a teacher who had used software (in this case MAGpie) to synchronise video and subtitles. This offers an excellent way to introduce children to the written word in MFL and to work on phonics at the same time (by highlighting elements of the words of the song). As one teacher commented:

> I think mp3 mics (e.g. Easi speak) are great for voice recordings. At a younger age, I think children are less 'hung up' and more interested in having their voice recorded. The UK–German Connection website has encouraged sending in mp3 recordings of traditional songs. Our children were highly motivated to practise and record songs for this website. Children are then more likely to visit the website at home and share with parents.

This level of involvement in the creation of multimedia resources will require some coordinated training and at least some of this training should be subject-focused for those who are not familiar with the necessary software. But teachers can also acquire the necessary skills by taking part in collaborative projects with colleagues or seeking appropriate training courses as part of their continuing professional development (see Chapter 11). Teachers we spoke to recently are no longer reticent about using technology and once they had gained in confidence and technical know-how, they were amazed at how much fun they and the children had working with MFL and multimedia.

Creating resources collaboratively and exchanging ideas

There is a lot of potential to forge electronic links between teachers and to share ideas about resources and good practice in MFL teaching. Random searches will throw up many excellent ideas for resources, even lesson plans, as well as official websites such as the ALL's Primary Resources site (http://www.all-languages.org.uk/resources/primary-resources). Indeed, since finding time is an issue for all teachers, the primary MFL support (e.g. coordinator) might well take on the responsibility for providing an illustrative list. The potential for pupil links is discussed below, but for staff, national and international cooperative projects offer a way of sharing ideas and building links that may lead to future collaborations at all levels: professional development, pupil links, whole-school twinning, even personal friendships can emerge from such partnerships. MFL plays a key role in establishing such social networks.

125

As well as connecting teachers in school, there is scope for integrating this type of exchange in initial teacher training programmes, which is precisely what we have done with two types of link between King's College London and primary-teacher trainees at the IUFM (now called ESPE) de Paris: we cite this as an example of active practice in initial teacher training. First, French and English student teachers communicated via video-conferencing about a range of professional topics, from different national developments in MFL to broader whole-school issues such as ways of teaching literacy, involving parents in school life, special needs education, etc. The exchanges were held in both languages so there were clear linguistic benefits, but trainees were also led to think about different ways of educating and the degree to which assumed practices are often culturally determined.

The following year, we went a step further with another type of exchange, this time based on regular email communication – again around different topics but with a stronger focus on MFL resources for early learners. The correspondence led to the creation of a simple multimedia resource centred on the theme of Red Nose Day and its associated language and cultural characteristics. While this web-based resource was created principally for French primary-school children learning English, the collaboration gave UK trainees opportunities to practise their French by email and to develop technical know-how by providing input at each stage of the resource design.

The internet: a window on the world

The internet as a source of information for teachers

For teachers of MFL, the internet represents a rich source of information on several levels. As mentioned above, it has become a well-established forum for exchanging ideas about resources, views about teaching MFL and lesson plans. Within the context of professional development, the internet keeps teachers informed of the latest developments concerning subject, teacher, and broader educational issues and offers links to professional bodies such as ALL. Many sites have message boards where teachers can seek technical advice about the use of technology or professional support for MFL teaching or, indeed, make any specific requests to colleagues in cyberspace. The message boards, usually informative and often great fun, illustrate the sense of camaraderie and the spirit of mutual support and understanding that emerge from sharing thoughts and experiences within a 'community of practice' (discussed in Chapter 11).

The internet has revolutionised access to ready-made resources for language learning and teaching. Many are free and just need to be downloaded, and some are sold online. Often, however, resources will need to be adapted to suit specific learning contexts. We suggest that the internet works well as a pool of inspiring ideas for teachers to create their own material as well as a bank of ready-made resources.

Children using the internet

The internet offers great potential for children to develop investigation skills. In primary MFL this is naturally restricted by pupils' limited knowledge of the foreign language, especially in the written form. Furthermore, as with internet use across the curriculum, early learners will need very clear signposting when doing internet searches. Quite apart from the possibility of accessing inappropriate sites that have slipped through the filter, too much time can be wasted on fruitless searches if children are not led to specific websites that have been selected beforehand by the teacher. Once specific websites have been chosen and vetted, it is generally advisable to list them on the school intranet site.

Official tourist board websites are a good, authentic source of target language in use and provide a stock of cultural knowledge that is often presented in simple tabular form, ideal for cross-curricular exploitation. An example of this is to look up town population numbers for an English town and a French town or the translated title of a well-known film. Pupils' actual use of the target language here is very limited but they are nonetheless engaging with an authentic French-language website. This is a confidence boost and leads pupils to pick out and retrieve specific information from a text: a valuable information skill put to use in a genuinely communicative context. Other information-retrieval research tasks that are appropriate for primary children include finding the capital of a region in Spain, finding out who the goalkeeper of a French football team is, and changing a sum of pounds sterling to euros or another currency using a currency converter website.

For some activities, especially with younger children, the target language use in such activities will be minimal, maybe just focusing on one or two key words, but the value in cultural learning and developing information and thinking skills within a cross-curricular context is enormous. (This is the broader definition of MFL for which we make a plea in Chapter 5.)

Twinning and virtual exchanges

Technology has opened up several ways of corresponding with partner schools and has led to possibilities for redefining our relationship with the world. While school trips abroad continue to have immense value in terms of linguistic, cultural and personal developmental gains, technology can open new pathways for children to engage with one another across nations, forging new types of identity within a global dimension. The social and psychological benefits of involving the school in international projects are discussed in greater detail in the next chapter, but here we suggest practical ways to approach virtually managed projects and exchanges.

Exchanging information over the web

Some teachers have told us that they did not believe email exchanges were appropriate for primary-school pupils because of the emphasis on writing in the target language. While we would suggest that KS2 pupils can, in fact, handle an exchange by each partner writing in their mother tongue, we accept that other forms of exchange that are less text-based and so privilege oral and aural skills development work best with early learners. Some of the options available do require a certain degree of technical handling and many teachers will need technical support in the early stages. However, as we have said above, the initial effort and extra time needed to develop know-how pay real dividends in terms of adding value to the children's experience of MFL.

The exchange of sound or video files is highly motivating. Children use simple phrases to tell their partners about an ordinary day at school or about a celebration that takes place in their country, etc. In terms of technical requirements, the use of a piece of sound-editing software (such as 'Audacity', which is free) to record sounds is very simple since it follows the same principle as a camcorder. The sound files can then be attached to emails, posted on a web page or exchanged, and pictures can also be added. Many teachers find Dropbox the best way to exchange large files, especially video files.

Children from different partner schools in continental Europe or elsewhere can also digitally film their school environment and comment on it orally using a digital camcorder. This type of presentation will appeal enormously to children of the same age who share the same interests and concerns. The digital film thus produced can be integrated into a web page for easy access. No film showing children can be put on the web unless signed parental consent forms are held by the school; the website can be restricted to limited user-access only, for increased security. Technology facilitates this type of exchange inasmuch as it is faster in terms of transmission and compatibility of format, unlike, for example, DVDs. The technical requirements include the use of a digital camcorder; uploading the footage onto a computer; editing, if necessary; and then the integration of the film onto a web page and the upload to a server.

Such projects are well within the reach of teachers, and similar projects have already been carried out. For example, a project entitled 'I'm ten years old and I live in . . .' consisted of children from different target-language countries making web pages in their own language about agreed themes, like the means of transport for getting to school, food, etc. All the information was then gathered onto a single website, and this gave rise to very interesting comparisons and to increased intercultural and linguistic awareness. Originally, the objective was to motivate children to develop digital literacy skills by taking part in a project whose content could be shared with other children, but the cross-curricular dimension is obvious as children were encouraged to work on other subject content, such as geography. From the MFL perspective the website provided authentic material to develop oral comprehension and oral production, triggered by the sound files or the images. The technical requirement here is the know-how to make web pages, including work on integrating image and sound. There are many websites that can help schools find partner contacts abroad. Look through the British Council School Partnerships and the European Schoolnet sites, as well as websites for embassies and cultural and educational departments.

Video-conferencing

Video-conferencing has been used by schools in different countries to share information about their schoolwork and to learn about each other's language and culture. The main advantage of video-conferencing projects lies in the fact that they emphasise oral and synchronous communication. Equipment costs have decreased and video-conferencing via the web has become increasingly accessible. Skype provides a practical alternative, though its technical quality may be problematic. Indeed, it is important that any exchange with partners in the foreign language is not hindered by added comprehension difficulties caused by poor technical quality, so good sound quality is an essential criterion when setting up this type of face-to-face exchange. The quality of web video-conferencing, as well as its ease of use, is bound to improve in years to come and we should keep this option in mind. Such projects undoubtedly represent a considerable asset for the pupils involved, as we have seen where successful exchanges have taken place. Video files are a popular choice not only because they are readily exchanged via Dropbox, but also because they can be fully rehearsed and prepared in advance.

A project that we have seen using video-conferencing involved Year 5 children in their second year of learning Spanish linking to a Year 4 school in Spain where children were in their second year of learning English. The simple, well-prepared exchanges revolved around the following themes:

- individual presentations
- learning a song
- questions and guessing based on images of animals.

The children were thrilled to be in face-to-face contact with native speakers of their own age. As well as the linguistic benefits, the cultural dimension was also very much present. Indeed, the Spanish children told their UK friends that they thought their school uniforms were funny! Clearly, there is a lot of potential for following up the issues raised in these exchanges in other subjects, as this example from a teacher of primary German shows:

> Online webcams are great for looking at the weather! To have learnt the phrase *Es regnet*, for example, and then to find it actually is raining that very morning in our twin town of Rinteln, is somehow exciting. During certain months a webcam in the south of Germany near the mountains might even show us *Es schneit*! This can also help with discussing climate differences between Germany and the UK. With digital advances, it is now relatively easy to video a child in front of a map of Germany giving their weather forecast (just like a real German TV weather presenter!), and then show it to the class on the whiteboard!

One of the key advantages of video-conferencing is that it combines sound and images in real time, which helps in terms of the motivation to communicate in a realistic exchange. Before taking part in such a project, teachers need to consider the following points:

- It is important to find a reliable partner and to make sure that the partnership is fair on both parties (depending on what the objectives are for each).
- No matter how smoothly the real-time exchanges seem to go, they require minute preparation. Pupils at this stage of learning – and even older children – cannot use the target language spontaneously and will need thorough preparation for the exchanges. This preparation includes coordination with the other teacher beforehand as well.

■ Logistically, it might be advisable to have children working together and presenting in pairs – i.e. two at each end. Mutual support then operates when necessary: this is less stressful at the beginning for children who might feel insecure speaking to the camera.

Video-conferencing represents the ultimate interactional opportunity in terms of communication between children of different mother tongues. In fact, it could be what all the other MFL activities lead to and it endows such activities with meaning since it results in children's concrete use of the foreign language in a real communicative context and in real time. In practical terms, there are obstacles that may delay its use for some, but other new technologies that facilitate high levels of authentic communication between pupils, such as email, message boards and sound and video files, are already accessible to all.

Conclusion

In this chapter we have considered the important and dynamic role of technology in primary MFL teaching and learning. Technology offers much more than a new way of presenting traditional resources, though its highly efficient function as on-hand illustrator, support assistant, marker, display board, storage cupboard, etc. is not to be underestimated. Engagement with technology also leads to new ways of engaging with the foreign language and culture and can provide new ways of learning – even new forms of knowledge – through increasing pupil ownership of the learning process (autonomy) and allowing greater levels of differentiated participation, for example in whole-class formative assessments.

We have looked at how technology can support the teacher as a pedagogic resource in whole-class teaching and how it can be a powerful learning medium for pupils of all abilities and a support for children with a wide range of special educational needs (see Beltrán et al. 2013). We have suggested specific activities based on our observations in schools but these can only give a flavour of what can be done as the rate of change in technology is increasingly fast and we believe that each localised context must appropriate technology to suit the specific purposes of different teachers and pupils. For instance, schools are increasingly embracing the potential of mobile technology and we have seen iPads and iPhones used effectively in schools as digital dictionaries and as hand-held audio and digital camcorders as well as for target-language searches. One principal theme that remains perennial, however, is the role of the teacher in primary MFL, and this is equally important when integrating technology. As extensive research, cited in the chapter, has indicated, the attitudes of the teacher and the teacher's willingness to experiment with and engage with technology are crucial factors in ensuring the effective deployment of digital technology.

Questions on which to reflect

■ How are your pupils engaging with digital media? Does their experience in school build on their use of technology away from school?

- Is there a colleague in school (computing coordinator or MFL specialist) with whom you could collaborate to exploit technology more fully in delivering MFL (e.g. through joint planning, writing a development action plan, team teaching)?

- Do you think an electronic link with a school in France/Germany/Spain etc. would be feasible and beneficial for your pupils or for a whole-school link? If you have a link already, what are the benefits?

Cultural learning: opening the classroom door and broadening horizons

In this chapter we will examine the vital role of primary MFL in 'opening the classroom door' to encourage pupils to look beyond their own physical and psychological borders, both by forging different types of international links and by celebrating difference. Case studies and examples of materials will suggest ways in which pupils can be led to reflect on their own language use and cultural norms and to enjoy and value other linguistic and cultural experiences. We look at how patterns and practices in EAL support for purposes of integration might dovetail with the expansion of MFL early learning, and how the often untapped linguistic and cultural resource of increasing numbers of bi- and multilingual pupils can enrich intercultural learning. We also look at how MFL can help achieve curriculum goals for citizenship.

Key issues

■ MFL has a key role to play in broadening pupils' cultural horizons.

■ Intercultural learning can take place both by extending the scope of how we interpret language teaching and, ultimately, by forging links with children from different countries.

■ The inclusion of historical, context-specific developments of a language enriches the language-learning experience and lifts it above abstracted technical coding of words and sentences.

■ Difference is all around us and is to be celebrated. In any primary classroom there is a rich diversity of cultural and linguistic heritage that can be drawn on to support language and intercultural learning.

■ There are also universal experiences and global challenges that can be linked to the primary MFL curriculum in order to forge overlapping, shared identities based on inclusiveness and common goals.

■ MFL encourages a broader concept of citizenship, extending beyond political and geographical boundaries.

Introduction

Cultural enrichment has long been seen as a key benefit of language learning, and 'intercultural understanding' was listed as a key objective in the Key Stage 2 Framework for primary modern languages. Although explicit reference to *intercultural* learning is absent from the 2014 NC, the opening statement makes a clear case for MFL to provide 'an opening to other cultures'.

In this chapter we look at how 'culture' can be defined in the primary MFL classroom and how we can systematically integrate elements of intercultural learning as we develop pupils' language competence. We emphasise the importance of examining cultural differences through looking at the lives of children of the same age living in different countries and the habits, symbols, rituals and artefacts that constitute their cultural life. We also believe it is essential that our pupils examine their own environment and recognise their own cultural experience. Accepting difference has never been more important, given our task of preparing children for a fast-changing world of cultural mixing and global communication where the need to adapt to changing circumstances and different social contexts is essential. In many schools, especially in urban areas, children live with cultural difference all around them and this experience is to be celebrated. Indeed, MFL builds on this diversity and embraces difference. In other schools, where the ethnic and cultural make-up of a school population seems fairly homogeneous, intercultural awareness is all the more important as it opens the door on the differences 'out there' that pupils will one day confront.

Assessing the role of 'culture' in primary MFL

Throughout this book we emphasise the multidimensional role of teaching and learning modern languages. We believe that learning languages is so much more than developing a technical linguistic skill. The social and cognitive processes involved in language learning do support other curriculum subjects but they also enhance whole-child development, as language and culture intersect. We embrace a broad vision of MFL and believe that it is only where language learning is narrowly defined as a technical skill that pupil disaffection results. Rather, MFL can be viewed as a study of culture, and cultures, where language is a cultural code that embodies specific world-views and historically shaped behaviours and preferences. In fact, it is somewhat unfortunate that, by definition, the name MFL suggests a language-only focus. It might be better to have a subject name with a wider focus to take into account the cultural dimension. For example, we can envisage MFL being rebranded as International Studies, French Studies, European Studies, Languages and Culture, or some other such title. While language study remains the key staple in MFL, it is essential that language is viewed as an evolving social practice, rooted in a community of speakers with specific historical and geopolitical identities. To divorce these cultural aspects from the study of a language can only be reductive and, ultimately, alienating.

It is through the study of, and interaction with, 'the other' that children become aware of their own cultural selves. In schools where there is little ethnic diversity, MFL and other such educational experiences have the potential to steer children away from a restrictive monocultural/monolingual view of the world. In areas where there is already ethnic diversity in the school, intercultural learning can encourage children to embrace variety and be flexible in their burgeoning world-view.

Claire Kramsch, who has written extensively on the intercultural dimension in language learning, suggested the metaphor of a 'third space' (1993) occupied by the language learner, that is the 'in-between' space between two languages and cultures. MFL teaching is situated in this metaphoric third space as it seeks to bridge the known and the unfamiliar through language and intercultural learning. More recently (2006, 2010), Kramsch has revised this 'third space' concept as it implies that cultures are solid, immutable entities that can be distinguished from each other. She suggests instead that intercultural learning develops a 'symbolic competence', an ability to apprehend and negotiate a complex system of processes that overlap – and possibly conflict, since different world-views might not neatly mesh. We hold with this latter view as we acknowledge that intercultural learning is anything but straightforward. However, for teaching purposes, we believe it is useful to conceive of cultural learning as having certain, discrete phases:

1   Starting point: using pupils' knowledge of and assessment of first-language culture;

2   Interaction with the new culture and language (the input phase);

3   A phase of comparison between 1 and 2;

4   A reassessment of the initial position 1.

These four phases provide a useful teacher checklist when integrating intercultural work in language teaching and learning.

Let us now turn to the parallel processes, expressed as pupil learning objectives, that are seen as requisite skills in developing intercultural competence.

Developing intercultural competence

The word 'intercultural' emphasises that cultural learning is about linking or reconciling different starting and end points: that is, it is more than just learning about how things are done differently 'over there'. Developing intercultural competence in primary language contexts requires developing a set of skills in the same way we aim to develop children's thinking skills and language skills. Michael Byram (1997: 89) lists the following five *savoirs* to describe the skills used in intercultural projects (the paraphrasing is our own):

- intercultural attitudes/predisposition (*savoir être*)
- critical cultural awareness (*savoir s'engager*)
- knowledge (*savoirs*)
- skills of interpreting and relating (*savoir comprendre*)
- skills of discovery and interaction (*savoir apprendre/faire*).

These *savoirs* relate to the four phases of planning we have listed above, though Byram is writing specifically about preparing for intercultural *exchanges*, either real or virtual.

Such exchanges or visits are an ideal goal to work towards but are not always possible, and the absence of genuine interaction with foreign native speakers should not be seen as a bar to effective intercultural work.

Many of the children we spoke to when writing this book answered the question 'Why do you think it's important to learn a foreign language?' with replies such as 'So that we can buy food when we go on holiday' and 'Because my uncle's got a house in Spain'. While these answers are perfectly legitimate, and we have no reason to dispute that learning a foreign language for such purely instrumental purposes is anything but well-grounded, we believe that motivation to learn language(s) needs to be understood in much broader terms, both from the perspective of those who implement MFL provision and from the pupils' point of view. For a start, if MFL learning is only understood as connected to concrete, instrumental outcomes, it becomes increasingly difficult to justify its presence in the UK curricula in the face of global English use. After all, we may tell children that they need to use Spanish to buy an ice-cream on holiday, but this message is often incompatible with their own experience, given that English is widely understood and used within the tourist industry they come into contact with when on family holidays. Similarly, we may tell children that having competence in foreign languages will improve their job prospects in the future, but most of the adults they know fare well enough in the UK labour market without using French or German, and so there is another discrepancy between the reasons given for MFL learning and the experience of the child.

Furthermore, such an instrumental view encourages attachment to a particular language and its spatially situated usefulness – for example, French for use in France and Italian for use in Italy. In this book we are arguing for a broader definition of MFL learning as language and cultural awareness with the development of transferable skills and strategies. If MFL needs to justify its presence at all in the curriculum we suggest that its *raison d'être* as a vital school subject is grounded in two bold yet overlapping strands. (See Chapter 1 for a discussion of the rationale for early language learning.) First to be cited are the cognitive benefits and skills associated with learning a new language (discussed in Chapter 5), but equally important is the developing awareness of language as a social practice, a cultural behaviour.

Which 'culture'?

The term 'culture' is often used to denote a fixed or clearly defined entity – a community seen from the outside which we associate with certain sets of practices, particular languages, types of food, housing and so forth. This has important implications for the intercultural dimension of language teaching, for it raises the question: Which 'culture' are we to assume a language embodies? Brian Street, an anthropologist turned education-alist, renowned for his pioneering work in new literacy studies, claimed that 'culture is a verb' (Street 1993) to emphasise the fluid, transient nature of what we call 'culture'. Street reminds us that 'the storage and transmission of both language and cultural knowledge . . . appear to involve a number of processes that are not captured by the study of language alone' (1993: 42).

Let us consider for a moment what type of culture we are referring to when speaking about teaching it in an MFL context. Firstly, we could distinguish between 'Culture' with a capital 'C' and 'culture' with a small 'c', meaning the day-to-day habits and customs of the target-language community, although in fact this becomes something of a false dichotomy because the two are linked in the way we perceive ourselves as belonging to a nation. In the case of 'Culture', we are speaking about the historical, national emblems of a country or language community, such as famous writers, philosophers, saints, artists, explorers, etc., but also national events that are still commemorated. For example, the Gunpowder Plot, the French Revolution and the more recent reunification of Germany are all remembered with national celebrations or holidays. These historical events and famous figures are often a source of traditional national pride and, in time, become woven into the grand narrative of a nation, which binds together a collective consciousness and forges the notion of a shared identity. Within this definition of culture, exploring different ways of celebrating shared and different feast days in the calendar can provide a stimulating and enjoyable springboard for looking at difference.

The following is an example of effective intercultural language learning with a Year 1 class, combining the excitement of games and holidays with the enjoyment of singing (and the universal love of chocolate).

Year 1 Topic: Easter

Just before the Easter holidays, and following a topic on colours, I hide some mini chocolate eggs round the classroom before the children arrive, enough for one for each child. When the German class begins, I say an Easter rhyme to the children (*In dem grünen Gras sitzt ein kleiner Has, legt ein rotes Ei, und du bist frei!*). I ask the children if they can hear any words they know? (Colours, cognates.) I show the children an image of the scene in the rhyme, with a removable bunny, which reveals a red egg! We practise saying the rhyme together, with my cardboard bunny acting out the scene. I explain to the children that this rhyme is used sometimes by children in playgrounds, to decide who is going to be 'on' in a chasing game, and that we are going to use it to decide who can go looking for chocolate eggs in the classroom! I talk about how German children celebrate Easter and tell them of the tradition in Germany of the *Osterhase*, hiding eggs in the garden, or in the woods, or in the flat where they live. The children sit in a large circle on the carpet, and join in with the rhyme, as I point to each child using the rhythm of the rhyme. Whichever child I point to on the word *frei* gets up and goes to look for a chocolate egg hidden in the classroom. We agree they will put their egg on the carpet in front of them until the game is finished, so it is easy to see which children are still waiting for their turn (nobody gets two turns!). I think it is important for young children to know traditional rhymes that would be familiar to German children of a similar age. The children soon pick up the rhyme (well, we do repeat it about 30 times!) and join in with me, though occasionally a few of them 'forget' to join in because their thoughts are overwhelmed by whether or not it will be their turn next!

This type of activity resonates with Byram's *savoirs* inasmuch as this enjoyable game is allowing the children an insight into a (slightly) different cultural practice so that their system of reference points, in this case in relation to Easter, is broadened. It also fits clearly with many of the objectives of the KS2 NC, including:

Pupils should be taught to:

- ■ Explore the patterns and sounds of language through songs and rhymes.
- ■ Appreciate stories, songs, poems and rhymes in the language.

In our second definition of 'culture', we are referring to daily habits and routines such as eating habits and ways of dressing. Even in a global world, many of us cling to what we consider essential elements of our shared culture and continue to ritualise aspects of our Englishness or Frenchness. Let us take, by way of an example, eating habits. Although few British people actually eat fish and chips more than occasionally, we may feel that there is something comfortingly 'British' about this dish, as if it really were part of a shared cultural understanding and more than a serving of fried fish and potato, which only fairly recently came to be regarded as a 'national dish'. In fact, many such 'traditions', which bind us to a sense of shared identity, are of recent origin, many consciously constructed to give an illusion of longstanding tradition. One example of this, described in Hobsbawm and Ranger's (1983) *The Invention of Tradition*, is the 'ancient' tradition of Scottish clan tartans, which, upon closer inspection, can be deconstructed as a romantic myth invented in the nineteenth century.

It is useful to keep this relativism in mind when introducing 'Culture' and 'culture' in MFL lessons. Indeed, teaching children about where our customs and the iconography that constitutes our Britishness originated represents useful, important work on understanding identities. If we ignore the historico-geographic dimension when discussing difference(s), young pupils only see the end point of a complex chain of localised circumstances and so view different habits or beliefs as innate characteristics rather than behaviours and viewpoints developed over time to deal with specific contexts. Younger children naturally have a keen curiosity and a flexible, adaptable mind, and it is this *souplesse d'esprit* that makes them such good intercultural language learners. As they develop a more centred sense of self and position in the world, in relation to their own cultural context, it is important to encourage ongoing reflexivity so that children think about their own immediate experience and maintain openness and flexibility to new ideas. This reflexivity is an important opening-up phase when embarking on intercultural work, leading pupils to examine the specificity of their own beliefs and practices. We have seen some wonderful examples of this type of intercultural study woven into MFL learning and other areas of the curriculum.

At a Roman Catholic primary school in East Anglia, where prayers were often said in Italian, the staff had an open, really rather progressive attitude to the geographic origins of the school's faith. For example, the school was named after an Italian saint and children performed, in assembly, a sketch portraying one of the legends of the saint's life (St Francis talking to the wolf and to the townspeople) in 'original version' by using simplified Italian with a side-of-stage narrator interpreting:

San Francesco: È vero che vuoi uccidere la gente del villaggio?
St Francis: Is it true that you have tried to kill the townspeople?

Il lupo: Sì, Signore
The wolf: Yes, Sir.

San Francesco: Perché?
St Francis: Why?

Il lupo: Perché ho fame.
The wolf: Because I'm hungry.

There was also a map display in the hall showing where the saint had lived and where key events in his life, such as his conversion, had taken place.

At the same school there was an art wall featuring images of Jesus, including an early Byzantine Christian Italianate Renaissance Jesus, an Ethiopian black Jesus and the blue-eyed, white Christ of a Hollywood film. Although not necessarily linked to the teaching of Italian (the principal foreign language taught in this school), this display, prepared by pupils, was a clear demonstration of how interpretation is culturally subjective. This important intercultural project allowed pupils to understand how widely shared beliefs – in this case the Christian faith – are also experienced differently at an immediate, local level. The Key Stage 2 Framework (2005: 75) identified as a key objective that children should be able to recognise how symbols, products and objects can be representative of specific cultures, and this has been achieved in this example by supporting both the faith-based ethos of the school and its mission to be fully inclusive and to acknowledge difference. The headteacher of this school also regularly invites speakers of different faiths to speak in assemblies as she believes that pupils 'living in a multicultural, multi-faith world have to learn to get along with other people who might not have had the same cultural and religious background as theirs.' She added, 'They often realise that many faiths are actually saying the same thing, spreading the same message.' This headteacher, like many others we have spoken to, recognises the key role that MFL has to play in this kind of education, whether it be called 'spiritual' or 'cultural', which aims to broaden the child's view of the world and to engender interest in, and tolerance of, difference.

Similarly, although Spanish is increasingly the language of choice in primary schools, the historical and geographical lineage of the language is often omitted so that it is taught only as representative of a modern holiday destination (beaches and tapas!). This aspect of Spanish appeals to both pupils and parents and so increases motivation to learn: it is a pity not to capitalise on this motivation by exploiting the opportunity to broaden pupils' understanding of what constitutes Spanish culture. One school we visited in the East Midlands, where Spanish had been voted the school MFL by parents and pupils, had set about engaging with Spanish language and culture – especially the important Moorish influence on Spanish language, food and architecture (see the box on p. 139) – by integrating Spanish culture in this broad sense across the curriculum.

These projects exemplify Byram's *savoir être* because they broaden children's understanding of what 'Spanish' means in relation to their own British perspective; *savoir apprendre* because the children are set a research task to find out about given everyday objects as cultural artefacts; and *savoirs* because the children see how these items contribute to a collective, historical identity of Spanishness. The work on the Moors' influence in Spain not only encouraged a broader understanding of the Arabic Islamic heritage in Europe but also affirmed the vitality and richness of Islamic culture, a particularly worthwhile objective in today's climate of suspicion and intolerance towards followers of the Islamic faith.

Durante la época de expansión del islam los árabes introdujeron muchas cosas en España (estabán en España del año 711 hasta 1492). Así que quedan muchas palabras de origen árabe en español, por ejemplo.

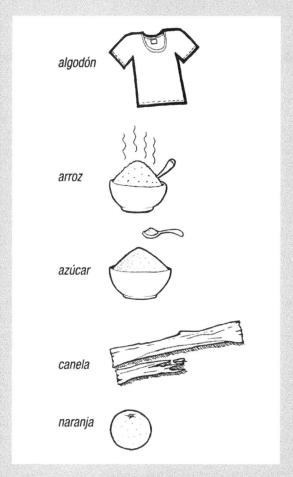

FIGURE 9.1 Five pictures of items with Spanish labels

Year 5 pupils were each asked to bring in an example of the item and to find out something about how it is used, e.g. for making clothes or for flavouring food. Children then learnt how the item was cultivated and how it was processed for consumption. Although the task was mainly conducted in English, the impetus was awareness of cross-cultural etymologies in language and a sensitivity to the richness of cultural mingling. The Year 5 teacher who set up the project told us how surprised he had been that pupils had such little awareness of the Muslim Empire compared to, for example, the Roman Empire, and hoped that this project would go some way towards redressing the balance. In the same Year 5 classroom, pupils had each designed an *azulejo* ceramic tile (though drawn on paper) and a lower part of a wall had been covered with their designed squares in the Moorish style still popular in Spain (*un zócalo*).

Many from mixed-heritage backgrounds feel alienated by narrow cultural epithets such as 'English', 'British' and 'European', and so we believe a key objective of inter-cultural education is to redefine these terms to include pupils rather than to describe given characteristics. In this respect, the relatively new subject area of Citizenship Education links naturally to the intercultural strand of primary MFL.

Citizenship and MFL

The 'non-statutory' framework for Citizenship was introduced into English and Welsh primary schools in 2000 with provision becoming statutory in 2002. The latest National Curriculum (2014) has reverted Citizenship Education to non-statutory in primary schools though still statutory in Key Stages 3 and 4. We believe that MFL has a key role to play in broadening the scope of citizenship beyond the limits of national boundaries. Research led by Coffey (2005) into London schoolchildren's perceptions of Europe and European citizenship revealed that many children from minority ethnic backgrounds equate European identity and languages with white, Christian populations that they may feel excluded from, often preferring instead to align themselves with their parents' place of origin – 'I'm Jamaican', 'I'm Somali'. Many schoolchildren questioned were unaware of the Muslim contribution to cultural life, not only historically but in modern-day France, Germany and Spain. The more pupils learn about the multicultural make-up of all modern European nation states, the greater their affinity for a shared European identity, not at the exclusion of other identities but, rather, as another strand to their integrated identity.

With a truly global language such as French, spoken over different continents as a mother tongue, it is relatively easy to present examples of different cultural and geographical contexts and many good coursebooks now address this broader definition of a French speaker by showing, for example, French-speaking Canadians enjoying winter sports in Quebec, a Martiniquais child helping his father with the fishing catch, a Côte d'Ivoirien school room, a French Polynesian girl helping her mother cook the family meal, and so forth. These images are interesting and help show the diverse contexts in which French is present, but there is also a risk that they become internalised as romanticised snapshots of a different, exotic way of life unless there is some *intercultural* preparatory and follow-up work. For example, as suggested above, an important initial phase for children confronting difference is that they are led to frame their own customs and way of living not as the indexical 'norm' but as one way of managing specific contextual circumstances. This allows greater objectivity when learning about how people in different social and geographic contexts manage the same universal challenges of eating, learning, making a living, maintaining relationships, finding spiritual fulfilment and having fun. Follow-up work might consist of comparing pupils' own lives with what they have learnt about other children's lives, but it is important that this is set up, as much as possible, as an unbiased analysis with the aim of providing a shared experience.

As with all intercultural learning, the ultimate goal is actual dialogue between pupils from different countries (more on this below), yet intercultural work can still be managed successfully within the class group, using images and information from the internet and from other sources such as embassies and cultural institutes. The following example illustrates how an object as mundane as a school bag can represent a cultural artefact for different uses in intercultural learning.

Schulranzen

Year 2 children are the same age as school-starters in Germany, so it is a particularly appropriate time to look at the topic of 'schools'. The language learning in this topic revolves around revision of greetings and new classroom commands (*Schau her, hör zu, steh auf*, etc.), which appeals to their more 'bossy' natures! Towards the end of the topic, I bring in a real German *Schulranzen* and we compare this satchel to the kinds of bags British children bring in to school. The discussion and ideas from the children are often very rewarding. They notice how many reflectors it has on it and suggest they are to help keep the children safe in the dark. This leads into a discussion of lessons starting in Germany at 7.30 to 8 am, often when it is still dark, and the fact that many more primary children walk unaccompanied to school in Germany than in Britain. They comment on the large size of it and wonder whether that is so it can fit in a big packed lunch! This leads to a discussion of German children needing a *zweites Frühstück*, but finishing lessons in many schools in time to go home for a midday meal, which in turn leads to a discussion of the recent present of the *Schlüsselanhänger* sent to us from our partner school, and why children might be more likely than my Year 2s to wear a house key round their neck. We also look at the fact that the *Schulranzen* is designed to stand squarely next to the children's tables in class and, yes, that leads to yet another discussion, this time on how children in Germany are required to equip themselves with stationery, etc., and have it readily to hand in class. Using the *Early Start German* DVD, we look at scenes of children setting off to school with their *Schulranzen* and having them next to their tables in a classroom. I ask the children to look out for certain things when watching the DVD, e.g. 'Can you spot a *Schulranzen*? Where in the classroom do the children store their bags? How do their classroom tables and chairs compare to ours? Look out for the delicious cakes in the bakery!' We watch the DVD together, and then discuss what they have seen. The children are always full of questions. They are fascinated by the differences and reassured by the familiarities (the 'They look just like us!' feeling). Then we watch the DVD again to remind ourselves of what we have discussed. Watching a DVD is second best to the children actually experiencing Germany but miles better than me just talking to them about it. At the end of a very busy, chatty lesson, which usually has the children buzzing with questions, I leave the *Schulranzen* behind for the children to try on over the next few days, they love this!

The activity described above clearly illustrates how many perspectives can be exploited from a single item. The use of the authentic material incited interest and the children's natural curiosity led to further discussions. Although English was used in these discussions (other than for the vocabulary for the main items being discussed) the cultural input provided a highly motivating frame for the planned language work relating to school and classroom language use.

As well as learning about different ways of life in 'exotic' locations, it is important to represent the reality of cultural diversity in modern Western societies. For example, learning about the colourful cultural landscapes of French-speaking societies across the continents should not exclude the enormous cultural range within any French metropolitan city. Pupils are often surprised by the cultural, ethnic and religious mix of neighbouring European countries, which are often represented in advertising and published material by quaint, old-fashioned stereotypes. Young learners experience cultural diversity in their everyday lives, and seeing that diversity in countries like France or Spain gives them a more realistic picture of life in those countries.

EAL pupils and bilingualism: building on diversity

Many modern classrooms are characterised by rich and diverse cultural and linguistic heritage. Even in all-white, seemingly monocultural areas, there are often interesting family histories of immigration or other geographic movements that can be uncovered two or three generations before. Until recently, children who spoke another language at home, especially if it were not one of the Western European languages, were considered disadvantaged at school, their bilingualism often seen as a drawback rather than an asset. This 'deficit' perspective has changed radically in recent times and now children are encouraged to celebrate their linguistic and cultural backgrounds. Indeed, this development was enshrined in the Key Stage 2 Framework as a key learning objective:

> IU3.1 Children should be taught to learn about the different languages spoken by children in the school.
>
> (Key Stage 2 Framework 2005: 76)

This objective has been continued by removal of any stipulation of specific languages to be taught in the KS2 NC (2014), even though, for obvious reasons, most schools have continued with the main foreign languages, especially French and Spanish. Increased awareness of the varied needs of EAL children has led to effective, differentiated support strategies in language coaching that take into account different starting points in terms of age and previous exposure to English, but also with reference to first-language experience. For example, some pupils may already be successfully reading and writing in their first language and whether or not this is a language using Roman script will affect the transition to English. Many of the strategies employed in EAL tuition are transferable to the primary MFL teaching context, where reference to existing knowledge of language is made explicit and built upon. Making links explicit in this way is a development reminiscent of Eric Hawkins' forward-thinking work in the 1980s on raising 'language awareness' across the curriculum (Hawkins 1984) and ties in today with the call to embed literacy across the curriculum through a SPaG (spelling, punctuation and grammar) approach to all language learning, including English, MFL and ancient languages. Seen in this light, MFL is redefined as more than foreign language teaching and becomes part of the child's whole-language awareness, whether that child is a first-language English speaker or an EAL pupil.

In cases where pupils' first language corresponds to the MFL of choice, they can be a rich, natural resource in primary MFL teaching, providing authentic language models and peer-coaching other pupils. We believe that this not only provides linguistic benefits but can also be a cultural enrichment and a celebration of diversity. One cautionary word we might add here relates to the potential reluctance of some EAL pupils to use their mother tongue with peers as they may feel this makes them stand out as different when they really wish to just assimilate. Such reticence may be linked to parental pressure to 'get on' and assimilate through English or may result from some confusion themselves in regard to language use. After all, bilingual pupils are still young children and, especially if they have spent a long time in the UK, their productive skills in the mother tongue may well be underdeveloped even if their aural understanding is instinctive.

By way of an example, let us cite two Spanish-speaking identical twins who one of the authors (Coffey) met recently in Year 4 of a London primary school. The two brothers were asked, separately, to recount the story of Little Red Riding Hood using pictures only. The boys were addressed in Spanish but were not asked to respond in any particular language. One of the boys told the entire story in English with only one or two difficulties in vocabulary gaps, which he tried to explain in English or asked 'What's that?', but his brother switched freely between languages several times throughout the story, calling the grandma *the abuela* and the wolf *the lobo*. Whenever he was unsure of a word or expression he used Spanish. The different responses illustrate how motivation to use English versus the mother tongue varies even between children with almost identical environmental influences and how these translate to different communicative strategies.

In a multilingual classroom there is space for a variety of strategies to be developed and these can be adapted freely by first-language English speakers as they engage with MFL learning.

Celebrating diversity or language teaching?

In many schools, especially where there is a sizeable cohort of bilingual children, cultural diversity is celebrated throughout the school by respecting different religious feast days, greeting children in a different 'language of the week' or by talking about different cultural traditions in assemblies, etc. We fully endorse these affirmative enterprises, which are both culturally enriching and encourage children to accept difference; however, such initiatives are not to be confused with MFL teaching and learning. For MFL to be effectively taught, a clearly structured programme of study is required that sends consistent messages and is pedagogically sound. Culture has a vital part to play in the success of this language teaching, but again, this needs to be structured and planned to fit a scheme of work. Anecdotal and ad hoc exposure to words and phrases of different languages may serve to bond the school community and engender tolerance but, alone, it does not constitute effective MFL teaching. Instead, what we are proposing is that planned language development is dovetailed into intercultural work throughout the MFL schemes of work and that both strands are underpinned by whole-curriculum links.

Making friends across the world

The ultimate goal of intercultural language learning is to arrange actual or virtual exchanges between schools. The pathways opened up by digital technology have made such exchanges increasingly manageable (see Chapter 8 for a discussion of the different ways these can be arranged). The benefits of having a partner school in a target-language country are enormous, because they represent a source of material and a window on the parallel lives of pupils of the same age. For staff, too, partner schools offer great opportunities for teacher exchange (both for language and cultural enrichment). Within the EU, funding is available for teachers to spend time in a school abroad or to attend language courses, and there are also wider global links available for school global citizenship facilitated through schemes such as Connecting Classrooms (managed by the British Council) and the UK One World Linking Association (UKOWLA).

Where we have seen MFL most successfully embedded in the cultural life of the school it has been underpinned by some form of partnership abroad, not necessarily between pupils, maybe only between teachers, often led by the MFL coordinator or a visionary headteacher. Initial contacts can be provided by such agencies as the European Schoolnet site, the British Council, foreign embassy cultural and educational departments, or by informal word-of-mouth networks, but the ongoing success of links is only sustained through effective personal relationships, clear joint planning and flexibility. Although this chapter has dealt primarily with developing cultural awareness in pupils' learning, it is essential that teachers also develop their own 'interculturality', and learning from visits to schools abroad, where culturally different ways of teaching and learning are experienced, provides enormous value in terms of professional and personal development.

Conclusion

Language learning and cultural awareness are inextricably linked. This has been recognised in the current KS2 NC for Languages, where cultural learning constitutes a key rationale. In this chapter we have considered how culture can be defined within a language-learning context to meet the needs of children today: that is, to understand and to accept the differences that surround them as natural and enriching. The whole-curricular dimension of cultural learning is emphasised, as is the importance of self-reflexivity if children are not simply to learn that foreigners do things differently but rather that differences are understood contextually as rooted in specific historical and geographic circumstances. In this light, cultural awareness becomes truly 'intercultural' as children have a broader understanding of their own emerging identities. Embracing cultural diversity is important, both for schools where ethnic and cultural mix is evident and also for those where the pupil cohort appears to be culturally homogeneous, because all children need to develop flexible and adaptable ways of engaging with others in a world of change and increasingly globalised identities contending with locally framed experiences. MFL has a vital role in the school in developing empathy. As one Year 6 girl in East Anglia told us about her MFL learning: 'It's fun, you get to feel like you're French or German when you speak the words.'

Questions on which to reflect

- Is the cultural diversity within your school/class already recognised and celebrated?
- Is there any linguistic diversity among pupils (are there EAL pupils, etc.) which can be exploited for MFL learning?
- How is the ethos of your school embedded in school traditions and practices? Is there scope for extending these to draw on a wider range of cultural and linguistic sources?

10

Transition from primary to secondary: continuity, cohesion and progression

In the same way that it is important that children's learning trajectories provide continuity from their primary schooling into the secondary phase in all subjects, it is vital to ensure that the initial interest in and enjoyment of primary MFL is maintained, and that primary and secondary teachers work together to ensure that learning is sequential and coherent. Transition needs to be seen and understood in a wider context. The concept is based on liaison (defined as discussion and other links between primary and secondary schools) and transfer (understood as the actual move from one phase to the other). Liaison, transfer and an awareness of needs and expectations of all parties involved are the key elements of a structured dialogue on issues of the process of transition enabling stakeholders to develop a suggested framework. Transition, then, is the concept that embraces all the cross-phase deliberations and procedures. It comprises mini-transitions throughout the primary phase as well as the major point of transition from KS2 to KS3. Transition and its aspects are the focus of this chapter.

Key issues

- Primary and secondary teachers of MFL need to conceptualise the foreign language learning pathway as a continuum of learning.

- MFL teachers in both phases benefit from a mutual awareness and understanding of teaching and learning approaches appropriate to the age level and from working in collaboration.

- Cross-phase liaison between teachers is essentially concerned with the continuous and continuing development of the whole child in their language learning.

- Transfer documentation on children's primary MFL learning needs to be informative and useful to all readers to provide a bridge for progression.

- Liaison provides an opportunity for teachers to show leadership on a cross-phase basis. The headteacher and senior leadership team have a role to play in supporting primary–secondary liaison in their school organisational arrangements.

■ Primary and secondary MFL teachers and other relevant parties need to put in place a regular and open dialogue to plan the progression of pupil learning and the enhancement of teacher subject knowledge.

Introduction: avoiding 'horrible things'

> At secondary school, the French teacher might say horrible things if we get on to harder things and we have no idea what they are talking about.
>
> (Year 6 boy at end of summer term)

The genuinely felt fear of 'horrible things' anticipated by this pupil can be prevented when modern foreign languages teachers from the primary and the secondary sectors communicate with each other. Such communication between teachers will open opportunities to provide a joined-up approach to primary and secondary MFL learning.

As a subject, primary MFL requires special attention, given its recent statutory status in the curriculum at primary level (and variable position at secondary-level KS4). Furthermore, primary MFL is not just a question of learning 'a little French' but a part of the child's whole language and literacy development project, and therefore liaison is essential.

There are actually many points of transition as the child moves through her or his school career (and indeed in life outside of school), not just one solitary transition at the end of primary and beginning of secondary schooling (although this is a very obvious and critical one), as Figure 10.1 shows.

We see primary MFL as a foundation stone for ongoing learning and an important step in preparing pupils for the progression from primary to secondary, as does the KS2 National Curriculum (2014). Secondary schools can also benefit from a structured, joined-up approach in that they have the opportunity to build on previous learning outcomes and ensure that appropriate challenges for pupils are set from the start. Teachers need to consider the primary to secondary transfer within the context of a series of transitions that make up the child's school career.

Issues of transition, then, are about more than communication and collaboration between teachers at the surface level – they are about the whole child and their long-term development at a deep level of consideration. This perspective will form a basis for planning a coherent, if not always entirely seamless, continuum of learning, for learning is never without its surprises, challenges and deviations. Learning, like a tree, grows up towards the light but develops interesting side branches and complex root systems as learners engage in different language-learning experiences in different contexts. One very obvious example is that some pupils will take up a different language at secondary level to the one, or those, offered in the primary school.

A la recherche du 'tronc commun'

Transition was the focus of research by Erika Werlen and colleagues at the University of Tübingen. In collaboration with several other institutions during the period 2001–2006, they undertook some large-scale research into primary English as a foreign language

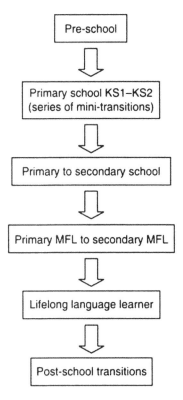

FIGURE 10.1 Points of transition

learning context and progress made in early foreign language learning. The pupils were aged from six to nine and were learning English or French as a foreign language. Werlen's intention was to try to identify apparently significant factors promoting the progressive learning of a foreign language at primary level, leading to the identification of what she calls a *tronc commun*. Some 470 primary schools in Baden-Württemberg were involved in this comprehensive exploration of teaching approaches and learning styles, infrastructures of MFL provision and their impact on learning, and issues of progression and transition to higher year groups. A great many classroom interventions were planned as part of this research, including older, more advanced learners coaching younger, less proficient learners.

Although this research was devised for, and conducted in, a different context, we consider it useful for the UK as it focuses on transitions and coherence throughout the child's school career. Werlen (2005) considers that the focus on learning needs to take a long-term view of the child's whole school life, a perspective of long-term learning that she plots onto a model comprising vertical and horizontal axes (see Figure 10.2) designed to mesh flexibly in order to promote cohesion on the *tronc commun* at various points.

The vertical cohesion axis is concerned with transitions of the traditional kind and easily identifiable ones such as moving from one year group to another (and ultimately from one school to another), but also transitions from systems and routines such as the inevitable shift from informal holistic assessment by the teacher of younger pupils to more

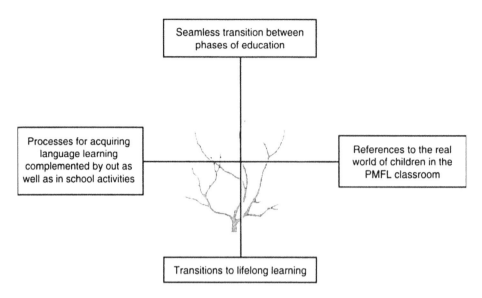

FIGURE 10.2 Cohesion model of learning and transition

formal assessment of the older ones. Such transitions are tangible, visible and manageable; they comprise the organisational stuff of school life and how primary MFL is managed across the whole school, as discussed in Chapter 2 about primary MFL as a whole-school learning project; they are about systems, structures and procedures.

The horizontal axis focuses more on the children, their development and their needs. It emphasises the classroom as one site of learning among a myriad of others outside of school, and on how primary MFL teachers should, according to Werlen, create classroom language-learning contexts that reflect the children's life experiences. This could be through the everyday life in school or by exploring the realms of the children's imagination with storytelling in the foreign language, for example. The curriculum, while rich in different topics, subjects and approaches, has cross-curricular dimensions and internal cohesion. The transitions on this axis are individualised, learning-centred and negotiable; they focus on children's needs and their growth.

As a primary school deputy headteacher with responsibility for early years commented, demonstrating an awareness of the horizontal axis:

> There are many mini-transition points, starting with the transition from home to school. This transition is huge, especially if the child has not had the opportunity to attend nursery school. You can see this sometimes when a child has been accus-tomed to baby talk at home and then has to use more formal language at school. Within the KS1 stage, there is a major transition from the Foundation Stage, which is play-based, to the National Curriculum, which is more formal, subject-based, structured and includes literacy and numeracy, although the current trend is back to more cross-curricular and more creativity. This provides a structure for KS2 which also provides new opportunities such as after-school clubs, sports,

networking with other schools, community activities, more work in the arts and so on. Oddly enough, when I first started teaching, the third year was called the transition year between infants and junior classes, but the immediate jump from KS1 to KS2 makes that transition more difficult now. The whole thing is like the change from nappies to trainer pants and then ordinary underwear, thank goodness.

It seems to us that much of the teacher-transition discourse, where it takes place, focuses on issues arising from the vertical axis, such as schemes of work, resourcing and assessment. There is scope for extending the transition discussion agenda to include issues deriving from considerations on the horizontal axis as well as exploring, more comprehensively, points of crossover. As Pagden writes (2001: 9):

> For a child to succeed there are some things that should stay the same throughout their time at school: most obviously, the combination of physical and social factors which ensures the child's right to feel safe and cared for. Other things should change progressively in order to support the child's growing competence and maturity; for example, the complexity of texts designed and/or chosen to foster the development of literacy skills.

Such issues would include pupil comfort level in primary MFL lessons and whole-school curriculum mapping and collaboration with colleagues. Indeed, we need to think about transition not just at the crucial KS2–KS3 stage, but as a series of mini-transitions that dot the primary-school child's career on a continuous basis.

Hold the teddy, pass the teddy – mini-transitions in the primary MFL classroom

In a primary MFL context, children go through a number of mini-transitions, comprising changes in classroom organisation and in expectations of social behaviour. Teachers teaching throughout the whole school are aware of these and integrate them into their teaching. One teacher of primary MFL throughout the whole school, who is thus responsible for learning transitions on the vertical axis, demonstrates sensitivity and awareness of these transitions, and in doing so takes into account both the vertical and horizontal axes. The following are examples of the many transitions children have to make as they progress through the key stages.

Organisational skills

These skills refer to the children organising their day, tasks and materials.

■ From carpet to sitting at a table:

> I teach Years 1 and 2 on the carpet, as it's much easier for them to easily stand up, but sitting at a table is easier for playing Question and Answer catch, as their

coordination is better developed and less time is spent dropping the toy used for this activity, the *Grüne Spinne!*

■ From group work at tables to individual seat, and a tray for their material:

> At KS2 I can easily play two minutes of number Lotto, without preparing for it . . . they grab their rough books and a pencil from their trays under their table, and off we go! At KS1, I would need to be resourced fully in advance to do this as the children sit on the carpet with no equipment to hand. Having said this, I've done Lotto with Year 2, using a pre-prepared grid and handing out photocopies and pencils. Year 1 tends to be equipment like multilink or number bananas, which have to be given out by passing along the rows of children.

■ Coping with time and timetable: from having an afternoon playtime, to working right through from 1pm to 3.15pm:

> Year 3 can get very tired in the afternoon, and also before lunch they get jaded. I swapped my Year 3 German slot with my Science slot to avoid MFL coming just before lunch when they were fading. It was Science 9 to 11.30 (with assembly and playtime breaks), German 11.30 to 12. Now German 9 to 9.30 and Science 9.30 to 12. German lessons were much more sparky as a result, and Science hasn't suffered.

> In PMFL in Year 1, 'evening' is new English vocab for some children, so *Guten Abend* means nothing until they are clear on the idea of 'evening'. I put it down to the fact that at that age, once the afternoon is over, it's tea and bath and bed, with no real evening to speak of – i.e. straight from *Guten Tag* to *Gute Nacht!* Older children need to be secure in reading a clock before introducing telling the time in German. I would usually expect a fair few Year 5 children to be wobbly on time-telling still.

Social skills and growing up

■ From responsible for self to showing responsibility for others:

> These include forming relationships with other pupils, moving from classroom to whole-school assemblies, taking responsibility for other children. Our older children have opportunities to be responsible for younger or more vulnerable children – e.g. sitting among the little ones in assembly as good role models, or shadowing a vulnerable boy at playtime, or helping a wheelchair-bound child with her coat etc. . . . some older children might sometimes sing a PMFL song when playing with the younger children at break.

■ From being relatively uninhibited at KS1 to the beginning of adolescence in Year 6:

> Silly songs can still work at Year 6, providing the atmosphere in the classroom allows for this. Silly songs at Year 1 are a must! Some of my current Year 6 are

becoming shyer at doing role plays for the class. I know they are capable, but one or two are starting to be less willing to 'perform', more 'cool', so it is harder to assess what they can do.

- Linked to the above, some children are becoming less comfortable with the opposite sex:

  A lovely 'touchy-feely drawing weather symbols on backs' lesson would go down a treat in Year 3, but in Year 6 some girls would not wish to be partnered with a boy, only a best friend for such an activity.

Learning skills

- From thinking of oneself to thinking in a group/class about tasks. The children move from being lone players to knowing the sort of behaviour required to play a group board game (MFL dice/snakes and ladders work best after Year 3):

  At KS1 when the children are passing e.g. a teddy to say *Guten Morgen* to, they are still learning to pass an object, to be fair, to take turns, not to snatch, etc., and are largely oblivious to the other children if they have hold of a particularly lovely teddy! My Year 2 topic on toys was most enjoyable, but passing them round sometimes took ages, as children gently rocked the dolly, or vroomed the toy car! By KS2, they pass things round quite quickly and efficiently. At Year 1, I once had a disastrous lesson with large, 12-sided foam dice to help learn numbers. The children were so fascinated by the dice, and had to put so much concentration into rolling them, and were so hopeful that the dice would come to them next from across the circle, that any language learning was swamped by all these other things! I tend to keep equipment and activities really simple at KS1, whereas at older KS2, sometimes you have to pull out a few stops to 'wow' them and grab their attention!'

- From doing the best for the teacher to being more responsible for their own learning, their targets:

  PMFL at KS1 is a lot about them looking forward to me coming, and enjoying making lots of lovely German sounds, and I almost always tell them how brilliant they are at some point. With Year 6 the other day, they knew their aim was to use good pronunciation for and confidence with numbers to 36, and they were responsible for asking me for help with the bits they needed to improve on. Praise plays a large part here too, but it's also important they know when it's not up to scratch, and what they have to do to get there.

- From individual to recognising 'the other':

  A child moves from being a person who thinks of number one to maturing to include consideration for number two and number three. MFL links with use of first, second and third person. With the little ones, emphasis is on *ich*, moving to *du*, eventually onto *er/sie/es* and then to *wir* as group belonging is important and for example with the topic of *Meine Familie*.

■ Transitions also occur at the level of motor skills when learning to write:

Using a pencil to being allowed to write in pen.

■ From being a non-reader to a reader:

With obvious implications for differentiated tasks in reading and writing.

In this way, Werlen's theoretical axes of cohesion translate to the practical transitions from home to school, nappies to trainer pants then pants, hugging the teddy to passing the teddy, pencils to pens, primary MFL for pure enjoyment to learning targets, unbridled exuberance to incipient 'uncool', cuddly toys to board games, and so on. Add to this the potentially seismic transition from primary to secondary school and conversation between all parties involved becomes urgent, in order to embrace the well-being and continuing and progressive learning needs of the children as well as to enhance subject dialogue between the language teachers concerned. The key purpose of such a dialogue is to continue to close the gap between the two phases as far as primary MFL is concerned and to build on the mechanisms for general primary–secondary transition procedures that have been developed over the years.

Mind the transition gap! The current situation

Any transition is, as can be seen from the examples provided in the previous section, a complex situation consisting of many aspects and different stages. Within the context of the transition from primary to secondary school, the concerns and needs of all need to be heard and attended to. Lorraine Flynn – then headteacher of a secondary school with a successful languages bias and a strong promoter of primary MFL and its links with secondary school – referred to this need as 'opening dialogue, closing the gap' between teachers in the two phases, stressing that 'Effective dialogue, which takes in the generalists' skills and knowledge (for example, those of the literacy coordinator), is vital to developing successful models to ensure our primary children remain motivated as they move through the Key Stages' (Flynn 2005: 4).

The current situation, although improving, is still fraught with difficulties, as the concerns expressed by the stakeholders involved show. There is a primary-school teacher who regrets missed opportunities for visits from her school to a secondary school due to financial and geographical factors:

We have an open invitation to visit a secondary school but no visits yet due to distance, cost and time.

And one of her colleagues is concerned about secondary MFL imposing their scheme of work on their colleagues in primary schools:

They ask us to use a certain scheme of work to suit them.

This one-directional dialogue can lead, in some instances, to secondary schools simply ignoring the foundation that has been laid in the subject area and teaching MFL as if the children were new to the subject, as one primary headteacher observes:

> In spite of the good work of some really enthusiastic colleagues in both primary and secondary schools, too many of the secondary schools just start at the beginning again and ignore what the children have done.

This statement could, however, also be interpreted as secondary MFL teachers' attempts to ensure that the children from different feeder schools start from the same level in the subject.

There is clearly a need for support for primary MFL from the leadership level in secondary schools, as one experienced subject leader pointed out:

> For me it is a question of leadership at secondary level. We need support for primary languages from the top and it isn't always forthcoming. There are issues to do with school organisation such as choice of language, groupings and the strategic overview of the place of MFL.

Even more disconcerting than the criticism made by the members of the professional group are the fears and concerns expressed by parents whose children have learning difficulties. This parent of a Year 7 child anticipates an increase of difficulties for her son:

> My son struggled with French at primary school as he is dyslexic and is having a really hard time at secondary school.

And children who, like this Year 6 child, found the subject hard at primary level, and fear a lack of support and extra help:

> If we are struggling at secondary school, it will be even harder and we won't be able to get extra help in groups like we do here.

A coherent scheme of transition from primary to secondary MFL needs, as can be seen by these comments, to be transparent to all parties concerned. Devising a model for an effective dialogue on the issues relating to the process of transition will have to start, in our view, with the ultimate beneficiaries – the pupils.

Scary and hard work to come

If given the opportunity, pupils can provide insightful views on the subject of their learning and express their own, sometimes strong, views about their experiences of MFL learning. Interestingly, a striking consensus emerged from two Year 6 pupil focus groups in London that we organised at the end of a summer term and a third group organised one autumn term in a school in the south east. All the pupils thought that MFL would:

- get harder
- involve more writing
- involve less speaking.

Asking the pupils in the focus-group discussions to elaborate on what they meant by 'hard', they linked 'hardness' to: 'scary' textbooks that they had seen; writing, 'like describing yourself – my brother had to do a whole page of writing'; fearing that they might not understand what the teacher would be saying when speaking the target language; and, by extension, 'getting homework that we might not understand and we would get a detention'. Some pupils had heard through the peer or sibling grapevines that some of the work done at secondary school was the same as in primary school. All had, indeed, been warned about textbooks and those children who had seen the textbooks used by their friends or brothers and sisters thought they looked 'hard'.

Among the interviewees there was one boy who felt he was already 'rubbish at French' and was worried about how he would cope at secondary school, whereas the majority of children thought that having learnt French/German/Italian etc. might be useful. They saw that, in their own words, 'We will know what to do'; 'We know some of the language so we will recognise it'; 'Even if we do German, the French we have done will give us a clue about learning'; and 'We will know what the teacher is talking about'. This is an important point coming from the pupils about their primary language experiences serving as a 'learning to learn a language' experience. In spite of all the talk about MFL 'getting hard', the children exhibited determination and indomitable stoicism, and had good ideas, effectively about improving transition and closing the gap.

Closing the gap: opening the dialogue and moving towards a framework

Foundations of dialogue – perspectives from the teaching staff

The dialogue to close the gap has been ongoing among pupils, primary-school teachers, secondary-school teachers, parents, trainers, advisers and others with an interest and stake in the process.

In instances where heads and colleagues involved in the primary MFL adventure have planned primary MFL bridging activities and/or helpful transition arrangements, their enthusiasm and transition problem-busting skills are tangible. One head of MFL reported positive impressions gained on visits to primary schools and the extent to which this had had an impact on her planning:

> I went to visit one of our feeder primary schools and watched the PMFL teach and saw what they had covered over three years and realised we would need to change our scheme of work. We have since begun to amend our teaching approach with Year 7 to be more in line with what we saw at primary school. It was a revelation.

Visits to feeder schools can be extremely profitable for secondary-school teachers at an early stage of their career, as this newly qualified teacher (NQT) points out:

I go to teach Year 6 at one of our main feeder primary schools once a week and I can honestly say it is the highlight of my week. I love it. I try to do similar things with my Year 7 and 8 classes.

Lesson observations can be a very effective means of teacher learning and form an essential part of the dialogue on transitions, as one primary-school teacher comments:

The head of MFL from one of our secondary schools comes in fortnightly over the summer term and teaches Year 6. I find it interesting to watch her and the children can see that what they will do in Year 7 is not too different from what they are used to.

It is beneficial when a school has a member of staff whose enthusiasm can start the dialogue on transition using networking skills, as the following example provided by a secondary headteacher shows:

We have one teacher who is ideally placed to liaise on primary–secondary languages as she used to teach in a prep school and she is really keen to work closely with some of our feeder primary schools. In fact she has already made a start with the school just down the road as part of our school cluster arrangement.

Towards a structured dialogue

So what are the key elements for a structured dialogue between primary and secondary teachers from which both sides benefit? Our discussions with teachers show the following issues:

- Secondary teachers knowing what primary MFL content the primary school covers and which skills have been developed and to what extent (we think it would be useful for primary teachers to be acquainted with at least KS3 schemes of work, in particular Year 7);
- Discussion about respective teaching approaches (to identify the areas of expertise of each and to find common bridging ground);
- Consideration of the best possible permutations of languages on offer;
- Agreement on a baseline coverage (to which primary colleagues would be oriented and on which secondary teachers can build and ensure progression rather than use guesswork);
- Sharing of materials (in order to familiarise themselves with the resource bank and perhaps share these with the pupils (see 'Pupils' perspectives on transition', below));
- Problematic areas – and a search for solutions – and identifying what works well (how teachers can help each other and share good ideas);
- Agreement on primary MFL profiling data on pupils (to decide what transfer information would be useful and in what format, and to identify learning and other needs of pupils – one way to avoid 'horrible things'!).

Foundations of the dialogue: the family support group

The impact of the transition from primary MFL to secondary MFL reaches beyond the school, and pupils seek and receive help from their parents and siblings, as this Year 6 pupil states:

> I don't think it will get harder if we learn really hard at primary school and I have my brother and sister to help me when I am at secondary school. My dad got me a German dictionary.

A parent describes her experience with the transition from primary MFL to MFL at secondary school:

> My daughter always enjoyed French when she was here [at primary school] – and my son does too – and she is really enjoying French in Year 7 at the high school. I know a bit of French and the teaching seems to be really inspirational.

Pupils' perspectives on transition

In the focus-group discussions, pupils were asked for their ideas about improving their transition. Transition was explained to them as the move from primary to secondary school and what teachers might do to make it easier for them to continue to make progress and to know what they were doing. Among the pupils' ideas were:

- Looking at some of the textbooks they would be using at secondary school but with their teacher at primary school who would help deal with the 'scary' factor as they could see what would be expected of them.
- More regular French lessons, and French used by more members of staff across the school (see Chapter 2).
- More focus on writing and more opportunities to write as a way to prepare for secondary school. Even where the primary MFL teacher does not explicitly embrace this, we have seen children reading and writing in every school we have visited. Writing provides immense opportunities for extension and differentiation, and the former Key Stage 2 Framework that is still much used is inclusive in this respect (as are the myriad schemes of work available to be shared online).
- A suggestion from Year 6 pupils in one school that they might teach pupils in Key Stage 1 some basic language so that the younger ones would not be afraid:

> Our Y6 children plan and prepare to teach the Y1 children. I fill them in on the Y1 learning so far (numbers 1–7), and explain what their task is (teach 8, 9, 10). The Y6s have so much experience of learning German, it's good to give them the chance to use that experience to help others learn. Their creativity is wonderful! They make little flashcards, bring in lovely puppets from home, and one group even had a wand and top hat to add that extra sparkle! The Y1s were

enchanted! They duly learnt their three new numbers. The Y6s were extraordinary – they learnt an immeasurable amount!

As well as peer-teaching, the children enjoyed doing small amounts of homework for French and project work, and said they would like to do a bit more. Some children expressed an interest in independent study and suggestions included researching cultural information and making recordings of speaking. One child said it would be helpful if the teacher would ensure the pupils understood what they were saying, especially if they were always speaking in French 'as sometimes they sound like they are talking to other adults'. Above all, the children were anxious that teachers at secondary school find out what the pupils know and can, and conversely cannot, do. An 11-year-old girl said: 'Teachers need to get into the child's mind and see our problems.'

The observations and views put forward by the stakeholders show, we find, a remarkable consistency concerning the issues surrounding the transition from primary to secondary MFL teaching. These points need to be considered when devising a framework for transition.

A framework for transition

Taking the results of our findings and Werlen's research into consideration, it would be very short-sighted to focus on the KS2–KS3 transition only. In the light of the multi-transitional language-learning journey that the pupils have to undergo, we suggest that teachers take all four key stages into consideration. At the point of KS2–KS3 transition, it is vital that teachers plan transfer information that can guide and inform the next stage of learning provision. We have detected a certain vagueness in some instances, as Cynthia Martin, primary languages expert, put it in a personal correspondence: 'The information can sometimes be rather restricted to topic areas – greetings, ages, pets and colours, typical early Year 7 fare.' Some teachers have integrated MFL into the regular subject profiling of a child's progress, and transfer information includes a report as for other subjects. Children are often encouraged to take a folder or portfolio of work with them to their secondary schools, but we have no evidence yet of this sample being acknowledged at secondary school in any systematic way. We would assert that assessment is an important part of primary MFL provision within an 'assessment for learning' framework and can provide useful data on pupil progress for the secondary school (see Chapter 7).

In order to develop the transition framework, teachers need to visit each other's classrooms from time to time and to work collaboratively and in imaginative ways. They can create a forum on transition in which their opinions will be heard and where they are respected as experts in their own field and feel involved in a constructive dialogue. Lynne Jones (SCILT) says that in Scotland, although transition practice is not uniform and depends on working relationships between teachers across sectors:

> On moving from primary to secondary, e-portfolios covering all learning go with the learners, and may or may not include specific information about additional languages. SCILT is currently working to collect examples of existing practice, to develop an evidence-informed approach to transition and to support school clusters and LAs in developing their own transition practice.

FIGURE 10.3 A 'suitcase of primary children's skills and abilities'

We consider this good practice and annotated exemplification of assessment useful for transition is available in the National Assessment Resource on the Education Scotland website. Given the difficulty many primary teachers have in finding time to make contacts and undertake visits, sharing practice online is a practical solution.

It is incumbent on all teachers to take some responsibility for the continuing motivation, for the progression in learning throughout the child's entire MFL school career, and for her/his social progression in terms of self-confidence and self-efficacy. Joined-up thinking and collaborative action are thus important in establishing a foundation for language learning later in life on the basis of having been exposed to the skills required to learn an MFL. One headteacher in Jersey asserted strongly that secondary teachers needed to know, really understand and respect the 'suitcases of skills and abilities' that primary children take to their secondary schools in order to be able to build on these.

The following case study provided by a London headteacher shows how important this is when language learning begins at Key Stage 1:

CASE STUDY

Within the whole school adoption of an approach where kids are experts, we always have a commission in a project. In terms of MFL, we have a Spanish speaking doll called Cristina. The first lesson the pupils ever have involves the secretary coming in to the classroom with a parcel that says special delivery and has airmail written on it.

We open the parcel together and there are clues such as a map, a flag and some postcards. There is also a letter in Spanish with the doll that says *My name is Cristina. I have come to your school because I heard that you are very kind and can help me learn English. I do not know how to say anything at all but if you learn some Spanish I think we can work together to help each other. Can you help me?*

At times Cristina leaves messages in Spanish for them to introduce new objectives, taken with an iPad or written in her special handwriting, and we work out what she wants to learn next. At times, she will go home to someone's house for extra practice: it works well. We also use Numicon shapes to help her count – they use the scheme in maths. Some of my Year 1 are writing numbers one to 10 accurately from memory by Christmas and meetings and greetings phrases. I use Cristina to set really challenging goals and they really respond when she says she is not sure if they can all do it.

Some readers may feel this achievement is exceptional but we think it is feasible for almost all children by the end of Key Stage 1. There are clear implications for pupil learning and progression at Key Stage 2. A constructive dialogue between all parties involved will take the issues outlined above into consideration and a constructive dialogue between all parties can work towards resolution of these.

Frequently asked questions (FAQs)

Given the frequency of certain concerns, the key issues for conversation between teachers can be summed up in the form of frequently asked questions. The responses we provide are based on our discussions with teachers.

FAQ 1: Isn't it unfair that primary teachers have all the fun with oral methods and games and we (secondary teachers) have to do writing and grammar or we can't cover what we have to?
Some secondary teachers and also some Year 7 pupils have commented on this, but it can be avoided if primary and secondary teachers work together so that their teaching, especially in Years 6 and 7, demonstrates coherence and plans for progression across the phases. This needs to include reading and writing as well as speaking and also the learning of grammar, albeit in an appropriate way. That secondary teachers are sometimes aggrieved is understandable. It is they who have the task of responding to the needs of incoming children with their very varied primary MFL experiences. We suggest 'fun' is equated to engaging, active learning and there is no reason why writing tasks and learning grammar should not be learnt in a thoroughly engaging and fun way at both stages, using songs, for example, that the pupils enjoyed so much at primary school. Where this kind of pedagogy was in evidence, research by Graham *et al.* (2014) identified some modest progress in grammar and vocabulary over Years 5, 6 and 7.

FAQ 2: How are we at secondary school supposed to cope with children coming from over 30 feeder schools when some have done some French and some haven't? That's why we often start from scratch.

You have to start somewhere, so start with a small group of willing schools on very practical planning issues, then spread this to others or, at the very least, disseminate your planning and create email and intranets. Schools working in clusters, learning groups or other networks have a mechanism for conversations to take place as well as for organising peer observation. It is, ultimately, vital not to destroy children's sense of achievement or enthusiasm by not acknowledging and validating what they have done.

FAQ 3: We really want to liaise with our colleagues but how do we find the time?
It is useful to construe time as a flexible resource. The introduction of statutory primary MFL into primary schools needs some prioritising on the part of primary and secondary teachers in order to make it a success. Time can be found by creative timetabling and through leadership decisions that enable teachers to undertake the necessary visits and networking.

FAQ 4: (From pupils) Why do teachers, when we go to secondary school, start all over again when we did a lot of the topics at primary school? It's boring.
It is indeed frustrating and disappointing. However, the message is getting through and secondary teachers talk much more about what pupils have done at primary school in their language lessons and will be able to build on at secondary school. Sometimes secondary teachers perceive the need to revise and review 'shaky' or insecure learning but many secondary-school teachers are impressed with the work being done in the primary school, which means that they can move ahead at a faster pace. It might be an idea to tell your Year 7 teacher what you have done and can do when you meet them and take your primary MFL folder/portfolio with you to show them. Sometimes, teachers do not know about these.

FAQ 5: Who should be in charge of coordinating transition?
Leadership is of the essence (see Chapter 2) and the role of headteachers in their management and support of primary MFL is crucial. It requires shared leadership from primary MFL coordinators and secondary teachers with responsibility for liaison. Recent restructuring arrangements of posts of responsibility in English schools, adaptable in any school context, have seen a shift to whole-school and team leadership roles that provide an opportunity for enhanced dialogue within the primary school and between primary and secondary schools. Coordination requires the engagement of all those involved in the school community who can have a role in supporting transition arrangements. The coordinator role is actually a very good role for an early career/almost-new teacher to take on.

FAQ 6: I am a Year 7 teacher. What can I do to build on what the pupils will have done but that I don't necessarily know about?
Overall, we feel that the really important issue is for teachers to know about the children's learning backgrounds and to build on, validate and progress their learning in terms of content, teaching approach and formative assessment. We suggest that you consult the primary–secondary coordinator in the school to see what transfer information has been sent. Ideally you would be able to organise a visit to a couple of feeder primary schools

to see what is going on generally with primary languages and to discuss and share teaching, learning and assessment approaches. Most importantly, you need to talk to your Year 7 pupils about their primary experiences and make a simple audit of what they have learnt and know. These can be the basis of some really useful early lessons with Year 7 that will provide you with some baseline information about what has been taught and how, and enable you to validate the children's learning. Our research shows clearly that the pupils will appreciate this and such information will be useful to inform your lesson planning.

Conclusion

Taking all the issues, opportunities and challenges the transition provides into consideration, it seems to us that the transfer from primary to secondary MFL needs to be seen within the context of whole-child development and whole-language policies, especially English/Literacy. It is incumbent on all the partners involved in this process to close the transition gap. There are also many simple common-sense solutions for all schools that do not have a huge cost element, such as making contact with colleagues, making occasional visits to each other, swapping materials and looking at each other's schemes of work to see where adjustments can be made. This is especially important in the last term of primary, e.g. practising some of the 'scary' things associated with secondary school such as elementary writing, and the first term at secondary school, e.g. setting a range of challenges as a means to consolidate and assess work covered, as Jones and McLachlan (2009) exemplify. Some schools jointly plan special thematic and cross-curricular MFL events as bridging activities (e.g. language-learning days and MFL treasure hunts): these are time- and cost-effective as well as memorable for all concerned. Recent suggestions from King's College London secondary PGCE students who were reflecting on how to bridge the gap for Year 7 pupils in the early weeks of the autumn term include:

- Pupils making posters/mind maps of what they have done in their primary schools, either individually, in pairs or in groups, as part of a learning dialogue.
- Organising the classroom by making labels and instructions in French to put around the room, and putting pupil portraits with self-descriptions in French on the walls to maximise use of the target language.
- Creating a large learning tree for the wall to which the pupils can add 'leaves' to show what they have learnt and can remember. This can be added to as they remember more items.
- Creating a town brochure naming places, opening times and things to do, drawing on vocabulary and phrases learnt in primary school and extending these with new items.
- Making individual passports with personal details that can be used for pair work and information gap questioning.
- Writing mini-books – just a couple of pages based on what the children know, with pictures and activities. These books can become a class library, so that children coming from different schools with different language-learning backgrounds can consolidate and extend their knowledge.

- Doing lots of little quizzes and testing games to see what pupils already know.

- Putting on a kind of Languages Show where groups of pupils present items to their peers about what they feel confident about.

- Pairing up the pupils with learning buddies so that they can peer-teach and peer-assess each other.

- Planning the teaching around various pupil dialogues/conversations using the vocabulary and phrases pupils know.

- Doing peer assessment – two stars and a wish – at every opportunity as the pupils are good at this and they really learn from each other. AfL techniques give the teacher the chance to find out what the pupils know, and also give continuity of learning from the primary school.

Planning on such a basis where shared with colleagues provides a platform on which a structure for continuous professional teacher learning based on mutual trust and a willingness to learn from each other can be developed. In the words of Cable *et al.* (2010: 149):

> This issue needs to be prioritised if continuity and progression are to be ensured. As Hunt *et al.* (2005) noted, an emphasis on transferable language-learning skills may help improve performance where children begin a new language at secondary school. This development needs to be nourished across the whole secondary sector.

The KS2 NC 2014 highlights the Key Stage 2 learning phase as a 'foundation for learning further languages, equipping pupils to study and work in other countries'. In their Language Trends survey, Board and Tinsley indicated that the secondary-teacher respondents were 'sceptical of many primary schools' ability to deliver what they regard as a worthwhile level of language knowledge that pupils can apply to their studies in secondary school' (Board and Tinsley 2015: 7). Whilst the 2015–16 Survey (Tinsley and Board 2016) found some small modifications in Year 7 MFL teaching, it shows that many of the respondent secondary teachers are still not convinced that the primary experience provides a sound platform for secondary language learning.

We commend those secondary teachers who take the time to engage with primary colleagues and respect the groundwork done, planning in terms not just of transition from KS2 to 3 but *across* both key stages. It is, quite simply, imperative that children go to secondary school with their achievements recorded and acknowledged in order to enable their progression. The children should not in any way be 'scared' about the prospect but should go with a sense of excitement and looking forward to their continuing and expanding languages learning, from the primary stage through both KS3 and, indeed, KS4.

Questions on which to reflect

- What creative solutions can be found to confront the logistical problems of time, funding and an apparently unmanageable number of primary schools needing support from secondary schools?

- To what extent are primary-school children's fears of 'horrible things' and 'hardness' at secondary school real or unfounded?

- What might constitute an ideal primary MFL transfer pack of information to support transition?

Professional development, teacher learning and research: developing a community of learning and practice

Over recent years, primary MFL practitioners have enjoyed great success in achieving their mission to make the subject a welcome and essential fixture in the primary curriculum. Enthusiasm and a deep-rooted belief in primary MFL as an entitlement for young learners have been vibrantly felt in the whole MFL community of practice. While secondary MFL has a strong and recognisable identity, the primary subject identity has been in transition as it has been framing its practice and defining appropriate well-grounded pedagogical principles and practices within the context of lively subject debate, work that is still in progress. The professional development/learning needs of teachers and others in the developing community of practice are the focus of this chapter. In our view, professional development (PD) is an essential tool to empower all primary teachers, already expert in general primary pedagogy, to undertake their role as confident and competent MFL teachers. This can be achieved by adopting a creative, eclectic approach when devising plans using teachers' prior knowledge and experience, and, very importantly, their individual PD needs and wishes as a starting point. Above all, teachers need to have ownership of their own PD plans.

Key issues

- There is a need for a supply of well-qualified teachers to sustain effective primary MFL provision and to ensure enjoyment and confidence in teaching.

- The fundamental subject knowledge areas of language competence, cultural knowledge and pedagogical practice on a cross-phase basis are cornerstones of the professional learning agenda.

- PD needs will be varied and will need to be varied and tailored to build on existing expertise, prior experiences and knowledge, age and preferred learning style. It will address the needs of teaching assistants, governors, foreign language assistants and others engaged in the planning and delivery of primary MFL.

- Training forms an essential part of the development and enhancement of the subject community of practice.

- A wide variety of continuing professional development (CPD) and teacher-led learning opportunities are available to select from, ranging from provision from external providers to internal formats that include peer coaching, networking and teacher research.

- Coordination and support from those with leadership roles is crucial in creating a school culture that encourages a vibrant and empowering teacher learning community.

- Teachers need to take agency to consider their own professional development needs.

Introduction: a community of learning – and some unlearning?

A German Landseer dog we know named Ossi undertook behaviour training and was duly, if rather incomprehensibly, awarded a certificate, yet he still behaves disgracefully in the house and equally appallingly when out for walks. His training was evidently inadequate and the core principles of appropriate dog behaviour were not sustained nor internalised. Ossi has much unlearning still to do. In a similar vein, one secondary colleague, in discussion about the impact of primary MFL for him at Key Stage 3, commented: 'It [primary MFL] requires some unlearning of habits of a lifetime.'

There clearly is a need for a sustainable supply of confident, competent and adequately qualified teachers. We would suggest that, alongside the CPD that will be required, in certain instances some unlearning may be necessary as MFL primary and secondary teachers work within an ever-evolving paradigm of MFL teaching that requires some adjustment to certain established constructs of, or perspectives on, teaching.

Recognising that statutory primary languages needs a supply of qualified teachers, government has funded various kinds of training programmes (such as specialist Post-Graduate Certificate in Education routes) and other initiatives. There has been a range of training opportunities provided by national language organisations, some LAs, embassies, the British Council, EU projects and promotions, and other international agencies in the larger international community, in addition to a plethora of private consultancy offers. This chapter does not advertise, describe in detail or evaluate these initiatives but considers more broadly the professional learning needs of teachers and others associated with the primary languages, which will support the development of a well-defined and well-grounded community of practice.

Such a community provides dynamic and flexible parameters for teacher learning, acknowledging the varied strengths, needs, experiences and motivations of the participants in MFL. We loosely associate such learning with Lave and Wenger's (1991) seminal work on the concept of the 'community of practice', drawing on their notion of 'situated learning' through participation in professional activity in which participants

FIGURE 11.1 Ossi the dog

have a shared understanding about what they are doing (see Chapter 6). Much effective primary MFL practice has grown in a 'bottom-up' way from experimentation in classrooms and dissemination of such practice. Its learning-centredness, we consider, is at the core of our primary MFL learning community. Primary MFL practitioners, alongside secondary specialists or the increasingly common cross-phase practitioners, can enjoy a shared and evolving discourse concerning subject knowledge and pedagogical expertise.

The learning-centred approach needs to be enhanced by professional development opportunities suited to teachers at different stages of their career. This would be achieved by, in Lave and Wenger's terms (1991), a process called *legitimate peripheral participation*. In this process, newcomers to the community – i.e. inexperienced teachers – move from peripheral to full participation via a wide range of activities, resources, arenas of mature practice, other learners and ample opportunities for practice. Learning in this sense is experiential rather than abstract.

We find the 'community of practice' metaphor a useful and relevant learning perspective for primary MFL, given its natural vibrant coaching context for language teachers. We would contend that not all teacher learning is socially situated and that cognitive styles of learning and individual reflection, for example, also have their place. Teachers learn in their own individual ways, as do their pupils. Furthermore, abstraction and generalisation have important roles to play in the theorisation of what makes effective primary MFL practice and ensure an adequate theoretical foundation for it. We suggest that training should comprise learning opportunities of the widest kind and that providers, be they external agencies, training institutions or in-house agents, bear in mind that learning and training needs differ from individual to individual. We would assert that Lave and Wenger's perspective, in its emphasis on top-down induction, does not give due credit to two-way learning, with experienced teachers learning from and refreshing their knowledge from more inexperienced practitioners. A very experienced generalist and primary MFL teacher shows how this reciprocal learning can work:

> I have considerable experience and have built up quite a stock of songs, materials, activities and the like over the years but I am still learning. I enjoy being in the classroom with our NQT who trained on a specialist primary MFL course and I pick up something from her every time I watch her. She switches from language to language and the children do too. I would never have thought to do that. But then I don't really know another language apart from French, but I have picked up the songs from the Reception class children.

In considering PD needs, it is always useful to identify and audit the varied needs of individuals as a starting and monitoring point. This can be done in a simple way such as devising, for example, a questionnaire (as we did to illustrate this point) to capture teachers' individual needs and concerns regarding PD and using them as a basis for a scheme of school-wide PD or personalised teacher learning.

Auditing primary MFL teachers' PD needs

We asked the primary MFL coordinators of two primary schools, one in the north of England and one in the south, to audit the PD needs of the staff. This included all teachers and TAs and any other helpers who might need to make a teaching and/or support contribution to the primary MFL provision. The coordinators used a questionnaire to elicit information about perceived foreign language capability and the capacity to contribute to the teaching of primary MFL.

The results gave a clear message that there is a great deal of goodwill on the part of non-specialist teachers who teach, or will teach, some primary MFL. Most teachers evaluated themselves as having basic knowledge of a language, mainly French. Of 19 teachers who responded to the questionnaire, 12 had various levels of qualification in French, five had some knowledge of German and two had basic Spanish. They indicated in their answers a high level of confidence to be able to teach simple structures and notions such as numbers, colours and greetings, reflecting the strength of the primary generalist, although beyond this mini-survey, on our visits to a wide range of primary schools, there was widespread lack of confidence, as expressed by this teaching head: 'For those primary teachers who had no French to start with (I know a few) they still lack the confidence to teach French to their pupils and are often teaching words incorrectly.'

The teacher highlights the anxiety about their language skills felt by many teachers. This can be quite acute when associated with accountability and performance manage-ment, when a teacher might be fearful about getting it right in a formal observation situation. Confidence is also an issue when it comes to looking at preferred PD options, and many teachers we consulted expressed a preference for peer coaching and one-to-one in school. Some teachers told us that they needed a coaching situation with which they would feel comfortable as opposed to language tuition where, in the words of one teacher, 'I might be pounced on.' This is an interesting comment in the light of similar feelings expressed by some older adolescent pupils who also dislike being 'pounced on' in language lessons. There were, as always, time issues for teachers about twilight meetings held off-site, but bespoke training by an adviser/expert in school was much appreciated, as was intranet sharing and dissemination of information and materials. The massive range of online resources and sharing via social online networking must now comprise the number one training slot and provide instantaneous self-training. This range of resources, taken together, can ensure some personalised PD for all according to need and preference. The question then arises: What makes an effective primary MFL teacher so that continuous professional learning can be oriented towards a construct of effective practice?

The review of research conducted by Driscoll and one of the authors of this book (Driscoll *et al.* 2004), explored the characteristics of effective primary MFL practice. The potential of the primary generalist teachers to exploit their skills and knowledge as active participants in the primary MFL community of practice was found to be very important. Such teachers are able to provide an enjoyable and, at the same time, challenging primary MFL learning environment and adopt an appropriate teaching approach that relates to the learning needs of pupils. The review also highlighted the importance of the skilful and selective use of resources, especially visuals that provide a powerful support for the young learner. Cable *et al.* (2010) commented on how pupils found interactive resources very motivating. The research by Graham *et al.* (2014) showed that the teachers who best motivated children's learning were those who promoted interactivity, creativity, cultural contact and purposeful learning.

The research of Erika Werlen (2005) has also contributed to a definition of effective primary MFL teaching practices. Teachers, Werlen suggests, should be able to provide good language models themselves and make use of, and build on, the children's experiences as core 'content'. Using authentic materials (in the sense of materials that are meaningful to children), the teachers will help the children to see parallels with their mother tongue. Werlen also suggests that pupils' mistakes, e.g. from carelessness and errors based on a child's inter-language, provide a valuable learning and teaching opportunity and can make children feel secure in their learning. Good communication about learning that takes place with other teachers, TAs and parents would also indicate quality of practice.

PD needs, then, would seem to focus on certain key skills and knowledge areas:

- linguistic competence, including the confidence to use the language;
- an ongoing interest in target-language culture(s) and in developing an intercultural perspective (see Chapter 9);
- aspects of methodology including assessment (see Chapter 7) appropriate to the age range;
- an understanding of children's learning and language-learning strategies (see Chapter 6);

- knowledge about foreign language learning;
- the critical reviewing of materials and an understanding of their role as a resource (see Chapter 3).

Graham *et al.* (2014) highlighted key 'teacher factors' that included time for teaching, the teacher's linguistic competence and the quality of the teacher's training in language-teaching pedagogy as crucial to effective pupil learning and progression. HEI training programmes have made a huge contribution to the training and upskilling of primary languages teachers with their imaginative and comprehensive provision, including intensive language-learning opportunities abroad. Skilled training of this kind has shifted the focus from a rather narrow range of teaching techniques of the 'fluffy bunny' kind to a consideration of a more principled pedagogical context.

The course information we have investigated – and there are a great many offerings – indicate a wide variety of models for teachers, TAs and other non-specialists to choose from. The concept of 'andragogy', i.e. adult learning, implies, in Law and Glover's (2000: 249) words, 'an acceptance of the importance of more focused and individualised learning strategies, rather than simply treating everyone homogeneously, as a group with common needs and experiences.' This does not mean an end to collective learning and shared reflection, which are very important, but means that it is also important to recognise ages and stages in teachers' lives and career cycles when considering professional learning needs and ways to meet them. Online learning and sharing caters for this in enabling teachers to do their learning as and when it suits and as needs be.

Horses for courses and courses for horses

Higgins and Leat (2001) introduce this colourful metaphor to distinguish between a 'one size fits all' type of training (prevalent in the past and largely of the differentiated 'one shot' type of course) and longer-term differentiated courses or other training provision. The 'one shot' course is largely discredited now since research has shown such courses have very little impact on teacher learning. However, the occasional 'one shot' course, if well-targeted and prepared (intensive days such as are provided by embassies, for example, and engaging experts who can inspire) can serve as useful triggers for an engagement with a more continuous and sustained type of professional learning and provide an opportunity to network as well as to browse through available materials. We are recommending such an eclectic and individualised approach, based on the auditing of a teacher's needs, preferences and interests – which should, of course, mesh with the training needs of the school as a whole and its School Learning Plan, but key in to as many formats as possible.

There are a great many types of PD available in addition to the format of 'the course'. These formats include peer coaching, the network concept and practitioner research, all suitable for developing the primary MFL community of practice in that they continue to develop a bottom-up approach and encourage continuing teacher ownership on the basis of school need.

FIGURE 11.2 Horses for courses and courses for horses

Peer coaching

Peer coaching, or classroom support, crucially recognises the expertise of one's colleagues and acknowledges the usefulness of exploiting the internal know-how in the school. Peer coaching can usefully feature as part of staff-development activity. We have found, in practice, examples of successful peer-coaching formats that include the following:

- Some of the outreach work of 'leaders of learning', for example, where secondary teachers team-teach with primary colleagues to develop the capability of the latter, and vice versa. We recommend a two-way transfer of learning so as to achieve maximum benefit and to avoid top-down classroom 'takeovers' by secondary colleagues where the primary teacher is little involved.

- Primary languages coordinators providing customised support for their peers in school on a needs/request basis; for example language pronunciation, introducing a particular song or game, demonstrating some use of technology, and ideas for embedding the target language into another subject.

- Peer coaching by the MFL coordinator/lead teacher, providing professional development for the whole staff to promote a common understanding.

Primary MFL has, with its more flexible approach to early language learning, used the opportunity to unlock the subject leadership of a great many talented teachers, and peer coaching is fundamentally about sharing, empowering and promoting subject leadership. In this way, subject leaders develop as leaders of learning in what Lingard *et al.* (2003: 50) refer to as 'productive leadership' that 'creates an environment for teachers, and others within the schools, that is intellectually challenging, that is replete with professional development opportunities that connect with teachers' concerns and interests'. It is a form of CPD that is so much richer when it can be shared for the benefit of the many rather than the few or hidden under a bushel in one classroom! It also fits with the knowledge-sharing vision of society, developing communities of learners, both teachers and pupils.

The power of networked learning

Whilst in-house peer support formats are invaluable, it is essential to be aware of colleagues' practice in other contexts and to network outside of one's own learning locale. In the spirit of cooperation, schools can network or cluster together, either informally or through the platform of a formal school cluster or arrangement, and ideally involve primary and secondary colleagues working together to share and develop effective languages provision across the sectors. Most school clusters/hubs have an intranet for teacher discussion and for the posting of materials to share.

Newer to the teacher learning options are Teachmeets. Teachmeets are innovative networked face-to-face meetings promoted by social media as well as word of mouth; structured but informal meetings with the aim of sharing innovative practice and teaching insights. Volunteers lead the sessions and organise a range of 'show and tell' type presentations and sometimes speakers. In some cases, those not able to attend can follow proceedings on Twitter via synchronic reporting from attendees or live via an app such as Periscope. The modern social media age has generated networked learning as an essentially social experience in online thematic discussions such as on Twitter (Jones 2014b). These discussions can be open, or can require some kind of signing up, or may comprise a well-organised collaborative blog designed for teachers to share good practice and learn from each other. Teachers will also find on Twitter a variety of general MFL chats and blogs, materials and Virtual Learning Environment (VLE) resources, handbooks, toolkits, interactive wikis and offers of customised support and training from experienced practitioners. There are webinars on a variety of topics that can either be joined in real time or viewed when convenient via logs of the discussion. These initiatives are PD opportunities designed by teachers for teachers. There is also a wide variety of online language courses for teachers to undertake language-upskilling. Online provision has the additional advantage of opening up a global network for the MFL community.

Networking, however tightly or loosely, provides an opportunity to share not just good practice or practice that works (and in what circumstances), but also the processes that lead to such practice. It shifts the learning mindset from what Huberman (1993) calls the 'lone wolf' style of working to a 'pack of wolves' collaborative effort that can synergise efforts and activities, perhaps integrated in research projects, thereby cutting out time-wasting and unnecessary 'wheel reinventions' – very important for busy teachers everywhere.

Practitioner research

It is but a short step from the classroom investigations mentioned previously to something a little more structured that would merit the description of practitioner research. Our concept of practitioner research involves teachers, alongside other colleagues, researching their own practice in classroom contexts that are meaningful to them. Working with a definition of research as 'systematic self-critical enquiry', the primary MFL community of teacher learning, no less than any other subject, has embraced research in this sense and includes a nucleus of teacher research in various forms, such as:

- Educational research events held in schools and universities that aim to support, promote and disseminate evidence-based teacher research at the chalkface, with workshops and a variety of speakers from the 'Edusphere';

- Teacher learning communities/groups in a school or across a group of schools as a way to support structured teacher enquiry;

- Individual teacher research in teachers' own classrooms as they research their own practice in an informal way from the 'inside out', as Cochran-Smith and Lytle (1993) call it. Such research activity could be a choice of PD that remains with the individual, is shared with colleagues or is formalised in study for an MA or a PhD.

Individual research: examples

Examples of individual primary MFL teacher research that we have come across include:

- An investigation into children's learning preferences in the primary MFL classroom that involved lesson observation, interviews with teachers and pupils, and question-naires to teachers, pupils and parents. The data sets enabled the teacher-researcher to draw tentative conclusions about what was working well and to suggest areas for development. A staff meeting presentation and discussion led to an action plan (which included improved planning, more formative assessment practices and a focus on creative use of the target language). This was then included in the School Learning Plan as a whole-school learning objective for primary MFL.

- A small-scale research project into the extent to which children with EAL backgrounds might be enabled by their existent bilingualism/multilingualism to learn a language in school. This study for an MA dissertation found that the EAL learners benefited enormously in many ways, making good progress and, with support, also making strategic use of linguistic knowledge that may not be available to their monolingual peers.

- A primary languages specialist explored early language learning policy across the EU for her PhD to see how different countries interpret the language learning expect-ation of the EU's policy of '1+2' languages at the primary level (routinely the case in Spain and Italy, for example). The research indicated how the '1+2' could be managed in primary schools. (See Chapter 1 for the case of Scotland in this respect.)

Teacher learning communities/groups and research: examples

Teacher learning communities (TLCs), also known as learning groups or learning circles, are a fairly recent trend in CPD (Bolam *et al.* 2005; DuFour 2004) and would seem an ideal strategy to support collaborative professional development in primary MFL. They involve the creation of a group of teachers meeting regularly to collaborate on a topic of interest and importance, share effective practice, identify common areas of concern and seek workable solutions, sometimes consulting the pupils as part of the learning conversation. The group can then spread the learning to the wider school community or network as part of whole-school development of language provision.

There are certain conditions to ensure an effective learning community, including dedicated and protected time and space, and clear, focused questions to guide the enquiry. It is important to create working norms for collaboration and areas of responsibility, and, above all, to proceed in small steps, planning and evaluating try-outs and developing confidence to make decisions about best provision and practice.

This approach can be a very productive way for teachers to reflect on their practice and, we suggest, is especially suitable for the collaborative development and embedding of a whole-school primary languages policy of teaching, learning and assessment. Such enquiry might involve school visits, peer observation and agreed classroom try-outs, followed by analysis and discussion about a chosen focus.

Examples we found of such learning groups included:

- A group of teachers trying out, evaluating and planning assessment schemes. This project included the pupil voice – i.e. asking young children their opinion of how helpful to their learning they found the assessment they were asked to undertake.

- In another case, a teacher learning group in one school had successfully planned its primary MFL provision across the whole-school curriculum map, thereby solving the seemingly tricky issue of 'finding time in an overcrowded curriculum for primary MFL.'

- In one central London primary school that has a group with a twin focus on whole-school embedding of MFL and transition involving secondary colleagues, French (the language of choice and taught by a specialist working with her colleague teachers and TAs), has been elevated to the equivalent status of core subject.

One teacher, who had experienced the pioneering work on Cognitive Acceleration (CASE in Science and CAME in Maths) by Michael Shayer and Philip Adey (see Adey 2004) and colleagues at King's College London, suggested that the format used could be useful for clusters of schools to develop their primary MFL together:

> Groups of schools had, for example, trainer input in the morning then worked in one of the schools in the afternoon. Teachers paired up and observed each other or were observed by the trainer followed by feedback and then embedding into our lessons. This went on over a period of time. I think this sort of collaborative learning for primary language teachers could work really well.

173

While teachers may think research is something only academics engage in, they are in fact, as Brighouse and Woods (1999: 42) write, 'natural researchers, in the sense that all teaching is based on enquiry and the response of the pupils provides ready evidence as to the effectiveness of various teaching and learning approaches', as the above examples show. Over the last 50 years, primary MFL teachers have demonstrated an immense capacity to be deeply reflective practitioners in research into what makes effective primary MFL practice. The 1960s/70s Primary French experience, it could be said, was never a failure but a challenge to the community of practice to persevere with primary languages for all and maintain the sense of enquiry.

Conclusion

There are training implications for both primary and secondary colleagues in ensuring a supply of effective MFL teachers within the evolving context of cross-phase learning. Primary schools need support to enable them to embed sustainable learning arrangements within and across the whole curriculum, and PD to support this. In Scotland, where the 1+2 languages model is being rolled out at varying paces across the country, Lynne Jones of SCILT explains that training is eschewing:

> the drop-in expert model . . . in favour of capacity-building across the primary sector with the expectation that all primary teachers will be teaching/facilitating the learning and teaching of at least one language in addition to English with their learners.

There are organisational and infrastructural implications for secondary colleagues as well. They will need, for example, to rewrite at least parts of their schemes of work and adapt assessment and teaching to ensure continuity and progression of MFL throughout the pupil's school career. There is evidence of some progress here, as mentioned in Chapter 10. Effective and continuous MFL provision will require teachers to adopt new 'ways of knowing' (e.g. about children's learning in age ranges other than those they teach), and, indeed, new habits (e.g. a reappraisal of how grammar is taught). It will also be important to keep up to date with technologies that can enhance language teaching and learning, especially for children with special educational needs, and with research and developments in early language learning in other cultural contexts. These will, in turn, require PD opportunities tailored, as emphasised in this chapter, to individual teachers' professional learning needs. It will also be important to provide focused training for others in the community of practice, such as TAs and foreign language assistants, who can have a very positive impact on learning, to enable them all to make a well-informed and appropriate contribution as effective primary MFL practitioners. The range of training and professional development options for primary teachers is substantial and caters for every learning preference and need; such options give teachers choice, agency and ownership of their professional development (Mehta 2016).

The role of leadership, as stated in Chapter 2, is vital, and where professional development is concerned there is need for careful coordination, budgeting and monitoring.

As one primary teacher commented: 'The head needs to support us by being in lessons, providing/arranging appropriate training and being fully supportive of staff teaching MFL.' Subject leaders need their own leadership training, such as courses for aspiring leaders, in-house peer leadership coaching/shadowing and visits to other schools to learn alongside experienced subject leaders.

Where the subject is developed in a web of shared leadership with teachers fully involved, then the exciting primary MFL project – for it is an ongoing, open-ended learning project for pupils and teachers alike as lifelong learners – is increasingly sustainable and, as a whole-school project, an essential part of the modern inclusive primary-school curriculum. This requires a collaborative school culture that promotes teacher, as well as pupil, learning with 'time for teachers to reflect and develop ideas and resources' (a further comment by the above teacher). We know that teachers are generally keen to continue their professional development, shown, for example, by the healthy take-up of Master's level study and the participation of teachers in EU-funded research projects. We commend especially participatory and social-learning approaches such as those proposed by Carr and Kemmis (1986) and Earley and Porritt (2009), which engage teachers in shared collaborative enquiry and action research projects.

Primary MFL is not only rather special, but it has also developed in a special way, building a substantial knowledge and skills base that also needs to be taken into consideration by secondary schools. It is a chance not to be missed if continuity and progression are to be assured. We wish to stress our hope that expert primary-school teachers will not feel anxious about developing their foreign language subject knowledge, but will enjoy upskilling their language competence alongside their pupils. We would encourage primary colleagues to enjoy upskilling their language competence in the same way as their pupils, in a way that is manageable and fun for them, too, and in a way that gives them the agency to take a creative lead in developing the pedagogy in the primary MFL project. Secondary MFL teachers, it is acknowledged, are, de facto, the principal language specialists, but it is a primary languages teacher to whom we give the last word. She emphasises how primary MFL is the start in a longer learning journey for all involved:

> Secondary teachers need to view primary colleagues as experts in their field and from whom they can learn. When secondary teachers do visit, they often change perception when they see our skills. In fact primary language teachers lead the way in strengthening the basis of the KS2 to not just KS3 but forwards on the KS4 continuum.

Questions on which to reflect

■ Undertake a simple primary MFL training needs audit in a school, with the whole staff, a key stage or a group of teachers and compare your results with those in this chapter and with the results in the DfES (2004) survey into training needs. What progress has been made?

- Devise a TLC/group collaborative learning format and research questions that would take on board the identified training needs. How could this then be taken forward as an action research project?
- What is your own personal teacher learning plan?

References

Adey, P. (2004) *The Professional Development of Teachers: Practice and Theory*. Dordrecht: Kluwer Academic Press.

Alexander, R. (2006) *Towards Dialogic Teaching: Rethinking Classroom Talk*. York: Dialogos.

Anderson, J. (2011) Reshaping pedagogies for a plurilingual agenda. *Language Learning Journal*, 39 (2): 135–47.

Barth, R. (1990) *Improving Schools from Within: Teachers, Parents and Principals Can Make the Difference*. San Francisco, CA: Jossey-Bass.

Barton, A. (2002) The gender effect. In Swarbrick, A. (ed.) *Teaching Modern Foreign Languages in Secondary Schools*. London: RoutledgeFalmer.

Becker, C. (2015) Assessment and portfolios. In Bland, J. (2015) *Teaching English to Young Learners: Critical Issues in Language Teaching with 3–12 Year Olds*. London: Bloomsbury.

Behrman, E. H. (2002) Community-based literacy learning. *Reading: Literacy and Language*, 36 (1): 26–32.

Beltrán, E., Abbott, C. and Jones, J. (2013) *Inclusive Education, Languages and Digital Technology*. Clevedon: Multilingual Matters.

Black, P. and Wiliam, D. (1998) *Inside the Black Box*. London: King's College London.

Black, P., Harrison, C., Lee, C., Marshall, B. and Wiliam, D. (2003) *Assessment for Learning. Putting it into Practice*. Buckingham: Open University Press.

Bland, J. (2015) *Teaching English to Young Learners: Critical Issues in Language Teaching with 3–12 Year Olds*. London: Bloomsbury.

Board, K. and Tinsley, T. (2015) *Language Trends 2014/15: The State of Language Learning in Primary and Secondary Schools in England*. Reading: CfBT and The British Council.

Boekaerts, M. and Corno, L. (2005) Self-regulation in the classroom: a perspective on assessment and intervention. *Applied Psychology: An International Review*, 54 (2): 199–231.

Bolam, R., McMahon, A., Stoll, L., Thomas, S. and Wallace, M. (2005) *Creating and Sustaining Effective Professional Learning Communities. DfES Report 637*. London: Department for Education and Skills.

Brighouse, T. and Woods, P. (1999) *How to Improve Your School*. London: Methuen.

Bruner, J. (1960) *The Process of Education*. Cambridge, MA: Harvard University Press.

Burstall, C., Jamieson, M., Cohen, S. and Hargreaves, M. (1974) *Primary French in the Balance*. Windsor: NFER.

Busher, H. and Harris, A. (2000) *Subject Leadership and School Improvement*. London: Paul Chapman Publishing.

Byram, M. (1997) *Teaching and Assessing Intercultural Communicative Competence*. Clevedon: Multilingual Matters.

Cable, C., Driscoll, P., Mitchell, R., Sing, S., Cremin, T., Earl, J., Eyres, I., Holmes, B., Martin, C. and Heins, B. (2010) *Languages and Learning at Key Stage 2: A Longitudinal Study. Final Report. RR198*. London: DCSF Publications.

Carr, W. and Kemmis, S. (1986) *Becoming Critical: Education, Knowledge and Action Research.* London: RoutledgeFalmer.

Cheater, C. and Farren, A. (2001) *Young Pathfinder Series (9). The Literacy Link.* London: CILT.

Cochran-Smith, M. and Lytle, S. (1993) *Inside Outside: Teacher Research and Knowledge.* New York: Teachers' College Press, Columbia University.

Coffey, S. (2005) A cross-cultural framework for citizenship training within the MFL PGCE. *CILT LINKS,* Spring, 4–5.

Comenius, J. A. (1657) *The Great Didactic* (trans. Keatinge, M. W. (1967). New York: Russell and Russell.

Council of Europe (2001) *Common European Framework of Reference for Languages: Learning, Teaching, Assessment.* Cambridge: Cambridge University Press. http://www.coe.int/.

Cox, M. J. and Webb, M. E. (2004) *ICT and Pedagogy: A Review of the Research Literature.* Coventry: BECTA/London: DfES.

Coyle, D., Hood, P. and Marsh, D. (2010) *CLIL: Content and Language Integrated Learning.* Cambridge: Cambridge University Press.

Cullingford, C. (1995) *The Effective Teacher.* London: Cassell.

Day, C., Hall, C. and Whitaker, P. (1998) *Developing Leadership in Primary Schools.* London: Paul Chapman Publishing.

DfE (2011) National Curriculum Review. Available: www.education.gov.uk/schools/teachingand learning/curriculum/nationalcurriculum [accessed 16/4/2016].

DfE (2014) Languages programmes of study: Key Stage 2, GOV.UK – DfE (Adobe pdf file) http://www. gov.uk/government/uploads/system/uploads/attachment_data/file/239042/PRIMARY_national_ curriculum_-_Languages.pdf [accessed 16/4/2016]

DfES (2004) Driscoll, P., Jones, J. and Macrory, G. *The Provision of Foreign Language Learning for Pupils at Key Stage 2. RR 572.* London: DfES Publications.

DfES (2005) Key Stage 2 Framework for Languages, Parts 1 and 2. Nottingham: DfES Publications.

Driscoll, P., Jones, J., Martin, C., Graham-Matheson, L., Dismore, H. and Sykes, R. (2004) *A Systematic Review of the Characteristics of Effective Foreign Language Teaching to Pupils Between the Ages 7 and 11.* London: EPPI-Centre, Social Science Research Unit, Institute of Education.

Drummond, M. J. (1993) *Assessing Children's Learning.* London: David Fulton Publishers.

DuFour, R. (2004) What is a professional learning community? *Schools as Learning Communities,* 61 (8): 6–11.

DuFour, R. and Marzano, R. (2011) *Leaders of Learning: How District, School and Classroom Leaders Improve School Achievement.* Bloomingdale, IN: Solution Tree Press.

Dugard, C. and Hewer, S. (2003) *New Pathfinder (3). Impact on Learning: What ICT Can Bring to MFL in KS3.* London: CILT.

Dweck, C. (2012) *Mindset: How You Can Fulfil Your Potential.* London: Robinson.

Earley, P. and Porritt, V. (2009) *Effective Practices in Continuing Professional Development: Lessons From School.* London: Institute of Education.

Earley, P. and Weindling, D. (2004) *Understanding School Leadership.* London: Paul Chapman Publishing.

Edelenbos, P. and Johnstone, R. (eds) (1997) *Researching Languages at Primary School: Some European Perspectives.* Scottish CILT.

Education Scotland: Supporting Curriculum for Excellence. Available: www.educationscotland.gov.uk/ [accessed 16/4/2016]. See this site for the National Assessment Resource (NAR).

Elliott, V., Baird, J-A., Hopfenbeck, T., Ingram, J., Thompson, I., Usher, N., Zantout, M., and Richardson, J. and Coleman, R. (2016) *A Marked Improvement? A Review of the Evidence on Written Marking.* London: Education Endowment Foundation.

European Parliament (2015) *Fact Sheets on the European Union.* Available: http://www.europarl.europa. eu/atyourservice/en/displayFtu.html [accessed 7/4/2016].

Flynn, L. (2005) Transition: opening dialogue, closing the gap. *Modern Foreign Languages,* 9, Autumn, 4–5.

Fullan, M. (1991) *The New Meaning of Educational Change.* London: Cassell.

Fullan, M. (1993) *Change Forces: Probing the Depths of Educational Reform.* London: Falmer Press.

Fullan, M. and Hargreaves, A. (1992) *What's Worth Fighting for in Your School?* Buckingham: Oxford University Press.

Gardner, H. (1983) *Frames of Mind: The Theory of Multiple Intelligences.* New York: Basic Books.

Gillespie, H. (2006) *Unlocking Learning and Teaching with ICT: Identifying and Overcoming Barriers.* Oxon and New York: David Fulton.

Goswami, U. and Bryant, P. (2007) *Children's Cognitive Development and Learning.* Primary Review Research Survey 2/1a. Available: http://image.guardian.co.uk/sys-files/Education/documents/2007/12/14/play.pdf [accessed 27/3/2012].

Graham, S., Courtney, L., Marinis, T. and Tonkyn, A. (2014) *Primary Modern Languages: The Impact of Teaching Approaches on Attainment and Preparedness for Secondary School Language Learning.* Project Report. University of Reading (Unpublished).

Grenfell, M. and Harris, V. (1999) *Modern Languages Strategies in Theory and Practice.* London: Routledge.

Hammersley-Fletcher, L. (2005) Leaders on leadership: the impressions of primary school head teachers and subject leaders. *School Leadership and Management*, 25 (1): 59–75.

Harris, A. (2003) Teacher leadership and school improvement. In Harris, A., Day, C., Hopkins, D., Hadfield, M., Hargreaves, A. and Chapman, C. (eds) *Effective Leadership for School Improvement.* London: RoutledgeFalmer.

Harris, V. (1997) *Teaching Learners how to Learn: Strategy Training in the ML Classroom.* London: CILT.

Hawkes, R. (2014) *Handout 1: Languages.* Available: http://www.rachelhawkes.com/PandT/2014_Curriculum/Handout_1_Curriculum14_Overview.pdf [accessed 4/4/2016].

Hawkins, E. (1984) *Awareness of Language: An Introduction.* Cambridge: Cambridge University Press.

Hawkins, E. (2005) Out of this nettle, drop-out, we pluck this flower, opportunity: rethinking the school foreign language apprenticeship. *Language Learning Journal*, 32: 4–17.

Heafford, M. (1990) Teachers may teach, but do learners learn? *Language Learning Journal*, 1: 88–90.

Herschensohn, J. (2007) *Language Development and Age.* Cambridge: Cambridge University Press.

Higgins, S. and Leat, D. (2001) Horses for courses or courses for horses: What is effective teacher development? In Soler, J., Craft, A. and Burgess. H. (eds) *Teacher Development: Exploring Our Own Practice.* London: Paul Chapman Publishing.

Hobsbawm, E. and Ranger, T. (1983) *The Invention of Tradition.* Cambridge: Cambridge University Press.

Hood, P. and Tobutt, K. (2009) *Modern Languages in the Primary School.* London: Sage.

Huberman, M. (1993) *Lives of Teachers.* London and New York: Teachers' College Press, Columbia University.

Hunt, M., Barnes, A., Powell, B., Lindsay, G. and Muijs, D. (2005) Primary modern foreign languages: an overview of recent research, key issues and challenges for educational policy and practice. *Research Papers in Education*, 20 (4): 367–85.

Hurrell, A. (1999) The four language skills. In Driscoll, P. and Frost, D. (eds) *The Teaching of Modern Foreign Languages in the Primary School.* London: Routledge.

Johnstone, R. (1994) *Teaching Modern Languages in Primary School: Approaches and Implications.* Edinburgh: The Scottish Council for Research in Education.

Johnstone, R. (2003) Evidence-based policy: Early modern language learning at primary. *Language Learning Journal*, 28 (1): 14–21.

Jones, J. (2005) Foreign languages in the primary school in England: A new pupil learning continuum. *Francophonic*, 3: 3–7.

Jones, J. (2010) The role of assessment for learning in the management of primary to secondary transition: Implications for language teachers. *Language Learning Journal*, 38 (2): 175–91.

Jones, J. (2012) Portfolios as 'learning companions' for children and a means to support and assess language learning in the primary school. *Education 3–13: International Journal of Primary, Elementary and Early Years Education*, 40 (4): 401–16

Jones, J. (2013) Languages as an inclusive learning opportunity for all. In Beltrán, E., Abbott, C. and Jones, J. *Inclusive Education, Languages and Digital Technology.* Clevedon: Multilingual Matters.

Jones, J. (2014a) Have developments in formative assessment been a retrograde step for languages teaching and learning? In Driscoll, P., Macaro, E. and Swarbrick, A. *Debates in Language Teaching: Research, Policy and Practice.* London: Routledge.

Jones, J. (2014b) Using Twitter for professional development. *School Leadership Today,* 6 (1): 70.

Jones, J. and McLachlan, A. (2009) *Primary Languages in Practice: A Guide to Teaching and Learning.* Maidenhead: McGraw Hill/Oxford University Press.

Jones, J. and Wiliam, D. (2008) *Modern Foreign Languages Inside the Black Box.* London: GL Assessment.

Knowles, G. (2009) *Ensuring Every Child Matters.* London: Sage.

Kohonen, V. (2004) How can the European Language Portfolio (ELP) promote transparency in FL education. *Associaçãao Portuguesa de Professores de Inglês,* 4 (2): 410.

Kramsch, C. (1993) *Context and Culture in Language Teaching.* Oxford: Oxford University Press.

Kramsch, C. (2006) From communicative competence to symbolic competence. *Modern Language Journal,* 90 (2): 249–52.

Kramsch, C. (2010) *The Multilingual Subject: What Foreign Language Learners Say About Their Experience and Why it Matters.* Oxford: Oxford University Press.

Krashen, S. (1982) *Principles and Practice in Second Language Acquisition.* Oxford: Pergamon Press. (Online version published in 2009 on www.sdkrashen.com) [accessed 8/4/2016].

Krashen, S. and Terrell, T. (1983) *The Natural Approach: Language Acquisition in the Classroom.* Oxford: Pergamon Press.

Lave, J. and Wenger, E. (1991) *Situated Learning: Legitimate and Peripheral Participation.* Cambridge: Cambridge University Press.

Law, S. and Glover, D. (2000) *Educational Leadership and Learning: Practice, Policy and Research.* Buckingham: Oxford University Press.

Learning and Teaching Scotland (2000) *5–14 National Guidelines Modern Languages Guide for Teachers and Managers.* Dundee: Learning and Teaching Scotland.

Leask, M. and Pachler, N. (eds) (2014) *Learning to Teach ICT in the Secondary School. 3rd Edition.* London and New York: Routledge.

Lee, J., Buckland, D. and Shaw, G. (1998) *The Invisible Child: The Responses and Attitudes to the Learning of Modern Languages Shown by Year 9 Pupils of Average Ability.* London: CILT.

Lee, W. R. (1971) *Language-Teaching Games and Contests.* Oxford: Oxford University Press.

Lenneberg, E. (1967) *Biological Foundations of Language.* New York: Wiley and Sons.

Light, P. and Littleton, K. (1999) *Social Processes in Children's Learning.* Cambridge: Cambridge University Press.

Lingard, B., Hayes, D., Mills, M. and Christie, P. (2003) *Leading Learning.* Maidenhead: Oxford University Press.

Macaro, E. (2001) *Learning Strategies in Foreign and Second Language Classrooms.* London: Continuum.

MacBeath, J. (1998) *Effective School Leadership: Responding to Change.* London: Paul Chapman Publishing.

Martin, C. (2000) *Analysis of National and International Research on the Provision of Modern Foreign Languages in Schools.* London: QCA.

Mehta, J. (2016) Let's End Professional Development As We Know It. *Education Week,* April 7th, 2016. Available: http://blogs.edweek.org/edweek/learning_deeply/2016/03/lets_end_professional_development_as_we_know_it_and_replace_it_with_teacher-led_professional_learnin.html.

Meisel, J., cited by Ludi, G. (2004) *L'enfant bilingue: chance ou surcharge?* Address to the Education Department of Basel, University of Basel.

Myles, F. (2016) *The learning of foreign languages in primary schools in England: issues and challenges.* Seminar. 18–19 March 2016, University of Essex (Centre for Research in Language Development Throughout the Lifespan). B.A.A.L./Cambridge University Press.

Nias, J., Southworth, G. and Yeomans, R. (1989) *Staff Relations in the Primary School.* London: Cassell.

O'Malley, J. M. and Chamot, A. (1990) *Learning Strategies in Second Language Acquisition.* Cambridge: Cambridge University Press.

Oxford, R. (1990) *Language Learning Strategies: What Every Teacher Should Know.* Boston, MA: Heinle and Heinle.

Oxford, R. (2011) *Teaching and Researching Language Learning Strategies*. London: Pearson.

Pagden, A. (2001) Continuity and progression from 3 to 11. In Cockburn, A. (ed.) *Teaching Children 3 to 11*. London: Paul Chapman Publishing.

Paige, R. and Meisterhauser, J. A. (1999) Internationalising educational administration. *Educational Administration Quarterly*, 35 (4): 500–17.

Piaget, J. and Inhelder, B. (1972) *The Psychology of the Child*. New York: Basic Books.

QCA/QCDA (2007, 2009) *Schemes of Work for Key Stage 2 Languages*.

Revell, P. (2005) Each to their own. *Education Guardian*, 31 May.

Senge, P. (1990) *The Fifth Discipline*. New York: Doubleday.

Sergiovanni, T. (2001) *Leadership: What's in it for Schools?* London: RoutledgeFalmer.

Sharpe, K. (2001) *Modern Foreign Languages in the Primary School*. London: Kogan Page.

Sharpe, K. and Driscoll, P. (2000) At what age should foreign language learning begin? In Field, K. (ed.) *Issues in Modern Foreign Languages*. London: RoutledgeFalmer.

Shaw, S. and Hawes, T. (1998) *Effective Teaching and Learning in the Primary School*. Leicester: Optimal.

Singleton, D. (1989) *Language Acquisition and the Age Factor*. Clevedon: Multilingual Matters.

Somekh, B. (2007) *Pedagogy and Learning with ICT: Researching the Art of Innovation*. London: Routledge.

Stoll, L. and Fink, D. (1996) *Changing Our Schools*. Buckingham: Oxford University Press.

Street, B. (1993) Culture is a verb: Anthropological aspects of language and cultural processes. In Graddol, D., Thompson, L. and Byram, M. (eds) *Language and Culture*. Clevedon: Multilingual Matters.

Tierney, D. and Gallastegi, L. (2005) Where are we going with primary foreign languages? *Language Learning Journal*, 31: 47–54.

Tinsley, T. and Board, K. (2016) *Language Trends 2015–16: The State of Language Learning in Primary and Secondary Schools in England*. Reading: British Council and Education Development Trust.

Torrance, H. and Pryor, J. (1998) *Investigating Formative Assessment: Teaching, Learning and Assessment in the Classroom*. Buckingham: Oxford University Press.

Trethowan, D. (1991) *Managing with Appraisal*. London: Paul Chapman Publishing.

Vilke, M. (1988) Some psychological aspects of early second-language acquisition. *Journal of Multilingual and Multicultural Development*, 9: 1–2.

Vygotsky, L. (1986) *Thought and Language*. Cambridge, MA: MIT Press.

Wade, P. and Marshall, H. with O'Donnell, S. (2009) *Primary Modern Foreign Languages Longitudinal Survey of Implementation of National Entitlement to Language Learning at Key Stage 2. RR 127*. London: DCSF Publications.

Werlen, E. (2005) Zwei Jahre Fremdsprachenunterricht an Grundschulen in Baden-Württemberg: Erste Zwischenergebnisse der Wissenschaftlichen Begleitung der Pilotphase Fremdsprache in der Grundschule. *Fremdsprachen praktisch: Beiträge und Mitteilungen aus dem Landesverband Baden-Württemberg des Fachverbandes Moderne Fremdsprachen*, 17: 63–76.

White, J. (2005) The myth of Howard Gardner's Multiple Intelligences. *Ioe Life*, 9 (1).

White, K., Lewis, K. and Fletcher-Campbell, F. (2007) *Raising the Achievement of Bilingual Learners in Primary Schools. RR 758*. London: DfES Publications.

Wingate, U. (2016) Lots of games and little challenge – A snapshot of modern foreign language teaching in English secondary schools. *Language Learning Journal*. (In press)

Wood, D. (2004) *How Children Think and Learn*. London: Blackwell.

Woolfolk, A., Walkup, V. and Hughes, M. (2007) *Psychology in Education*. Harlow: Pearson Education.

Index